Beauty

Onassis Series in Hellenic Culture

The Age of Titans: The Rise and Fall of the Great Hellenistic Navies
    William M. Murray

Sophocles and the Language of Tragedy
    Simon Goldhill

Nectar and Illusion: Nature in Byzantine Art and Literature
    Henry Maguire

Adventures with Iphigenia at Tauris: A Cultural History of Euripides' Black Sea Tragedy
    Edith Hall

Beauty: The Fortunes of an Ancient Greek Idea
    David Konstan

Onassis
Foundation **(USA)**

Frontispiece: Aphrodite's beauty attracts the erotic gaze of Pan.
National Archaeological Museum, Athens, Greece.

Credit: Marie Mauzy / Art Resource, NY.

BEAUTY

THE FORTUNES OF AN
ANCIENT GREEK IDEA

David Konstan

OXFORD
UNIVERSITY PRESS

OXFORD
UNIVERSITY PRESS

Oxford University Press is a department of the University of Oxford.
It furthers the University's objective of excellence in research, scholarship,
and education by publishing worldwide.

Oxford   New York

Auckland   Cape Town   Dar es Salaam   Hong Kong   Karachi
Kuala Lumpur   Madrid   Melbourne   Mexico City   Nairobi
New Delhi   Shanghai   Taipei   Toronto

With offices in

Argentina   Austria   Brazil   Chile   Czech Republic   France   Greece
Guatemala   Hungary   Italy   Japan   Poland   Portugal   Singapore
South Korea   Switzerland   Thailand   Turkey   Ukraine   Vietnam

Oxford is a registered trademark of Oxford University Press
in the UK and certain other countries.

Published in the United States of America by
Oxford University Press
198 Madison Avenue, New York, NY 10016

© Oxford University Press 2014

CIP data is on file at the Library of Congress
ISBN 978–0–19–992726–5

3 5 7 9 8 6 4 2
Printed in the United States of America
on acid-free paper

For Pura

CONTENTS

PREFACE AND ACKNOWLEDGMENTS

This book is in a sense an accident. I would never have thought of writing about Greek beauty, and when Pierre Destrée invited me, back in 2010, to contribute a chapter on beauty to a handbook on Greek aesthetics, my first impulse was to decline. But Pierre is persistent, and as I reflected further on the question, it occurred to me that there was a way of identifying more precisely how the Greeks conceived of beauty than I and others had assumed. Following out this path (the details are in Chapter 2), I began to see that the Greeks had rather a different view, or views, of beauty than I had supposed (see Chapters 3 and 4). What is more, the Greek vocabulary for beauty had parallels in that of other contemporary cultures (specifically, Hebrew and Latin, discussed in Chapter 5). Finally, the Greeks' way of thinking might even, it seemed to me, shed light on some still lively conundrums in modern aesthetics (Chapters 1 and 6). These problems have occupied my waking (and sometimes sleeping) thoughts for the past three years or more, and this book is the result.

Along the way, I had the good fortune to be invited by the Alexander S. Onassis Public Benefit Foundation to contribute a volume to the series on classical Greece that the Foundation sponsors and which is published by Oxford University Press. The process is exemplary: Oxford University Press vets the manuscript in its usual rigorous way, sending it to three readers for evaluation. The Foundation, in turn, provides the opportunity to discuss the book both prior to publication and after it appears. This experience, together with the practical, moral, and intellectual encouragement of the Foundation and of Stefan Vranka, the Oxford editor, was itself an inspiration. I am indebted to Stefan also for his acute sense of style, and I was wise enough to adopt all his recommendations. Thanks too to Sarah Pirovitz for essential help with images and other matters, and to Heather Hambleton for expert copy-editing.

Many people have heard or read parts of this project, and it is a great pleasure to thank them here. Over the years, I lectured on beauty in Novosibirsk (Siberia) and, courtesy of the Onassis Foundation, at the University of Minnesota, the University of California Santa Barbara, and Stanford University. I also presented talks on one or another aspect of beauty at the Universidad Nacional Autónoma de México, the City University of New York Graduate Center, the University of Western Australia, Hofstra University, the University of London, Columbia University, the University of Durham, the Université de Louvain-la-Neuve, Nottingham University, the University of St. Andrews, and the University of Edinburgh, and at conferences of the American Philological Association and the Sociedad Española de Estudios Clásicos. I am most grateful to the audiences at each of these occasions, who helped me in crucial ways to define and refine my thoughts. My dear friends Stavroula Kiritsi, Marty Wenglinsky, Andrew Ford, and Marco Fantuzzi read the entire manuscript, and I am deeply grateful for their reassurance (Stavroula also suggested the image for the frontispiece). Nico Momigliano read portions, as did Pierre Destrée and Penelope Murray. Saul Olyan provided invaluable help in the treatment of Hebrew concepts, and Daniel Picus prepared exemplary comparisons of Hebrew, Greek, and Latin terms in the several versions of the Bible. The readers for the press, Alexander Nehamas, Paul Woodruff, and a third who has remained anonymous, gave excellent advice at an early stage. Others too contributed ideas and suggestions, and if I have not named them, I hope they will understand that I am in their debt.

Scholarship is not an isolated enterprise, and I have been immensely fortunate in having friends and colleagues with whom to explore ideas and discover texts, ancient and modern, that would otherwise have escaped me. My family has been a great support, and I have been lucky to have their love and company.

Portions of the present book have appeared elsewhere, and I am grateful to the editors and presses for permission to use the materials. The articles in question may be found in the bibliography under Konstan 2012a, 2013a–d, and 2014a–b.

1

THE PROBLEM WITH BEAUTY

I. Beauty and History 🦶 The English word *beauty* is semantically rich; that is, it has a wide range of meanings and connotations. In everyday speech, this is not a problem: we can apply the noun, or the corresponding adjective *beautiful*, to a great variety of objects that do not seem to have much, or indeed anything, in common, and yet we know perfectly well what is meant. For example, we can speak of a beautiful woman, a beautiful child, a beautiful painting, a beautiful mathematical proof, and a beautiful catch in baseball. The expression "that's a beauty" can be said of almost anything at all. In some of the preceding examples, we might mean "attractive" or even "sexy," as when we use the term to describe a model or actress; in others, we may mean something more like "well executed," as in the case of a good play in athletic competitions. When ascribed to a work of art, the term may signify balance or proportion, or some other quality that we think of as aesthetic; in the case of mathematics, we perhaps mean that a proof is elegant because it is crisp and compact, or innovative in method. Very generally, *beautiful* is a term of approbation, and its precise sense depends on the context. However, it would seem to retain in most of its uses some connection with attractiveness, and its connotations do not overlap entirely or precisely with other expressions of approval such as *good* or *fine*. Upon reflection, one is naturally led to wonder whether all the different applications of *beauty* or *beautiful* really have a core quality in common, despite some outlying or marginal uses, or whether the term rather embraces a set of homonyms, in which the connection between the various senses is either thin or nonexistent, like *pool* when it bears the sense of a small body of water and then again when it refers to a game similar to billiards.

The nature of beauty became a central intellectual question with the emergence of the discipline known as aesthetics in the mid-eighteenth century, when the word was first coined. Aesthetics took beauty as its special province, above all in the domain of art. Why this interest should have arisen just then, and in Germany (or what is now Germany) in particular, is an intriguing issue in the history of philosophy, to which we shall return. From this point on, at any rate, serious thinking about beauty had to take account of well-developed theoretical positions and confront the paradoxes or difficulties that arose as a result of the umbrella character of the concept, which covered so great a variety of notions.

The present investigation is historical and looks to understand how our modern notions of beauty arose in relation to the prevailing ideas and accounts of beauty in classical antiquity, beginning with the Greeks. From this perspective, perhaps the quandary that most immediately presents itself concerning the nature of beauty is the apparent variety of forms that it takes across different times and places. This is evident in relation to the human form, the ideals for which may vary even in a relatively short period of time: for several recent decades, glamour was associated with models so thin as to appear anorexic. They would have aroused a certain revulsion in periods accustomed to more fulsome figures. The current practice of piercing and tattooing the body is another variation in the criteria for beauty, as is long hair or totally shaved heads for men compared to the trim haircuts of fifty or sixty years ago (I am not sure that younger people even know what a "part" is, in relation to a hairstyle). The ancient Greeks also had their preferences, which doubtless varied over time and in different locales. The same would be true for the Romans and the vast empire they eventually ruled. Although I mention, when relevant, the traits (for example, height) that counted as contributing to beauty, whether male or female, in antiquity, they are not the primary subject of the present book.[1]

II. Did the Ancient Greeks Recognize Art?   I propose rather to examine the kinds of things that were described as *beautiful* (Did the term cover the same wide range of objects that it does in modern English usage?) and what the typical response to beauty was understood to be (What did people feel or think of themselves as feeling, when they beheld something they called beautiful?). As I mentioned, one of the characteristic spheres in which the modern notion of beauty is applied is the aesthetic one, that is, as a response or relation to art. Yet some have claimed—with what validity we will examine in due course—that the ancient Greeks had no sense of art as a self-standing sphere of experience, any more than they had a word for "literature" in the way we understand it today.[2] Indeed, this is the dominant view today. As Elizabeth Prettejohn observes in her book about the reception of ancient Greek art, "ancient society, according to a prevalent view, did not have a 'conception of art comparable to ours.'" As a result, seeing ancient sculpture, for example, as part of a "chain of receptions is not just irrelevant to their contemporary context, but a positive falsification." As Prettejohn says, to scholars today "this sounds like common sense" (Prettejohn 2012, 98). The view was given its most influential expression in a well-known paper by the eminent historian of the Renaissance Paul Oskar

Kristeller, who affirmed that "ancient writers and thinkers, though confronted with excellent works of art and quite susceptible to their charm, were neither able nor eager to detach the aesthetic quality of these works of art from their intellectual, moral, religious and practical functions or content, or to use such an aesthetic quality as a standard for grouping the fine arts together or for making them the subject of a comprehensive philosophical interpretation" (Kristeller 1951, 506). According to Kristeller, an understanding of art as an autonomous sphere arose only in the eighteenth century, coincident with the rise of the new discipline of aesthetics.[3]

To be sure, there are also contrary voices. Perhaps the most incisive critic of the view associated with Kristeller is James Porter, who has turned the tables on Kristeller's picture of the ancient conception by asking: "Is it even true as a description of the state of the arts and their classification in the eighteenth century?"[4] But this still leaves the status of ancient art up in the air. Porter quotes a noted essay, in which Simon Goldhill and Robin Osborne signal "a danger in using the general word 'art'" in connection with painted images on classical pottery or friezes on temples, for example, insofar as "significant nuances of contextualization may be effaced."[5] Their basic thesis is, as Porter puts it, that "the term *art* risks misleading us into a false identification of the nature of ancient aesthetic production altogether." If it is "really the case that the ancients had no conception of art comparable to ours," then the question is, as Porter says: "Can we ever hope to approach their art on its own terms? Or worse still, in order to gain access to ancient culture, must we abandon all hope of approaching it through what we used to call its art?"[6] The question has an immediate bearing on the ancient conception of beauty. For if the ancient Greeks had no notion of "art" as we understand it, we may well wonder whether it makes sense at all to ask whether they thought of beauty as a feature of art itself as opposed to the objects—human or otherwise—represented in a work of art.

The question of whether spheres of life that we consider autonomous were also regarded this way in other cultures and more specifically in classical antiquity is not limited to matters of art or culture. Some scholars have questioned, for example, whether it is right to speak of an ancient Greek or Roman "economy" in the sense of an independent and self-regulating social domain with its own laws and history. They have argued rather that trade and other economic transactions were embedded in social relations generally, and only with the rise of modern capitalism did the economy as such emerge, distinct and separate from the wider social context that included family, religious practices, political formations, and so forth.[7] This view too has been challenged, and other scholars have seen in ancient banking and insurance practices ample evidence of strictly economic activity, in which people made investments with a view to profit and calculated gains and losses in relation to market values.[8] Efforts have been made in recent years to move beyond the polarity of embedded versus autonomous economies by paying closer attention to local behaviors, which may have varied from one place to another or even within different occupations in a single community.[9] The question continues to be disputed, but the debate itself is a salutary reminder of the need to avoid anachronism when we seek to understand ancient attitudes, values, and social categories.

III. Did the Ancient Greeks Recognize Beauty?

This book is concerned not with artistic beauty as such but with beauty more generally, which of course ranges well beyond the sphere of art. Even in the relatively narrow sense in which it is applied to visually attractive objects, beauty is perceived not only in paintings and sculptures but also in man-made items such as automobiles and furniture, which we would not necessarily classify as works of art. Still, it is hard to say just where the boundary is to be drawn between "art" and "design." But above all—and in some ways most fundamentally—beauty is an attribute of the human form and of certain objects in the natural world. We do not typically classify these under the rubric of art, although here again our notions of what a beautiful woman or beautiful landscape looks like may well be influenced by artifice, via the cosmetics and fashion industries or images of cultivated gardens and country scenes. Thus Lessing wrote in his classic treatise on poetry and painting: "If beautiful men created beautiful statues, these statues in turn affected the men, and thus the state owed thanks also to beautiful statues for beautiful men."[10] Our question, then, is whether the ancient Greeks had a well-defined conception of beauty in general, even if they did not "use such an aesthetic quality as a standard for grouping the fine arts together," in the words of Kristeller. It may seem even less likely that the Greeks lacked the idea of beauty than that they somehow failed to single out the more abstract notions of art or economy, which after all depend on the development of certain social practices that may not be common to all cultures. We can understand, for example, that ritual masks we gaze at in museums may not have been produced with an aesthetic purpose in mind but were intended to serve a religious function, and it is conceivable that images in a classical temple or on the altarpiece in a church were imagined as inspiring something other than an aesthetic response—at least in the first instance. So too, while we may think of the exchange of goods as strictly financial, we can recognize other contexts in which such transactions were primarily intended to promote solidarity and may have been the dominant form of exchange.

But beauty would seem to be a fundamental experience of human beings in any society, ancient or modern. Can there be a culture that has no such concept, or no term to express it? This would seem even more unlikely in the case of ancient Greece, with its brilliant art that to this day has set the standard for what we imagine to be the ideal representation of the human form. As Michael Squire has observed, "Like it or not—and there have been many reasons for *not* liking it—antiquity has supplied the mould for all subsequent attempts to figure and figure out the human body" (Squire 2011, xi). He adds, "Because Graeco-Roman art bestowed us with our western concepts of 'naturalistic' representation . . . ancient images resemble not only our modern images, but also the 'real' world around us" (xiii). Can the Greeks really have lacked the very idea of beauty?

Surprising as it may sound, leading scholars have in fact questioned whether any word in classical Greek corresponded to the modern idea of beauty. The absence of a specific term does not, of course, necessarily mean that the concept itself was lacking: languages, including our own, do resort to paraphrase after all, and we may recognize and respond to classes of things for which we have no special name.[11] The so-called Whorf-Sapir hypothesis, according to which the vocabulary and structure of a given language not only influence but in fact strictly determine how its speakers perceive the world, is hardly tenable in its strictest form, which would deny that people can even conceive of a class of things that has no name in their own tongue.[12] Edward T. Jeremiah has recently offered what he calls a "milder version" of the thesis that should "be uncontroversial." He writes, "What a culture does not have a word for is not important for them as an object of inquiry or socio-cultural signifier" (Jeremiah 2012, 12). Still, it would be no less shocking, perhaps, to discover that beauty was insignificant for the ancient Greeks as a "socio-cultural signifier," that is, a term charged with a specific meaning and value in their view of the world.

We shall take up in due course the question of whether there was a word for "beauty" or "beautiful" in classical Greek and Latin. For now, let me put the reader at ease and reveal that, despite the reservations entertained by serious scholars on this matter, I will argue that there was indeed a term for "beauty" in Greek and, what is more, that a proper appreciation of its meaning and use has something to tell us about our own ideas of the beautiful. The point requires argument, because if it were self-evident then it would not have been and indeed have remained controversial. But before tackling this debate directly, inevitably via an examination of the ancient Greek vocabulary, it is worth looking at some of the problems that beset the idea of beauty in its modern applications. For the idea of beauty, as we employ it, is not so simple or innocent a notion as it might seem. If beauty turns out to be a problematic concept for us, it may be less surprising to discover that some cultures may make do perfectly well without it or—if they do have such a notion (as I believe the ancient Greeks did)—may define and understand it in ways sufficiently different from ours to shed some light on our own difficulties and possibly on ways to resolve or circumvent them. Regarding the Greeks in particular, we may be able to see how the modern conception of beauty, with whatever baggage of contradictions and tensions it carries, emerged in the first place, since Greek works of art and Greek ideas about art had a massive influence on the Western tradition, even if they were sometimes misunderstood (not that this is necessarily a terrible thing: misunderstanding is one of the great sources of creativity).

IV. Beauty, Sex, and Virtue Before proceeding to the terminology for beauty in ancient Greek (in Chapter 2), we may consider for a moment the kinds of problems that may arise in connection with the way the word is employed in English today. There is a tension, for example, between two of the most familiar senses of beauty in English that is particularly relevant to theories of aesthetics. On the one hand, we commonly associate beauty with erotic attraction; on the other hand, as a category in aesthetics, beauty is a feature of artworks as well as of natural phenomena, and in these latter instances it is not necessarily presumed to excite desire in the beholder. On the contrary, at least since Kant's *Critique of Judgement*, and in fact even earlier, many critics have supposed that the proper response to such beauty is disinterested contemplation. What, if anything, do these two conceptions of beauty have in common?

Since Roger Scruton, in his recent book entitled *Beauty*, poses the question neatly, I take the liberty of citing his formulation.

> There are no greater tributes to human beauty than the medieval and Renaissance images of the Holy Virgin: a woman whose sexual maturity is expressed in motherhood and who yet remains untouchable, barely distinguishable, as an object of veneration, from the child in her arms . . . The Virgin's beauty is a symbol of purity, and for this very reason is held apart from the realm of sexual appetite, in a world of its own. This thought . . . reaches back to Plato's original idea: that beauty is not just an invitation to desire, but also a call to renounce it. (Scruton 2009, 54)

Likewise, the beauty of a poem or an abstract sculpture is supposed to evoke something more like admiration, even reverence, rather than the kind of desire that can be described as erotic. As Scruton puts it, "In the realm of art beauty is an object of contemplation, not desire" (40).

But if this is the case, what are we to make of the kind of beauty that arouses sexual desire? As Scruton asks immediately following the above quotation: "Does this mean that there are two kinds of beauty—the beauty of people and the beauty of art?" Scruton rejects this solution, and I am inclined to agree with him. But a problem nevertheless remains, for even if we agree that we react differently, or might do so, to the image of a beautiful woman in art—whether the Virgin Mary or anyone else—than to a beautiful woman (or man) in real life, we still want to know why we do: what distinguishes the kind of beauty that holds us at a reverential distance and that which invites an erotic response? Scruton is alert to the issue, which he poses in terms of the beauty of children. He writes: "There is hardly a person alive who is not moved by the beauty of the perfectly formed child. Yet most people are horrified by the thought that this beauty should be a spur to desire, other than the desire to cuddle and comfort . . . And yet the beauty of a child is of the same kind as the beauty of a desirable adult, and totally unlike the beauty of an aged face" (53–54).[13] Scruton here sets aside the realm of art and differentiates the two kinds of beauty in respect to the live human form alone. We may wish to cavil at Scruton's example—is a child's beauty really like that of a sexually desirable adult, and if so, why don't we respond to children in the same way? Is it simply that we repress erotic desire in the case of children, or renounce it, as Scruton puts it (an imperative he traces back to Plato)?

We shall return to Plato, and to ancient Greek conceptions of beauty, in the following chapters, but I should like first to frame the problem that Scruton has posed in relation to a mediaeval work of art, which, I believe, will help to sharpen the issue. In his recent book, *A Cultural History of Pain*, Javier Moscoso raises the question of how we identify pain in someone else (Moscoso 2011; translation mine; for an English version, see Moscoso 2012). We may infer it if we see a person or a depiction of a person suffering what looks like physical harm, indicated by the presence of instruments of torture, for example. But conceivably the individual is insensitive to hurt. We might rely on familiar manifestations of pain such as a contorted expression or cries of anguish (in pictures, the mouth shaped so as to suggest a scream), but what if the posture and appearance of what we take to be the victim of torment are or seem to be perfectly serene, as is the case, for instance, in numerous images of Christian martyrdom, from Christ himself onward? Various documentary accounts affirm that the faith of some saints was so strong that they did not feel the pain inflicted on them; other accounts make it clear that pain was indeed experienced but was welcomed as essential to penitence, and so again it was in some form transcended or at least different from the way we habitually think of pain as necessarily producing aversion.

One illustration on which Moscoso dwells is a *retablo* or altar-piece that was originally in a church (long since destroyed) in Mayorga de Campos, a town in the province of Valladolid in Spain, but is now located in the Museo de Bellas Artes in Oviedo, capital of the province of Asturias. The altarpiece (Figure 1.1), which was created in the fifteenth century and is attributed to the so-called Master of Palanquinos (possibly Pedro of Mayorga), consists of a dozen paintings illustrating the life of Saint Marina (and six more on the life of Christ). There is some question as to the identity of the saint. The Marina who is the patron saint of Ourense in Galicia was born in the town of Bayona de Pontevedra around the year 119 and was the daughter of the Roman governor of the region. But there was another another Marina, who was martyred in Pisidian Antioch (in modern Turkey) in the third century; the story of this Marina is narrated in the *Legenda Aurea* or *Golden Tales*, a collection of hagiographies compiled in the mid-thirteenth

Figure 1.1 The Martyrdom of Saint Marina. Courtesy of the Museo de Bellas Artes de Asturias, Oviedo, Spain.

century by Jacopo da Varazze, the archbishop of Genova. This is undoubtedly the source on which the Master of Palanquinos drew.

This Marina was the daughter of a pagan priest named Edesius, who was the first to persecute her after she adopted the Christian faith. Subsequently, her beauty attracted the attention of Olymbrius, the local governor, who was prepared to marry her if she gave up her faith. Needless to say, Marina rejected the offer, and Olymbrius subjected her to terrible tortures, which miraculously failed to mar her beauty, before finally putting her to death by the sword. Moscoso observes:

> As opposed to the prefect . . . , her beauty depends on her strength
> of spirit and not on the configuration of her body. Her tranquility
> contrasts with the enraged and deformed faces of the torturers

who administer the punishment . . . The altarpiece exalts the spiritual beauty of the young woman by way of her body, which reappears intact and unaltered at the end of each torment and returns to its natural state after every blow. Her beauty, which is a constant point of reference in literary characterizations and pictorial representations, turns her body into a witness of the truth and a tabernacle of salvation. (28)

What interests me in this narrative and the corresponding pictorial representation is the double role assigned to Marina's beauty. On the one hand, this trait arouses the desire of the Roman prefect Olymbrius and so is clearly a carnal kind of beauty. On the other hand, her beauty is evidently supposed to be spiritual in nature and thus of the sort that demands contemplation: this kind of beauty, in Scruton's phrase, is not "an invitation to desire" but rather "a call to renounce it." In itself, Marina's beauty produces both effects; what is it that makes us, as readers of the narrative or viewers of the altarpiece, respond to her in a spirit of reverence rather than with sexual desire?[14] Indeed, can the two perceptions be reconciled, or are we obliged to respond in either one way or the other, a bit the way we see either a duck or a rabbit in the famous image made popular by the American psychologist Joseph Jastrow at the end of the nineteenth century (see Figure 1.2).[15]

The theme of the Christian who is persecuted not only for refusing to acknowledge pagan gods or the emperor's divinity but also—especially (but not only) in the case of women—for rebuffing the sexual demands of powerful agents was a popular one in antiquity and afterward. To take one example, in the *Acts of Xanthippe and Polyxena*, dated roughly to the early fifth century, Polyxena, a beautiful (*hôraia*, 22) young woman, dreams that she has been rescued from the jaws of a dragon by a handsome youth (*neanias eueidês*), understood of course to be Christ. She is then

Figure 1.2 Duck-Rabbit.

abducted from her native Spain by a vicious man, who is a rival
to her suitor (*mnêstêr*, 23). In the course of her adventures, in
which she crosses paths with no fewer than four different apostles,
Polyxena lands in Greece, where the apostle Philip rescues her and
hands her over to the care of a holy man. The abductor, nothing
daunted, raises an army of eight thousand men to retake the girl,
but they are defeated by thirty servants, and in the meantime
Polyxena escapes. After an encounter with a lioness, which spares
Polyxena on the grounds that she has not yet been baptized, she
receives baptism at the hands of the apostle Andrew. Later, a kindly
ass driver counsels Polyxena to adopt the appearance of a man, so
that her beauty may not attract unwanted attentions (33), but a
wicked prefect sees her and carries her off. When he calls her to his
bed, however, Polyxena convinces his servants to pretend that she
has a fever. Meanwhile, the prefect's son, who has been converted
to Christianity by none other than Paul and Thecla, conspires to
escape with Polyxena to Spain. Their plan is discovered, however,
and the prefect orders both to be thrown to the lions, but the
lioness that is released against them—presumably the same one

that spared Polyxena earlier—merely licks their feet, at which the prefect and the whole populace are moved to adopt the new faith. The prefect arranges to have Polyxena and his son transported back to Spain, where the violent abductor, who intends to carry off Polyxena yet again, is also converted and baptized by Paul (as is Polyxena's original suitor).

This tale has much in common with a set of Greek romantic novels composed in the first three centuries after Christ. In them, an adolescent boy and girl of exceptional beauty fall deeply in love, are forcibly separated, and, in the course of many misadventures, are assailed by rivals who are smitten by their nearly divine good looks. Despite all hazards and temptations, they remain faithful to their original passion and are reunited in the end, though they may, under duress or in the belief that their partner has died, have consented at some point to sexual relations with someone else. I have suggested elsewhere that the fidelity of these lovers is analogous to Christian martyrs' commitment to their faith despite all threats and torments. Indeed, the expressions of spiritual integrity in these genres are remarkably similar.[16] Take this declaration on the part of Leucippe, the heroine of Achilles Tatius's novel, when she has been enslaved to a brutal master: "Take up all your instruments of torture, and at once; bring out against me the whips, the wheel, the fire, the sword . . . I am naked, and alone, and a woman. But one shield and defense I have, which is my freedom, which cannot be struck down by whips, or cut by the sword, or burned by fire. My freedom is something I will not surrender—burn as you might, you will find that there is no fire hot enough to consume it" (6.21).[17] The words of Anthia, heroine of the novel *Ephesiaca* by Xenophon of Ephesus, are another example. Reunited at last with her husband Habrocomes, Anthia affirms,

Husband and master, I have recovered you after wandering much
land and sea, having escaped the threats of bandits, the designs of
pirates, the outrages of brothel-keepers, bonds, graves, manacles,
poisons and ditches, and I come to you, despite all, O Habrocomes
lord of my soul, as I was when I first went from Tyre to Syria,
and no one induced me to sin, not Moeris in Syria, nor Perilaus
in Cilicia, nor Psammis and Polyidus in Egypt, nor Anchialus
in Ethiopia, nor my master in Tarentum, but I have remained
holy [*hagnê*] for you, having practiced every device of chastity
[*sôphrosunê*]. (5.14.1–2)

Habrocomes himself, when threatened with torture by Manto, who
is in love with him (he is at this point in the narrative the slave of
her father, the pirate chief), declares, "I am a slave, but I know how
to keep my promises. They have power over my body, but I have
a soul that is free. Let Manto threaten me, then, if she wishes,
with swords and nooses and fire and everything that can compel
the body of a slave; I will never be persuaded willingly to wrong
Anthia" (2.4).[18] It is easy to cite parallels in Christian literature,
such as this from the *Passio Anastasiae* (17.10–20), in which the
soon-to-be-martyred Irene declares, "Just as my flesh would endure
beasts, fire, beatings, or any other punishment, so too it will endure
a fornicator, a dog, a bear, or a serpent ... For the soul cannot be
faulted for impurities to which it does not consent ... Willingness
brings with it punishment, but necessity brings the crown."[19]

However, neither in the case of the classical novels nor in the
acts of Polyxena is the beauty of the protagonist treated as a symbol
of virtue or spiritual purity. The reasons why will be discussed
in the following chapters, but here we may observe that physical
beauty is sometimes seen as the opposite pole to saintliness. Thus,
it has been observed that in the *Acts of Paul and Thecla*, a novelistic
narrative dating to the second century, Thecla is represented as

charmed—*seduced* would not be too strong a word—not by the physical appearance of Paul but rather by his words, which she hears while seated at her window, though she does not see the apostle.[20] In Christian texts, women tend to lament the beauty that attracts the unwanted attentions of men. They see beauty as a curse rather than a blessing and sometimes resort to mortification of the flesh that is the locus of sin; beauty is hardly an unequivocal good.[21]

Let us return, then, to the dilemma posed by Roger Scruton and more radically by the narrative and iconic representation of the life of Saint Marina, at least as it is interpreted by Javier Moscoso—a dilemma that may not, as we have seen, have arisen in precisely this form in ancient tales of lust and fidelity. One strategy, which had its roots in Plato or at least in his followers, the so-called Neoplatonists, is to see in the beauty of the Virgin, or that of Marina, a kind of emanation of Beauty itself, which is made manifest in the human form but represents a higher order of being to which we are spiritually attracted.[22] We shall examine the origins and subsequent trajectory of this view later, as we investigate the fortunes of the Greek conception of beauty. Here, we may note simply that the attempt to combine beauty as physical attractiveness with beauty as a sign of divine purity would seem to run into trouble with stories such as that of Saint Marina, in which it is impossible to see her simultaneously as sexually desirable (yet she must have been to have attracted the attention of the Roman governor) and a symbol of purity by virtue of her beauty. David Freedberg cites an episode from the childhood of Maxim Gorky, as recounted in his autobiography, in which Gorky kissed an icon of the Virgin in a way his elders considered inappropriate.[23] Freedberg comments: "We may suppose that he, like everyone else in his culture, was accustomed to think of the Virgin as the most beautiful of all women; and so, instead of wanting to kiss her chastely, he kissed her more intimately, even wantonly"

(320–321). Freedberg observes that "we may have difficulty distinguishing between erotic and spiritual love," especially when "the Virgin looks like a living model of beauty. The problem recurs countless times in the history of art" (323). I may be permitted to cite a more recent illustration of the apparent fusion (if that is what it is) of the erotic and the spiritual that I myself have witnessed. Moreover, it is one that does not seem to bear the charge of shame or dread that accompanied Gorky's spontaneous expression of affection. In the processions of penitents that take place during Holy Week in Seville, the various confraternities or *cofradías* associated with the major churches bring out floats bearing magnificently crafted statues of Jesus, Mary, and at times other figures relating to the life of Christ. The Virgin is gorgeously adorned, and for all the grief that she may manifest, it is impossible to deny her beauty. Figures 1.3 and 1.4 and depict

Figure 1.3 The Virgin of La Macarena (Seville). © Shutterstock.

Figure 1.4 Holy Week in Seville. © Shutterstock.

the Virgen de la Esperanza Macarena, who is worshipped in the Basilica of La Macarena; the sculpture, whose artist is unknown, dates to the seventeenth century.

The grand image of the Virgin, borne on the shoulders of a dozen strong men, progresses in its stately march along the streets lined with worshippers, while others gaze down from the windows and balconies of their apartments. From time to time, a man, in the throes of rapture, will compose a spontaneous song to the Virgin, called in Spanish a *saeta*.

The word itself is an abbreviated form of the Latin *sagitta*, or "arrow" (hence Sagittarius), and evidently the songs were imagined as being shot forth. Indeed, they do give that impression. Others in the crowd, equally moved but perhaps less gifted poetically, shout out words of adoration. Frequent among them is "Guapa!," that is, "Beautiful!" Now, *guapo* or *guapa* (masculine or feminine) is a special term in Spanish: it refers only to human beauty and is never applied to such things as landscapes or works of art or creatures other than human beings.[24] This does not necessarily mean that it connotes sexual attractiveness (one can call a child *guapo*), but neither does it pertain to a special territory of artistic beauty, the sort that—according to Scruton—elicits contemplation rather than desire. Might it be that worshippers of the Virgin recognize that her beauty is not essentially different from that of ordinary women, and that sexual desire is repressed or absent not because she is perceived as having the beauty of a child but for much the same reason that we recognize sexual attractiveness in certain women—our mothers, sisters, daughters, or neighbors' wives— or, as the case may be, in certain men and yet discriminate between those who are legitimate objects of desire and those who are not?

Let me turn now to a sixteenth-century representation of the decapitation of Holofernes by Judith. The reader will recall that Judith, a beautiful Jewish widow, entered Holofernes's camp as he was preparing to force the Jews to worship Nebuchadnezzar, seduced the general, and beheaded him while he was drunk. As a result, the Hebrews defeated the enemy army.[25] This tale, like that of Marina, makes no sense unless we assume that Judith's beauty is more than simply spiritual. Here is how Judith is portrayed by Jan Massys, in a painting dated to 1543 and now in the Boston Museum of Fine Arts, where it arrested my attention as I was browsing the collection (see Figure 1.5).

How are we to understand her evident beauty? Was Massys being deliberately provocative? Have the perceptual codes changed over the past few centuries (i.e., exposure of women's breasts is more sexually charged in the United States today than it has been at many other times and places)? Is an erotic response to this image necessarily inappropriate, like the young Gorky's reaction to the icon of the Virgin?[26]

Figure 1.5 Jan Massys's Judith with the Head of Holofernes. Courtesy of the Museum of Fine Arts, Boston.

V. Beauty in Art and Life  I have been speaking so far as though the representation of a person in a work of art were equivalent to the sight of the living individual, and that the response to the image is not fundamentally different from that to a real person. Of course, we recognize the difference between a painting or statue and a real man or woman, although there may be extreme cases in which the distinction is blurred. If it is true that, thanks to the classical heritage, we think that a statue of a man or woman resembles a real man or woman, as Michael Squire argues, then we can perhaps the easier imagine a person falling in love with the statue as though it were a real person—this is the basis of the story of Pygmalion, after all, and there are other examples of such a perverse passion purporting to recount real events. There is even the word *agalmatophilia*, from the Greek roots *agalma* (statue) and *philia* (love); it is defined in the Wikipedia article as a perversion (*paraphilia* is the technical term used in the article) "involving sexual attraction to a statue, doll, mannequin or other similar figurative object."[27] The Wikipedia article informs us that "Agalmatophilia became a subject of clinical study with the publication of Richard von Krafft-Ebbing's *Psychopathia Sexualis* (1886). Ebbing recorded an 1877 case of a gardener falling in love with a statue of the Venus de Milo and being discovered attempting coitus with it." I doubt the gardener was aware that there was a Greek precedent for his behavior, but there was. Praxiteles created a nude statue of Aphrodite, which was enough of a scandal—we are told by ancient sources—in its own right (Figures 1.6, 1.7). But a man fell so in love with the statue that he attempted to make love with it, and left a stain on it that remained visible afterward (Pliny, *Natural History*, 36.21; cf. Lucian, *Images*, 4). Now, the question arises: did the man fall in love with a statue, and hence exhibit the perversion of agalmatophilia, or did he fall in love with the goddess represented

Figure 1.6 The Cnidian Aphrodite: Coin from Cnidos.

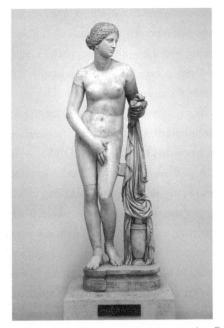

Figure 1.7 The Cnidian Aphrodite: Roman Copy. Credit: © Vanni Archive / Art Resource, NY.

by the statue and so coupled with it in the hope, perhaps, that it would come alive, like Pygmalion's sculpture, or in the belief that it was in some sense the goddess herself? Let us remember that the Greeks carried statues of their gods and goddesses in their religious processions, just as Christians do during Holy Week in Seville and elsewhere in Spain. The Greeks also worshipped them in various rites. When the Athenians wove the great robe or *peplos* for Athena and carried her, dressed to the nines, in the Panathenaic festival parade, they thought of the statue not as some inanimate stone but as a living symbol, energized in some fashion by the spirit of the deity (so too, the men who shout out *Guapa*! as the float bearing the Virgin passes by in Seville do not imagine themselves praising a statue but the Virgin herself).[28] Callistratus, who lived in the third or fourth century AD and wrote a set of descriptions of statues, explains in reference to a particularly fine statue of Paean: "What we are seeing seems to me to be, not an image [*tupos*], but a fashioning of the truth [*tês alêtheias plasma*]. For see how art is not unable to represent character; rather, when it has made an image of the god it passes over to the god himself. Though it is matter, it breathes divine intelligence, and though it happens to be handiwork, it does what is not possible for handicrafts and in an ineffable way begets signs of the soul" (Callistratus, *Descriptions of Statues* 10.2). Art opens a window on the true nature of things.[29] Clement of Alexandria, in his *Exhortation to the Greeks* (i.e., the pagans), observes that the pagan gods are recognized by their conventional attributes. Poseidon, for instance, is identified by his trident, "and if one sees a woman represented naked, he knows that she is 'golden' Aphrodite" (4.47.2). Clement goes on to explain that Pygmalion "fell in love with an ivory statue; the statue was of Aphrodite and she was naked" (4.57.3), and he went so far as to make love to it (*sunerkhetai*). He also mentions the man who was enamored of Cnidian Aphrodite and had intercourse, as he puts it, with the stone (*mignutai têi lithôi*). But Clement is puzzled by such behavior and ascribes it to the power of art to deceive (*apatêsai*). He goes on to affirm that effective as craftsmanship is, it cannot deceive a rational person (*apatêsai logikon*). He grants that stallions will neigh at accurate drawings of mares and that a girl once fell in love with a painting (*eikôn*), just as the boy did with the Cnidian Aphrodite, but he explains that "the eyes of the viewers were deceived by art" (4.57.4), since no human in his right mind (*anthrôpos sôphronôn*) would have embraced a goddess or fallen in love with a stone daemon (*daimonos kai lithou*, 4.57.5). It is all the more absurd, Clement concludes, to worship such things. Unlike many Church Fathers, Clement is hostile to graven images and fails to understand the subtle, even mysterious interplay between the work of art and the figure it reproduces.[30]

Today, we habitually ascribe beauty to works of art as such, and not just to what is represented in them. We might, then, prefer to say that the spiritual beauty that we perceive in a work like the altarpiece attributed to the Master of Palanquinos is to be found not in the figure of Saint Marina herself but in the work of art taken as a whole, distinct from any particular object represented in it, even though the painting also portrays the distorted and ugly expressions of Marina's tormentors. We may draw the same distinction, if we wish, in the case of Massys's portrait of Judith holding Holofernes's head. Judith's beauty is of the erotically attractive kind—as we should expect, given the role she plays in the biblical tale—but it is something in the composition of the entire painting, however we interpret this, that succeeds in producing what we think of as aesthetic beauty, the kind that invites not desire but rather disinterested contemplation. We shall consider in due course whether such a split between the beauty of the work and that of the object represented in it was recognized in classical antiquity. For now, we may observe that the question of whether or not a work of art has a beauty of its own, even though the figures in it are unattractive, continues to be debated among students of aesthetics. We may cite as an example of the clash of views the famous painting by Matisse entitled *Blue Nude*, dating to 1907 (Figure 1.8).

Matisse exhibited his painting a few months before Picasso composed his *Desmoiselles d'Avignon* (Figure 1.9); though Picasso's initial reaction to Matisse's work was negative, he soon came to appreciate its quality and found inspiration in it for his own creations: Is either of these paintings beautiful? The distinguished art critic and philosopher Arthur Danto affirms categorically that *Blue Nude* "is a good, even a great painting—but someone who claims it is beautiful is talking through his or her hat"

Figure 1.8 Henri Matisse's *Blue Nude (Souvenir of Biskra)*, 1907. The Cone Collection, formed by Dr. Claribel Cone and Miss Etta Cone of Baltimore, Maryland. Courtesy of the Baltimore Museum of Art.

Figure 1.9 Pablo Picasso's *Desmoiselles d'Avignon*, 1907. Courtesy of the Museum of Modern Art, New York.

(Danto 2003, 36–37). Danto indeed applauds the separation of aesthetic quality from beauty: "I regard the Intractable Avant-garde as having taken an immense philosophical step forward. It helped show that beauty was no part of the concept of art, that beauty could be present or not, and something still be art" (xv). And again: "I regard the discovery that something can be good art without being beautiful as one of the great conceptual clarifications of twentieth-century philosophy of art, though it was made exclusively by artists—but it would have been seen as commonplace before the Enlightenment gave beauty the primacy it continued to enjoy until relatively recent times" (58). Danto quotes (82) a remark by Roger Scruton: "If one finds a photograph beautiful, it is because one finds something beautiful in the subject."[31] Alexander Nehamas, however, objects to Danto's claim precisely in connection with *Blue Nude*, insisting that it is indeed beautiful as a work of art. Nehamas asserts crisply, "Beauty is not identical with an attractive appearance" (Nehamas 2007, 24), and he adds, "As long as we continue to identify beauty with attractiveness and attractiveness with a power of pleasing quickly and without much thought or effort, we can't even begin to think of many of the twentieth century's great works as beautiful" (29–30).

We shall return to the debate over the place of beauty in art and aesthetic theory in the final chapter of this book, after we have examined ancient Greek conceptions of beauty; we will thus be in a position to see how the modern conundrums emerged in the Renaissance and afterward. For it will emerge that they do not, in fact, have their roots in classical thought but rather represent a new complex—one that indeed looked back to and recuperated many classical ideas but reconceived or altered (not to say distorted) them in such a way as to give rise to problems that were moot in antiquity. It may be that, given the multiple senses of beauty that are current in English and many other languages today (but differently, as we shall see, in ancient Greek), there is an irreducible tension between the kind of beauty that might arouse the sexual desire of a Roman governor (as in the case of Saint Marina) and the beauty that invites disinterested contemplation, whether the latter is a quality of the work of art as a whole or is adumbrated in the serene expression of the martyr as she undergoes her ordeal. Is it even possible to separate the image of a beautiful woman from desire? Jerrold Levinson, in an essay that insists on the polyvalence of the notion of beauty, affirms, "I would deny that human physical beauty can be detached from sexual attractiveness" (Levinson 2011, 198). So much for what Javier Moscoso identified in the images of Saint Marina as "the spiritual beauty of the young woman by way of her body," or his idea that her beauty, in some fashion, "turns her body into a witness of the truth and a tabernacle of salvation." Ernst Gombrich, in turn, maintains that the notion of beauty as necessarily sexual goes back at least as far as the Renaissance (Gombrich 1990). Gombrich quotes a letter by the art historian Ulrich Middeldorf, published in *The Art Bulletin*, in which Middeldorf "took Otto Brendel to task for his symbolic interpretation of Titian's *Holkham Venus*":

> It is . . . inconceivable to me [Middeldorf writes] that a Venus by Titian should have only a profoundly philosophical meaning, while there is much evidence for the preoccupation of the Renaissance with quite different reactions to the beauty of women, and as long as even saintly men like Paphnutius are known to have succumbed to the charms of Thais.[32]

We shall examine in later chapters the connection between beauty and desire as it was construed in classical Greece and Rome, and also ancient views of the responses that art—or perhaps we should say "verbal and visual compositions"—might evoke. We cited Roger Scruton's affirmation that the beauty of the Virgin Mary "is a symbol of purity, and for this very reason is held apart from the realm of sexual appetite," and his further claim that "this thought reaches back to Plato's original idea: that beauty is not just an invitation to desire, but also a call to renounce it." Yet Alexander Nehamas, in his book on beauty and art, writes, "Plato and the ancients were not afraid of the risky language of passion because they thought that beauty, even the beauty of lowly objects, can gradually inspire a longing for goodness and truth" (2). According to Nehamas, modern approaches to aesthetics have separated beauty from goodness and in the process stripped beauty of desire, since desire is, as a consequence, deprived of a noble object. Nehamas insists, nevertheless, that "for Plato and the long tradition that came after him beauty is the object of love, the quarry of *erôs*" (9). Nehamas is aware that this thesis, stated in so bald a fashion, is likely to shock: "If beauty inspires the desire to possess and own its object or to use it for some further purpose, especially if it involves sex, it might seem reasonable to believe that those who value art for its beauty are either philistines or perverts" (11).[33] Well, I should hope that we are neither. But it is interesting, and perhaps surprising, to see that both sides in the quarrel over the relationship between beauty and desire feel comfortable appealing to the authority of Plato and via him to the ancient Greeks generally. Scruton finds in Plato "a call to renounce" desire, whereas Nehamas cites the philosopher for the idea that beauty is precisely an inspiration to *erôs*. It is tempting to speculate about who is right—if either is. A closer investigation of Plato's conception of beauty might be expected to shed light at least on the question of his own view and whether it conforms more closely to that of Scruton or Nehamas. And yet, if two major thinkers can disagree so radically about what Plato's view of beauty was, this may not be the most profitable route to take. This is yet another reason to investigate the more general question of what the ancient vocabulary for beauty was, before pronouncing on the attitude of Plato or other Greek thinkers.

We may conclude this chapter by remarking on Nehamas's suggestion, an intimation of which he finds in Plato, that beauty, even that "of lowly objects, can gradually inspire a longing for goodness and truth." To which we might reply: not in and of themselves. Nehamas concedes as much, in the end. "Unlike Plato, I don't believe that the pursuit of beauty leads necessarily to virtue and happiness, and for that reason I find in it an element of ineliminable risk. But, like him," Nehamas adds, "I am convinced that beauty is a spur to creation and sometimes results in its creators becoming beautiful themselves" (133). And sometimes, no doubt, it may result in the reverse. The attempt to identify beauty with the good requires Plato's transcendental metaphysics, which found its way into modern approaches to art, where it merged with other currents deriving from classical antiquity along with newer styles of thought, thereby giving rise to the kinds of problems that we have been pondering.[34] We shall discuss this process in more detail in Chapter 6, but it is now time to turn to the ancient Greeks and what they thought of beauty and its effects.

2

BEAUTY IN GREEK

I. Is There a Greek Word for Beauty? ✐ At the very start of our investigation into Greek ideas about beauty, we face a fundamental and well-known problem: did the ancient Greeks in fact have a concept analogous to our word *beauty*? Serious scholars of the classical world have argued that ancient Greek possessed no word that unambiguously signified "beauty" or "beautiful." The word that is most often translated as "beautiful," and that has been the focus of almost all studies, is the Greek adjective *kalós* (the root appears in the English *calisthenics* and *kaleidoscope*).[1] Now, although *kalós* can mean "beautiful" in particular contexts, it is also applied in the sense of "well wrought" to such items as clothes, armor, and manufactured articles. And it can be used to describe laws, knowledge, and other abstract notions. As the authoritative dictionaries of ancient Greek point out, *kalós* has a range of meanings broad enough to include "good," "of fine quality," and also, in a moral sense, "noble" and "honorable." If one adds the definite article to the (neuter) adjective, producing the phrase *to kalón* or "the beautiful," the sense is equally wide: the standard *Greek-English Lexicon*, edited by Liddell and Scott, indeed defines the phrase as "beauty" but also as "virtue" and "honor" (Liddell and Scott 1940).

Words in common use normally have ample connotations and subdefinitions, as one can see by consulting any major dictionary of English or other modern languages, and just because *kalós* covers a fairly wide semantic field does not in itself imply that the narrower sense of "beauty" was therefore nameless. Classical scholars are, of course, well aware of this. Nevertheless, in a recent issue of the journal *Classical Philology* dedicated to the topic, "Beauty, Harmony, and the Good," Aryeh Kosman, an expert in classical philosophy, affirms that Aristotle's observations concerning *kalós* and its congeners are only puzzling "to the degree that we render *kalon* as 'beautiful' and the *kalon* as 'beauty' or 'the beautiful.'" Kosman offers Aristotle's discussion of courage as an example and notes that when Aristotle writes that "a courageous person endures and acts as he does *kalou heneka*" (citing *Nicomachean Ethics*, 1115b23), translators quite correctly take him to mean that he or she does so "not for the sake of the beautiful, but for the sake of the noble" (Kosman 2010, 344–345). In connection with Plato's dialogue, *Hippias Major*, which is entirely devoted to defining *kalós*, Kosman affirms: "There is a deep history of uncertainty about how properly to translate *kalon*" (346), and he concludes that the ambiguities associated with the term "leave me with the urge, an urge that I will of course resist, to say that the Greeks had no concept of beauty. But this much is right: the concept of beauty is sufficiently different from that of the *kalon* to make the urge understandable." Kosman goes on to note (and this is particularly relevant to our concern with aesthetic beauty) that there are two features of the modern idea of beauty that "are not found in a comparable sense in the notion of the *kalon*: (1) Beauty critically involves the world of Art; (2) Beauty critically involves the world of nature" (351).

In the same issue of *Classical Philology*, Rachel Barney begins her paper by remarking, "How the fine (*kalon*) is related to the good (*agathon*) in Plato's thought is a puzzle" (Barney 2010, 363). Barney's use of the word *fine*, which is perhaps the most common rendering of *kalós* in English today, evades the problem of the connection between *kalón* and beauty, although Barney later wonders why, in that case, the response prompted by the *kalón*, according to Plato, "is *erôs*, not admiration" (375)—a point to which we shall return. Terence Irwin, however, is prepared to see ambiguity, or homonymy, in the meaning of *kalón*. As he puts it, "Aristotle uses *kalon* both to pick out beauty and to pick out moral rightness." But in Irwin's view, ethics concerns moral rightness only, without any suggestion that morality and beauty somehow coincide (Irwin 2010, 382). If one wants to employ a single term to cover all of Aristotle's uses of *kalón*, however, Irwin counsels against using *beautiful* and suggests that *fine* or *admirable* would be better (396). Anton Ford, in his response to Irwin's paper, quotes Aristotle's own definition of *kalón* in the *Rhetoric* (1366a33–34), which Ford translates, "That which is both desirable for its own sake and praiseworthy, or that which pleases because it is good" (Ford 2010, 400). This does sound as though Aristotle is at least associating *kalón* and desire, whatever he might mean by *praiseworthy*. A stricter rendering of Aristotle's words puts even this in doubt, for what Aristotle's text actually says is more like this: "*Kalón* is whatever is choiceworthy [*haireton*] for its own sake and praiseworthy, or that which is good [*agathon*] and pleasing [*hêdu*] because it is good." *Choiceworthy* is an ethical term very common in Aristotle and far from the notion of passionate desire; thus, in the *Nicomachean Ethics* (1097a30–b4), Aristotle explains that we choose happiness for its own sake. Finally, Umberto Eco, in his book *History of Beauty*, written in connection with a museum exhibition of works of art that have been deemed beautiful, states unequivocally, "In fact, Beauty had no autonomous stature in ancient Greece." He adds, "The very word *Kalón*, which only improperly may be translated by the term 'beautiful,' ought to put us on our guard."[2] That a specific term was lacking is not in itself evidence that the Greeks lacked a notion of the beautiful, but it does make it more difficult to isolate just what they thought it was.

There are, to be sure, contrary voices raised in defense of the idea that *kalós* meant precisely "beautiful." Drew Hyland, in his recent book-length study of Plato's conception of beauty, affirms that the word *kalós* "actually resembles the contemporary use of the English 'beauty' in the enormous range of its meaning. To be sure," he notes, "it means 'beauty' in the fairly narrow and standard sense that we have come to call 'aesthetic.' But the Greek especially shades toward the sense of 'nobility' .... In turn, the word can shade into the sense of 'good' in an extra-moral sense, as in 'that's a good idea' or 'you speak well,'" just the way the English word *beautiful* is used today (Hyland 2008, 4–5). Hyland notes that translators of works such as the *Hippias Major* often choose *fine* rather than *beauty* in rendering *kalós*, but he objects that the word thereby "loses the connection to the more obvious cases, as in the *Symposium* and *Phaedrus*, where 'beauty' is clearly the word called for." Hyland concludes by affirming, "Even when the meaning of the word is stretched, I shall translate *to kalon* and its cognates as forms of 'beauty,' occasionally adding 'and noble' when the term is clearly appropriate." But this final concession is telltale: despite a willingness to admit a rather wide semantic stretch, Hyland at least sometimes finds himself obliged to create a hendiadys, that is, the compound expression "beautiful and noble," in order to make sense in English of the way the term *kalós* is employed in Greek. And this raises the question of how one can be sure that, even in what may seem to be "more obvious cases," the term in fact corresponds to the English *beautiful*.

And yet, despite Kosman's and Eco's doubts about whether the very notion of beauty existed in classical Greece (and they are, as I have said, representative of a widely held view), there is in fact a classical Greek word that comes much closer to the modern notion of beauty. Indeed, if *kalón* is too broad in its signification, this other term is rather more narrow in its application than the English *beauty*. The word in question is the noun *kállos*, etymologically related to *kalós* but distinct from *kalós* in its usage. As it happens, there exists no detailed study of the meaning of this term, and yet it is crucial, I believe, to an understanding of how the Greeks conceived of beauty. The primary meaning of *kállos* refers to physical beauty, above all the beauty associated with erotic attraction. Like most fundamental concepts, however, *kállos* evolved and shifted meanings over time, and it was later applied to such things as works of art or rather specific aspects of artworks, as well as to certain kinds of speech. However, it appears not to have been used to describe a painting or poem as such, in the way we speak of a beautiful work of art today. Thus, I believe that art historian Jerome Pollitt overstates the scope of the word when he affirms in his brief treatment of the term in the glossary of *The Ancient View of Greek Art*: "The semantic range of *kállos* is as simple or complex as 'beauty,' 'Schönheit' or any other word denoting the same quality."[3] We shall come to the aesthetic sense of *kállos*, insofar as the term *aesthetic* is applicable at all to ancient ideas about art, in due course. It will be best, however, to proceed methodically, identifying to the extent possible the primary uses of the word and its relation to the adjective *kalós*.

II. Beauty: The Earliest Evidence   We may begin at the beginning. In the *Iliad* of Homer, the gods are said to have granted the hero Bellerophon *kállos* and *ênoreên erateinên*, "desirable manhood" (6.156); the adjective *erateinên* is related to *erôs*, and it is telling, since his host's wife will fall passionately in love with him (it is a Potiphar's wife type tale, and when Bellerophon fails to respond, the host's wife denounces him to her husband).

Enamorment is a characteristic response to *kállos*, and it is crucial to defining the term's role in Greek patterns of thought. Paris too is beautiful: after Aphrodite has whisked him from the battlefield, she tells Helen that "Paris is in your bedroom and your well-turned bed, glowing in his beauty and garments" (*Iliad*, 3.391–392); it was his beauty that caused Helen to run off with him, and the scene of her enamorment is implicitly repeated or reprised here in the *Iliad*. Helen is, of course, the paradigm of human beauty, whether in Homer or later literature. She is the standard by which all women are judged: other women may be described as being most beautiful—apart from Helen (*Iliad*, 9.140 = 9.282). In Euripides's *Helen*, Helen recalls the judgment of Paris concerning the *kállos* of the three goddesses (23), and her own fatal beauty (27; cf. 261, 304; Isocrates, *Helen*, 16, 58–60). When Agamemnon tries to woo Achilles back into battle by offering him a king's ransom worth of gifts, he includes seven women seized when he captured Lesbos, "who exceeded the tribes of women in *kállos*" (9.130 = 9.272; cf. 13.431–432, on the exceptional *kállos* of Hippodameia, the wife of the Trojan Alcathoos); Achilles, in turn, rejects marriage with a daughter of Agamemnon, even if she should rival golden Aphrodite in beauty (*Iliad*, 9.388–389)— Aphrodite is, of course, the epitome of beauty (the Hellenistic poet Theocritus describes Aphrodite as excelling all the goddesses in beauty, 17.45). In a touching scene in the *Odyssey*, Athena inspires Penelope to face the suitors in her house, and her nurse, Eurynome, urges her mistress to anoint her face and wash away her tears, so that she may appear more attractive. Penelope protests that she lost all her glow (*aglaíê*, 18.180) the day that Odysseus departed, but as she sleeps, Athena cleanses her fine features (*kalá prosôpata*) with ambrosial *kállos* (18.192–193) and renders her taller, stouter, and whiter than ivory (we shall return shortly the question of what the gift of *kállos* might have added to Penelope's already *kalá* countenance). Also in the *Odyssey*, the young companions of Nausicaa, the princess who meets Odysseus when he washes up on the shore of the Phaeacians, possess beauty granted by the Graces (6.18), whereas Nausicaa herself derives her *kállos* from the gods (8.457). Nausicaa is a potential bride (she has gone to the beach to wash her wedding garments), and her beauty underscores her desirability. So too, we are told that Neleus married Chloris because of her beauty (11.281–282). And indeed male *kállos* too is associated with youth in the Homeric epics. When Athena bathes Odysseus in *kállos* in the *Odyssey*, she also rejuvenates him, turning his hair dark as hyacinths (6.237; cf. 23.156), thereby making him attractive first to Nausicaa and later to Penelope. In the Homeric *Hymn to Aphrodite*, Aphrodite falls in love with Anchises, who has his beauty from the gods (5.77), whereas she herself possesses "immortal beauty" (174). Zeus, for his part, seized Ganymede because of his *kállos* (203); so too in the *Iliad* (20.232–235), Ganymede is described as the most beautiful or *kallistos* (superlative of *kalós*), placed among the gods on account of his beauty (*kállos*). The goddess Dawn, in turn, seized the youth Clitus because of his *kállos* (*Odyssey*, 15.250–251). In a passage to which we shall return later, Penelope affirms that Telemachus has now reached maturity, or at any rate adolescence (*hêbês metron hikaneis*, 18.217), and anyone can perceive his stature and *kállos* (219), though he seems not to have his wits about him.

The contrast between the noun and the adjective emerges clearly in a poem ascribed to Theocritus (23.32), in which the poet states the commonplace notion that "a boy's beauty [*kállos*] is a fine thing [*kalón*], but it endures a short while."[4] The epigrammatic observation would make no sense if the noun and adjective bore the same meaning. A similar distinction is apparent in 1 Esdras 4:18 in the Septuagint (there is no equivalent to 1

Esdras in the Hebrew Bible). In the Revised Standard Version
(RSV), the verse is translated: "If men gather gold and silver or any
other beautiful thing [*pan pragma hôraion*], and then see a woman
lovely in appearance [*kalên tôi eidei*] and beauty [*tôi kállei*]. . . ."
The expression "lovely in beauty" is redundant, and it is better
to take *kalên* in the sense of "outstanding" and render the phrase:
"excellent in appearance and in beauty." To take an example from
Christian literature, Clement of Alexandria reproaches Hadrian
for deifying his beloved Antinous and exclaims, "*Kállos* is shameful
when it has been shriveled by violence. . . Keep it pure, so that
it may be *kalón*," that is, "honorable," the opposite of shameful
(*aiskhrón*; Clement adds the he will venerate the boy's beauty when
it is "a true archetype of noble things [*alêthinon arkhetupon esti tôn
kalôn*]," *Protrepticus*, 4.49.2).

I may cite here a slightly more technical illustration of the
distinction between the adjective *kalós* and the noun *kállos*: in the
Homeric Catalogue of Ships, the obscure hero Nireus is described
as "the most beautiful [*kallistos*] man who came beneath Ilium
of all the Danaans after the blameless son of Peleus. But he was
weak, and a small group followed him" (*Iliad*, 2.671–675; for his
beauty, cf. Euripides, *Iphigenia in Aulis*, 204–205, etc.). *Kallistos*
is, as we have noted, the superlative form of the adjective *kalós*,
but here it evidently indicates Nireus's physical beauty rather than
his nobility of birth or character. So it was understood by later
commentators. The *Etymologicum Magnum* (a Byzantine lexicon)
reports: "*Kalliôn* and *kallistos*: not from *kalós*, but rather from
kállos. Both the spelling and the sense make this clear: the spelling,
since *kalós* is written with one lambda, *kállos* with two; the sense,
since the poet [i.e., Homer] usually applies *kalós* to manliness,
just as, on the contrary, he applies *kakón* [i.e., "bad"] to weakness.
The poet knows that Nireus is weak, but he nevertheless says
of him, " 'Nireus, who was the *kallistos* man who came beneath

Ilium.'" There is no basis to the argument that the comparative and superlative forms are derived specifically from the noun *kállos*, but the passage does show that whoever wrote this comment perceived that *kállos* generally indicated physical beauty and that the adjective *kalós* had a far wider range of meanings and most often connoted moral excellence or courage when applied to adult men. (Section III of Chapter 3 addresses why, if this is the case, the great warrior Achilles, "best of the Achaeans," is mentioned here as the handsomest or most beautiful of all the Greeks.)

But if *kallistos* means "most beautiful" and is in fact the superlative of *kalós* and not derived from the noun *kállos*, then the bare or positive form of the adjective can signify "beautiful." We have observed that this is the case, but I argue it is so because the basic sense of *fine* or *excellent*, when applied to physical appearance, naturally suggests the idea of beauty. To say in English that a woman looks "fine" can mean that she is attractive, but it may also indicate that she is healthy (she may have been ill before but seems well now) or well (or appropriately) dressed.[5] The context is what discriminates among the several senses of the term. Thus, we have seen that the noun *kállos* is ascribed to Paris, with whom Helen fell in love, and to only two other men in the *Iliad*: Bellerophon (also the object of a woman's passion) and the young Ganymede, whom Zeus carried off to Olympus. When Hector censures his half-brother for being a laggard in battle, he singles out his beauty and labels him "best in looks" rather than best in combat (the true test of a noble warrior), and also "mad for women" (*Duspari eidos aristos gunaimanes*, 3.39), which suggests a kind of sexiness. A few lines later, Hector reverts to Paris's handsome appearance (*kalón eidos*, 3.44–45); Paris looks good, and this is not necessarily a defect, but his appearance belies his sluggishness as a fighter. The sense is different when Priam, gazing out from the wall of Troy, asks Helen about the identity of a particularly impressive hero on the Greek side. Who, he asks, is that mighty fellow (*pelôrios*, applied to Achilles, Ajax, and Hector, as well as to Ares), that fine (*eu*) and large (*megas*) man, and "*kalós* such as I've never yet seen with these eyes?" (3.166–169). He is referring to Agamemnon, and there is surely no implication here of sexual allure but rather of an imposing figure who looks every bit the leader and general. Toward the end of the *Iliad*, when the Trojan Lycaon kneels before Achilles and begs for his life, Achilles replies, "Don't you see how *kalós* and big (*megas*) I am?" (21.108). He adds that, although he was born of a noble father and a divine mother, he too will die; Lycaon, then, ought also to be resigned to his fate. Again, Achilles is hardly pointing to his beauty in the ordinary sense of the word, though he is clearly referring to his physical appearance (the verb *see* guarantees this), and he is certainly not comparing himself to Paris in this regard. Presumably, he is pointing out that even a warrior of his stature will be slain, and so there is nothing surprising about this fate befalling a lesser fighter such as Lycaon. I expect that sentimental notions about death not sparing beauty are foreign to Achilles's thoughts at this stage. At any rate, the noun *kállos* is never applied to Achilles or Agamemnon in the poem, nor to deities other than Aphrodite; yet Ares and Athena appear dressed in golden garments, *kalós* (in the dual: *kalô*) and large (*megas*), in a scene on Achilles's shield (18.518).

The case is different, perhaps, with women, who might be prized for their beauty as well as their good sense or talent at weaving and other feminine occupations. But even here caution is advisable. Helen recognizes that the woman who commands her to join her husband Paris in their bedroom is Aphrodite when she perceives her supremely lovely (*perikallês*) neck (3.396), along with her breast that excites desire (*himeroenta*) and flashing eyes (*perikallês* is applied to the woman Eeriboia at 5.389, and Achilles uses it in reference to Briseis at 16.83). And yet, the same word (*perikallês*) is used of Paris's house (3.421 and 6.313–314), which is perhaps understandable by association with its owner, but it also describes Priam's house (6.242). It is applied as well to Apollo's lyre (1.603), Priam's chariot (3.262; cf. 4.486, 17.436), a tree (5.693), weapons (6.321), an altar (8.238, 249), a *temenos* or temple space (9.578), a cup (11.632, 12.234), a cauldron (23.897) that Achilles grants Agamemnon as a prize, and the robes (24.229) selected by Priam as part of the ransom for Hector's body. Nothing prevents us from regarding all these items as beautiful, but perhaps *splendid* or *exquisite* better fits the variety of objects so designated.

The simple *kalós* has an equally wide range of applications. The nymph Thetis takes her seat on a throne that is "chased in silver, *kalós*, and intricately wrought" (*daidaleos*, 18.388); so too, *kalós* is combined with *daidaleos* in the description of Achilles's gleaming shield (19.379–380; again at 22.314–315, where the horsehair crest of his helmet is also *kalaí*). Hector's infant son Astyanax is compared to a *kalós* star (6.400–401). In the scene where she is preparing to seduce Zeus, Hera is said to anoint her *kalós* skin (*khroa*, 14.175). This sounds sexy, perhaps, but the same expression is used of the skin of a wounded warrior (5.354, 5.858). Hera's veil is also so described (14.184–185), and so too her hair, which is "bright, *kalós,* and ambrosial" (*phaeinoi kaloi ambrosioi*, 14.177). A suggestion of "glinting" or "luminous" seems common to these instances.[6] The superlative, likewise, is applied to the water of a river (*kalliston hudôr*, 21.157–158), the evening star (22.317–318), and the robe that Hecabe picks out to give to Athena when she supplicates her favor against the besieging Greeks (6.294). *Kalliston* is also employed in reference to a large mixing bowl or *krêtêr* in the *Odyssey* (4.613–614). This last is a particularly interesting instance because such a bowl, made of silver, is the only object—apart from human beings—to which the noun *kállos* is applied in the Homeric epics (*Iliad*, 23.742). This bowl, which Achilles offers as a prize to the swiftest runner, is said to exceed all others in beauty and is given a special history to match: it was made by highly skilled (*poludaidaloi*, 743) Sidonian artisans, then carried overseas by Phoenician sailors who presented it as a gift to Thoas, whence it was given to Patroclus as ransom for Priam's son Lycaon (before he met his fate at Achilles's hands). We shall return to a consideration of this evidently highly desirable artifact.

In compound words, the root *kall-* is combined with stems meaning "hair," "cheeks," and "ankles" (*kallisphuros*), which are regularly used for women (e.g., 1.143, 310, 369 of Chryseis; 1.184, 323, 346 of Briseis; 6.298, 6.302 of Theano). Yet, when Menelaus is wounded, his thighs are said to be *euphuees* ("well formed") and his ankles (*sphura*) are *kalá* (4.146–147). Greece is *kalligunaix*, "with fair women" (2.683; so too of Achaea at 3.375, 3.258), but a river's flow may be said to be *kallirhoos*, "fair-flowing" (2.752).[7]

From the above survey, it appears that in the Homeric poems, at least, the noun *kállos* is used primarily for human beauty, generally with the implication of physical attractiveness, whereas the range of the adjective *kalós* is far wider. *Kalós* most often (but not invariably) refers to the visual appearance of things and seems to attach particularly to things that emit a kind of radiance. Two Greek warriors—the most important figures in the *Iliad*, Agamemnon and Achilles—are singled out as being especially *kalós*, whereas among males *kállos* is ascribed to good-looking youths such as Ganymede, Clitus (the beloved of Dawn), and Telemachus on the cusp of manhood, or to adults like Paris and Bellerophon, who are noted for their seductive effect on women. It is likewise applied to a rejuvenated Odysseus, after Athena intervenes to enhance his appeal to Nausicaa and Penelope.

The Byzantine lexicographer (or his source) who perceived a distinction between the application of *kállos* and *kalós* in respect to warriors—the former suggesting a feeble kind of prettiness, the latter heroic courage—was not entirely off the mark. For women too, *kállos* is the more specific term, particularly associated with Helen and Aphrodite (and with Penelope, thanks again to Athena's devices), whereas the adjective does not necessarily intimate allure (though it may) so much as a fine or shapely look, whether of hair and ankles (even those of Menelaus) or overall appearance, like the young and presumably marriageable Trojan girls at their washing wells, as dazzling as the stones on which they pound the clothes. For the rest, *kalós* can be said of anything that is fine or good-looking, from chariots and trees to shields and bread baskets, and by extension to deeds and the sound of a voice.

III. Beauty in Archaic Poetry   The subsequent history of the two terms follows in the tracks of the Homeric usage while developing some nuances in new directions. Broadly speaking, *kállos* comes more and more to be contrasted with virtue, just as the adjective *kalós* takes on a more distinctly moral flavor, though never losing its wider application to all things fine or brilliant. But the process is gradual, and the shift in significance of *kalós* becomes truly notable only in the literature of the fifth century BC and beyond. In Hesiod, for example, the god Eros is described as *kallistos* (*Theogony*, 120)— surely in the sense of beautiful and inspiring desire. The bare *kalós* is also associated with desirability (cf. *himeroentas, Theogony*, 8, of the chorus of the Muses; also used of items such as voices and houses), and indeed the term is applied to Aphrodite at the moment of her birth, though it is paired with *aidoiê* or "modest" (they are contrasting attributes). So too Himeros, that is, Desire personified, is qualified as *kalós* (*Theogony*, 201). Rivers flow prettily and women

have pretty cheeks, hair, or ankles (the same compound words with the stem *kall-* found in the Homeric epics); but women's appearance in particular is associated with sex and reproduction (e.g., *Theogony*, 238; Zeus experiences *erôs* for Mnemosyne of the fair hair [*kallikomoio*, 915]).[8] Pandora is described as a *kalón kakon anti agathoio* (*Theogony*, 585), a somewhat paradoxical expression meaning "a pretty (or fine) evil rather than a good." *Kalós* here clearly suggests a superficial attractiveness, but at the same time the juxtaposition with *kakón* activates the oxymoron "a good bad thing." So too, in the *Works and Days*, Pandora possesses "a *kalón* and desirable form" (*kalón eidos epêraton*, 63). In this case, the context makes the sense of the adjective clear. The Graces emit desire (*erôs*) from their eyes, and their glance is *kalón* (adverbial, 910–911). In a fragment of the *Oidopodeia*, the sphinx is said to have slain the boy (*pais*) Haimon, who is *kallistos* and "most desirable" (*himeroestatos*, fr. 1.1).

In the Homeric *Hymns*, which are on the whole later compositions than the poems ascribed to Homer and Hesiod, we find *kalós* used for *anthea* (flowers) in the *Hymn to Demeter* (6); it is also used for the pretty toy that seduces Persephone (11; same formula in the *Hymn to Hermes*, 32) and to describe sacrifices (*hiera*, 29; cf. *Hymn to Apollo*, 274; *Hymn to Aphrodite*, 101). When Demeter sheds her disguise as an old woman, her *kállos* blossoms around her (276); she is not a sexy goddess like Aphrodite, of course, but the contrast with her previously aged appearance highlights her divine beauty. When Demeter's eyes are said to be *kalá* (387), we may suppose that they are bright; Persephone herself is *perikallês* (405, 493), as befits a maiden pretty enough to arouse the passion of Hades.[9] In the *Hymn to Aphrodite*, we find *kalós* used for Aphrodite's clothing or *heimata* (64, 171), and for a mountain, groves, and bright golden jewelry that is compared to the moon (59). Overall, *kalós* retains a close connection with the visible and seems to hover between the notion of "excellent of its kind" and "visually attractive," often with a sense of brightness.[10]

When we come to the lyric, elegiac, and iambic poets, we begin to see some nuanced distinctions in usage. Sappho, in a well-known fragment (16), declares that what people take to be *kalliston* varies; in her view, she explains, it is whatever one is passionate about (*eratai*). She uses Helen, who far surpassed other human beings in *kállos* (16.7), as an example that confirms this proposition. Here, the connection between beauty and desire is manifest. Elsewhere, Sappho employs *kalós* of the moon (fr. 34.1) and *kallistos* of stars (104b1), where brightness would appear to be a relevant feature. Again, Sappho speaks of a girl as *kalê* (fr. 132): she has a figure (*morphê*) comparable to golden flowers, and she would not exchange her for all of Lydia or lovable— something; the word modified by *erannan* has fallen out. One two-line fragment (50) is illuminating though tantalizing for its poor state of preservation:

> ὁ μὲν γὰρ κάλος ὄσσον ἴδην πέλεται <κάλος>,
> ὁ δὲ κἄγαθος αὔτικα καὶ κάλος ἔσσεται.

> He who is *kalós* is <*kalós*> just to see,
> He who is also good will straightway be *kalós* as well.

The contrast in the first line is between *kalós* in the sense of "physically handsome" and *kalós* in the sense of "fine" or "good," assuming that the supplement is correct (others have been proposed). In the second verse, a good man will invariably seem fine, perhaps even attractive (cf. fr. 137, where Sappho speaks of a desire [*himeros*] for *esla* [good things] and *kalá*).

Archilochus, famous for his fierce invective, speaks of a *kalê* maiden who has a "faultless appearance [*eidos*]" and a "*kalón* body"

(196A).[11] Mimnermus (fr. 3), in his melancholy way, observes that the very one who was *kallistos* loses honor when the bloom of youth (*hôra*) has passed; that bloom is "pleasurable [*terpnon*] and *kalón*" (fr. 5) but passes quickly (fr. 26 speaks of women as *kalaí*). In his famous poem comparing women to various animals, Semonides notes how one husband boasts that no woman is either better (*lôïon*) or *kalliôn* than his wife (7.30–31); presumably, the latter term suggests "prettier," though it is possible that it simply repeats the idea of "better." The weasel-like lady (*ek galês*), in turn, has nothing *kalón* or *epimeron* (7.51), that is, "desirable." Again, the two terms can be taken either as equivalent or contrasted—a sign of the difficulty of deciphering the significance of *kalós* where the context does not disambiguate it. A little later, a woman is described as a *kalón theama* (sight) to others (7.67), and here the reference is clearly to her physical appearance. But when the good wife is said to have a *kalón* and distinguished (*onomakluton*) *genos* (lineage, 7.87), the primary sense must be something like "noble." Anacreon, for his part, speaks of hymns that are *kalá* (fr. 11b4–5; cf. 62.1.5 of song, fr. 41 of a lyre) and insists that what is just is *kalón* to the god Eros (fr. 57b): Anacreon is exploiting the two senses of *kalós* in a playful twist on the usual view that beauty inspires *erôs*.

The use of *kalós* in Simonides, famous for his historical and eulogistic verses, is more sober. Thus, a quotation from Homer is said to be *kalliston* (8.1); the term is applied to a witness (11.1); and the fate (*potmos*) of those who died in Thermopylae is described as *kalós* (26.1.2).[12] In a particularly interesting illustration, Simonides writes, "This is the *kalón* statue of *kalós* Milo, who once won seven times at Pisa [i.e., at the Olympic games] and never fell to his knees" (Μίλωνος τόδ᾽ ἄγαλμα καλοῦ καλόν, ὅς ποτε Πίσῃ / ἑπτάκι νικήσας ἐς γόνατ᾽ οὐκ ἔπεσεν, 16.24). The boy himself is no doubt handsome, but what of the statue? Is it handsome too, simply because the subject it portrays is so—in the spirit of Arthur Danto's view of art, according to which a painting such as Matisse's *Blue Nude* cannot be called beautiful just because the figure it depicts is not so, by any ordinary standard of human attractiveness (see Chapter 1)? I am inclined to think that this application of *kalón* signifies rather that the statue is a good or faithful representation of Milo, a sense of the word that is common, as we shall see, in reference to works of art.

The lyric poet Ibycus concludes a poem in praise of the greatest Greek and Trojan warriors by mentioning the most handsome of them, and he affirms that in respect to their "attractive figures" (*eroessan morphan*), both sides were equal. He adds that Polycrates too will have immortal fame (*kleos*) for his heroic accomplishments, together with *kállos* (1a46). Beauty is the complement to noble deeds, and lucky is the man (as Theognis says) who possesses both.

It will come as no surprise that in the political elegies of Solon, *kalós* assumes a clearly moral significance, modifying deeds (*erga*, fr. 13.21) and—if the supplement is correct—fine thoughts (<*kalá*> *noein*, fr. 9.6). The term is applied also to the power (*menos*) of the sun (fr. 13.24), in which case brightness is once more the relevant feature. Most saliently, Solon observes that a coward may seem to be a good man (*agathos*), but one who is *kalós* does not necessarily have a pleasing shape (*morphên khariessan*, 13.39–40); here character and appearance are sharply contrasted. Tyrtaeus recommends speaking *kalá* and doing *dikaia*, that is, things that are just (fr.4.7); the juxtaposition of the two words is telling. So too, it is *kalón* to die among the foremost in battle (fr. 10.1; cf. Alcaeus, fr. 400). Elsewhere, Tyrtaeus affirms that he is unimpressed by a man who is "more handsome in figure [*phuên khariesteros*, 5] than Tithonus," with whom the Dawn fell in love for his beauty, for the best and finest prize (*aethlon . . . ariston kalliston te*) for a young man is *aretê* (virtue, fr. 12.13–14). When Tyrtaeus states that a young man who has the bright bloom of lovable youth (*eratê hêbê*) and is the object of men's gazes and *eratos* (desirable) to women, is *kalós* when he has fallen in the forefront of battle (10.26–30), the meaning may be that "he is lovely yet" (as Martin West translates the verse, 24). But there may also be an implicit contrast between the youth's allure while alive and his noble appearance even in death: it is hard to imagine that the terms *eratos* and *kalós* could have been reversed.[13]

Theognis composed a series of poems in elegiac couplets in the sixth century BC, but the collection that has come down under his name contains verses written over a century or more, though in the style of the original compositions. They were evidently intended to be recited at symposia or other gatherings and are principally educative in nature. Theognis adopts the pose of teacher to a young man, after the idealized pattern of the pederastic relationship. He describes Apollo as *kallistos* (1.7) for his acknowledged beauty or more likely for his general excellence, especially in connection with song (cf. 1.16–17, where *kalós* is applied to poetry [*epos*], with the qualification that only the *kalón* is *philon*, that is, dear or lovable). So too, young men who are *eratoi*, that is, lovable or desirable, sing "noble songs" (*kalá*, 1.242–244). Theognis affirms that what is most just is *kalliston*, and health is best (*lôiston*, 1.255): the two terms are pretty much indistinguishable in this context.[14] A mare that is *kalê* protests at carrying a thoroughly base rider (*kakiston*, 257–258); again, the contrast is moral, or at least concerns value.[15] Theognis affirms that a good teacher is one who knows "what is good and noble" (*esthla kai kalá*, 652). Elsewhere, a man's *thumos* (roughly "heart" or "guts") tells him that he is not the only one who feels *erôs* (verb: *erâis*) for *ta kalá* (695–696). There seems to be a nice fusion here of the two aspects of *kalós*: the beauty that inspires erotic passion and the noble achievements that are the proper objects of a decent man's ambition (so too, Pindar will speak of passionate love [verb *eramai*] for *kalá*, clearly in sense of "fine," *Pythians*, 11.50). In later verses in Book 1 of the *Theognidea*, and in many of the poems in the second, shorter book, *kalós* is found in more openly erotic contexts, for example, in reference to the bloom (*kalón anthos*, 994) of a boy or the description, in a Mimnermus-type lament over old age, of youth as pleasurable (*terpnon*) and *kalón*, but short lived (1017–1022). More explicitly, a boy is described as *kalós* in regard to his figure (*tên morphên*, 2.1259), and that lover is called happy who can sleep with a *kalós* boy (2.1336; cf. 2.1350, where a man is conquered by *erôs* for a *kalós* boy; but at 2.1369, *erôs* for a boy is called *kalós*, that is, "good") in contrast to *erôs* for a woman, whose love is fickle. Ploutos, Wealth personified, is dubbed *kalliste* and *himeroestate* (vocatives), the most desirable of all the gods (1117), and the same formula is applied to a boy (2.1365): both passions are implicitly at odds with the aspiration to virtue.[16] In the entire corpus, the noun *kállos* appears only once, when Theognis affirms that not everyone possess both virtue (*aretê*) and *kállos*; fortunate (*olbios*) indeed is he who has both (933–934). The contrast or complementarity between virtue and physical beauty is clear.[17]

It is evident, then, that the adjective *kalós* continues to mean "fine," "noble," or "good" in a wide variety of situations, but may also refer to the physical appearance of things, particularly human beings, for whom the sense is often (though not invariably) erotically "attractive." This is the case when the reference is to a person's body or figure, or when the context is clearly amorous. The noun *kállos*, on the contrary, is far more restricted in its application and most often refers specifically to visible beauty, although it may, by extension or analogy, be applied to things that are not perceived directly by the eyes. Since beauty is not always coordinate with virtue, as Tyrtaeus, Theognis, and other archaic poets point out—indeed, the two qualities may on occasion be seen as incompatible—there is often a contrast between *kállos* on the one hand and deeds or personal traits that are described as *kalá*. I shall illustrate some of the uses of the two terms in later literature in a more cursory fashion and then look more closely at *kállos*, which captures more specifically the way the Greeks thought of beauty and its effects.

IV. The Classical Period It is perhaps remarkable that the word *kállos* does not appear in what survives of Pindar's poetry, although there are numerous uses of the adjective *kalós*. Since the excellent *Lexicon to Pindar* prepared by William Slater (1969) sorts out the various uses, there is no need to be exhaustive here, and it will suffice to pick out examples that are informative about Pindar's sense of the beautiful. Slater subdivides the meanings of *kalós* under various headings, including (1) "of actions, noble, honourable"; (2) "beautiful"; (2a) "of living things, handsome" (eight instances); (2b) "of things" (three instances); (3) substantival uses, under which come (3a) "work of beauty" (one example); (3bI) "blessings"; (3bII) "noble actions, achievements"; (3bIII) "what is fine, good to hear, see"; and (3bIV), "in wider sense, good, things noble." When Pindar declares in *Olympians* 1.84 that old age has no share of *kalá*, he means good or fine things, not beautiful ones.[18] When applied to trees (*Olympians*, 3.23), the idea of appearance is perhaps uppermost, as when Pindar affirms that an ape is *kalós* to children (*Pythians*, 2.72–73: perhaps "cute"?). The sense of physically attractive is clear when Pindar declares that Timosthenes was *kalós* to look at and in deeds (*ergon*) did not put his appearance or *eidos* to shame (*Olympians*, 8.19). Similarly, Pindar praises a lad who is *kalós* and whose deeds accord with his appearance (*morphê, Nemeans*, 3.20). There is a play on both connotations when a youthful (*hôraios*) and *kalós* athlete is praised for achieving things that are *kallista* (*Olympians*, 9.94). A boy—the son of Archestratus—who excites desire (*eratos*) is *kalós* in appearance (*ideâi, Olympians*, 10.103), and as though to remove any doubt about the meaning of the word, Pindar compares this youth to Ganymede when he was rescued from death by the power of Aphrodite.[19] Finally, Pindar asserts that in the old days, a youth who was *kalós* could gain the pleasurable harvest of Aphrodite (*Isthmians*, 2.4).

The noun *kállos* appears in the tragedies of Aeschylus twice. The first occurrence is in *Persians* (185), in connection with Atossa's vision of two tall women, faultless in *kállos* and dressed in Doric and Persian garb; they are symbolic of the two sides in the great conflict, and their beauty is presumably a sign of their divinity or at least supernatural status. The second is found in *Agamemnon* and is used in the plural of the embroidered carpet on which Agamemnon hesitates to tread (*en poikilois . . . kállesin*, 923), since to do so is to presume beyond what is right for a mortal. We have already seen in Homer that *kállos* can refer to an attractive artifact, and we may imagine that the term here suggests that it is inviting to step on, despite Agamemnon's doubts.[20] The adjective *kalós* most often bears the sense of "good" or "favorable" (cf. Linwood 1843, s.v.). For example, Aegisthus declares that death would be *kalón*, now that he has seen Agamemnon dead (*Agamemnon*, 1610).[21] The meaning is perhaps uncertain when Clytemnestra speaks of seeing a *kalliston* day after a storm (*Agamemnon*, 900)—a fine clear day seems to be the idea, with an implicit suggestion of brightness. In the same play, the chorus describe Artemis as *kalê* (or rather, in the Doric dialect, *kalâ*, 140) in a passage in which they are at pains to emphasize her tender concern for the young of every animal. The reference in this context is more likely, I should think, to her nobility or kindness than to her physical attractiveness.[22]

The noun *kállos* appears three times in the tragedies of Sophocles, always in connection with physical attractiveness. In *Women of Trachis*, Dejanira worries that her beauty may be a source of pain to her, as Hercules and the river-god Achelous fight to possess her (25). Later, Dejanira feels pity for Iole, the princess whom Hercules brought back as concubine after laying waste her city, and observes that "her beauty destroyed her life" (465). In an extraordinary phrase in *Oedipus the King*, Oedipus protests against the "beauty festering with foulness" (*kállos kakôn hupoulon*, 1396) that his foster parents raised, as he is now revealed as foul himself and of foul descent. Here *kállos* refers to his outward appearance, handsome and regal in contrast to the dark secret of his birth and destiny. The adjective *kalós* retains its wide application. For example, the law that children obey their fathers is dubbed *kalliston* (*Trachiniae*, 1171–1172; cf. 450 of knowledge, 667 of hope, etc.); Ajax can declare that he hated when it was *kalón* to hate (*Ajax*, 1347). The only occurrence of *kalós* in the sense of "physically attractive" in the tragedies is in *Oedipus at Colonus*, where Oedipus declares to Theseus that, despite his decrepit appearance, he bears a gift that is better than good looks (*kalê morphê*, 578); the term *morphê* ("shape" or "figure") specifies the sense of "excellent" that *kalós* conveys.[23]

We may pause from tragedy and, before examining Euripides's usage, glance at the historians Herodotus and Thucydides. The noun *kállos* is rare in both, occurring only a few times in Herodotus and once in Thucydides (3.17), in a corrupt passage that does not construe. In one Herodotean passage, it is employed in reference to a certain Philip from the city of Croton, an Olympic victor and the handsomest (*kallistos*) man of his time; indeed, it was on account of his unique *kállos* that the Egestans established a hero cult in his honor (5.47). In a second passage, the word describes a plane tree that Xerxes came upon as he was passing through Lydia en route to Greece, and which, on account of its beauty, he draped in gold and appointed a caretaker always to look after it (7.31). Herodotus offers what might seem like rare praise for Xerxes, when he affirms that "of all the tens of thousands of men who accompanied him on the expedition, for beauty and stature none was more worthy than Xerxes himself to hold this power," that is, of providing food and drink for the innumerable soldiers and camp followers (7.187). This is surely one of Herodotus's subtly ironic commentaries on the Persian king, given the general tension between *kállos* and masculinity in Greek thought, although some commentators—unconscious of this usage—have taken it as a sincere tribute. Thus, Reginald Walter Macan writes:

> A remarkable testimony and homage to Xerxes, at least as far as externals went, "every inch a king." Nor is it likely that Hdt. here means that in mind or character . . . Xerxes was unworthy his position . . . Xerxes looked the part he played, a tall and handsome man . . . There were probably, however, taller men in the army . . . , but Xerxes looked the god . . . This remark belongs to the more favourable strain of tradition in regard to Xerxes, but it does not prevent Hdt. from making game of him before and afterwards. (1908, ad loc.)

The same phrase, "on account of his stature and beauty" (9.25), is employed later in reference to Masistius, the leader of the cavalry under Mardonius, whom the Athenians succeeded in slaying despite his concealed golden armor (for the Persians' regard for height, see also 7.117). When they retrieved his body after a fierce fight in the Homeric manner, the Greeks gathered to wonder at it, "a worthy sight" (*theês axios*), according to Herodotus.[24] Once again, it is a Persian—and one most favored, after Mardonius himself, by Xerxes—who is recorded as outstanding in *kállos*. After the battle at Plataea, an Aeginetan approaches the Spartan general Pausanias with a proposal Herodotus labels as most unholy, namely that Pausanias augment his honor by mutilating the body of Mardonius. The Aeginetan begins by flattering Pausanias for "having performed a deed excelling in greatness and beauty" (9.78)—a word pairing we have seen twice now. There is one final appearance of the phrase toward the end of the *Histories* (9.96), where it is applied to Tigranes, the satrap, "excelling the Persians in stature and beauty," who had been left in charge of sixty thousand troops in Mycale on the Ionian coast at the order of Xerxes.[25] We may note too that the Athenians, in their passionate speech explaining why they would never desert the cause of Greece by making a treaty with the Persians, declare that there is no land "so greatly excelling in beauty and virtue [*aretê*]" (8.144) that they would barter it for the freedom of Hellas.[26]

Are the Greeks, then, less handsome than the Persians (apart perhaps from the extraordinary Philip mentioned above, whose beauty earned him a cult complete with sacrifices)? Callicrates, who was slain while attending a sacrifice, is described as *kallistos* of all the Greeks (9.72), but this term, as we have observed, is ambiguous and can mean either "most beautiful" or "most noble."[27] The Aethiopians, according to Herodotus, "are said to be the tallest and *kallistoi* of all human beings" (3.20; cf. 3.114, where they are said also to be the most long lived), and their customs differ from those of other people. In particular, Herodotus reports, they choose as their king the one among them they judge

to be tallest "and to possess strength in proportion to his stature."
After the Persians captured a Greek ship, they selected the
handsomest man on board (*kalisteuonta*, 7.180) and slit his throat
as a sacrifice, thinking it a lucky omen that the first of the Greeks
they caught was also *kallistos*.[28] Perhaps most telling, however, is
the stele that Darius himself erected when he reached the Tearus,
which those who dwell round it call "the best [*ariston*] of rivers"
(4.90). Darius's inscription reads: "The sources of the river Tearus
provide the best and *kalliston* water of all rivers, and the best
and *kallistos* of all men arrived there, leading an army against the
Scythians, Darius son of Hystaspes, king of the Persians and of the
entire continent" (4.91). Here, Herodotus is likely suggesting a
certain feminine quality in the Great King, evident in his vanity
and his concern with his appearance. For *kallistos* can certainly
connote erotic attractiveness: Candaules, who was "in love with
his own wife" (1.8), regarded her as *kallistê* of all women, and the
sense here is surely "sexiest." He went on to treat her as men were
wont to treat courtesans rather than spouses, by insisting—with
fatal consequences to himself—that his spearbearer Gyges view
her naked. The Spartan king Ariston was in love with the wife of
a friend (as Herodotus puts it, "*erôs* chafed him," 6.62) who was
"by far the *kallistê* of all women in Sparta" (6.61), though she
had been born exceptionally ugly. But her nurse brought her to
the temple of Helen (who was worshipped as a deity in Sparta),
praying that her disfigurement (*dusmorphiê*) be removed, and
her wish was granted: one day, as she left the temple, she met a
woman—clearly a stand-in for Helen herself—who stroked the
child's head and transformed her appearance. Herodotus seems
to be indicating a pronounced concern for physical appearance
among non-Greeks, and the Persians in particular, with a likely
suggestion of effeminacy. Although the adjective *kalós*, especially
in the superlative, may not in itself decisively indicate the sense

of a given reference, ascriptions of the more marked term *kállos*, which are clearly skewed toward non-Greeks, are revealing of Herodotean ideology. At the same time, they further confirm the special or more narrow sense of the noun in classical Greek.

I have mentioned that there is no secure example of *kállos* in Thucydides; insofar as his use of *kalós* is concerned, it tends naturally to the moral or evaluative sense, often in the predicative.[29] *Kalós* is paired with *khrêsimon* ("useful," 2.64.6) and *dikaion* ("just," 7.59.2; cf. 4.118; cf. the pairing of *to kalón* and *hê dike* at Euripides, *Orestes*, 417), and contrasted with *aiskhron* ("shameful," 5.107.1; cf. Euripides, *Hecuba*, 602). So too the superlative is paired with *arista* ("best," 1.129; cf. Aristophanes, *Thesmophoriazusae*, 300–301) and *asphalestaton* ("safest," 2.11). In his funeral oration, Pericles attaches it to the place reserved for the common burial ground for those who fell in battle (2.34), the noble danger for which they risked their lives (2.42), and the sacrifice that they made for the common good (2.42). It is used of reputation (*onoma*, 4.87; *doxa*, 5.9), of an army (5.60), and of a great deed or achievement (*ergon*, 6.33).

The tragedies of Euripides are particularly illuminating for the uses of the adjective *kalós* and the noun *kállos*. In the satyr play, *Cyclops*, the adjective modifies the flow of wine (148), its odor (153), and the cup and feast in which it features (399). When the Cyclops, in return for the wine, promises to eat Odysseus last of all, Silenus calls this a *kalón* prize (551; cf. *Heraclidae*, 297). He then excuses his sipping the wine intended for the Cyclops by claiming that the wine kissed him because he is so good-looking (*kalón blepô*, 553). When the Cyclops protests that Silenus likes (*philei*) the wine, not the other way around, Silenus replies, "No, by Zeus, it says it loves [*eran*] me because I am *kalós*" (554–555). The context thus activates the sense of "pretty" or "desirable" that is more consistently associated with the noun *kállos*. *Kalós* can be used ironically, as when Medea tells Jason that it will be "a fine reproach" (*oneidos*) to have beggared his own wife and children (*Medea*, 514).[30] The irony is dramatic—that is, perceived by the audience although intended by the speaker in earnest—when Medea applies the term to the news of the effects of her gift (1127).[31] The virgin who will sacrifice her life in *Heraclidae* declares that it is *kalliston* for a woman to remain quietly indoors (476–477; cf. 534): there is no hint here of beauty's allure; in turn, Alcmene inquires in all earnestness whether it is not *kalón* to kill one's enemies (965). In the *Hippolytus*, Phaedra censures those who prefer pleasure to *kalón* ("the beautiful," 382); clearly the sense is something like "honor" or "virtue," the opposite of sensual allure (cf. 403–404, 411–414, 431, 466 of moderation; but see 487 of deceptively fair words or speeches [*logoi*] that are pleasing [*terpna*] in contrast to those that earn one a good reputation; cf. 984–985). In *Andromache*, Hermione declares that it is not *kalón* for a man to have two wives (177; cf. *Iphigenia in Aulis*, 1209, where the chorus affirms with characteristically vacuous piety that it is good to rescue one's children). The slain body of Neoptolemus is said to have lost "its handsome form" (*demas to kallimorphon*, 1154–1155; cf. *kalliston demas* of Thetis, 1278). Only once does the noun occur in *Andromache*, when the title character declares, "It is not *kállos*, woman, but virtues that delight one's bedmate" (207–208).

We find *kállos* again in *Hecuba*, where—no surprise—it is used in connection with Helen. Hecuba declares that if a captive excelling in beauty must be sacrificed, it should be Helen, for she is most outstanding in appearance (*eidos ekprepestatê*, 267–269).[32] When the young Polyxena, on the point of being slain, pulls down her robe to reveal her bosom, *kallista* as that of a statue (560–561), the adjective suggests perfection of form but lacks, I think, the suggestion of sexuality that *kállos* would have conveyed. When Odysseus, on the other hand, refers to Achilles as *kallistos* (310), he has in mind Achilles's services to the Greek army not his looks (cf. *Hecuba*, 1225, *Troades*, 386, *Helen*, 941–942, and *Iphigenia in Aulis*, 357, with *kleos*). In *Suppliants*, the mothers of those who fell at Thebes exclaim that it is bitter to see their children's limbs, though they behold a noble spectacle (*kalón theama*, 635–637).[33] Electra protests that it is not *kalón* for a maiden to speak of Aegisthus's women (945; cf. *Orestes*, 26–27, and 108 on a girl appearing in public) and goes on to accuse him of arrogance on account of his own beauty: here the word is *kállos* (948), and Electra immediately proceeds to qualify his looks as effeminate (*parthenopos*, 949) rather than manly. Electra affirms that a woman who cultivates her beauty (*kállos*) while her husband is away proves that she is wicked (1072–1073). When the chorus in *Heracles* pronounces youth as *kallista* whether in riches or in poverty (646–648), they mean that it is the finest thing, but the association with youth also invites the idea of attractiveness as opposed to decrepit old age. In *Trojan Women*, Helen recalls, in self-defense, the competition of the goddesses for beauty (*kállos*, 931; cf. *Helen*, 23–24), a tale that Hecuba ridicules, asking why a married woman like Hera would conceive such a passion (*erôs*) for beauty (*kallonê*, a synonym for *kállos*, 976–977). Hecuba offers another explanation for Helen's elopement, namely that Paris was outstandingly handsome (*kállos ekprepestatos*, 987). As we have noted, Paris is typically cast as pretty, which explains Helen's enamorment. The term *kállos* is used of fair adornments for a funeral, such as are lacking to the Trojan women as they seek to bury the body of Astyanax (1200–1202); the usage is reminiscent of the reference to the rich carpet in Aeschylus's *Agamemnon*.

In *Iphigenia among the Taurians*, Iphigenia recalls that Artemis demanded the fairest thing (*kalliston*) born that year, and it was Iphigenia who won the award for beauty (*kallisteion*, 20–24). In

Ion, laurel trees are described as *kallistai* (113–114). Helen herself, in the play named for her, mentions the goddesses' beauty contest and goes on to remark that Aphrodite won by offering Paris Helen's own *kállos*, "if misfortune can be called *kalón*" (27; on the judgment of Paris over the goddesses' *kallonê*, cf. *Iphigenia in Aulis* 1307). The juxtaposition is illuminating: Helen is clearly playing on the two senses of *kalós*, as "beautiful" (in certain contexts), in which case affirming that *kállos* is *kalón* is mere redundancy and calling the equation in doubt smacks of paradox; and as "fine" or "good," and here Helen's beauty has obviously been a bane to all and so hardly *kalón*.[34] In *Bacchae*, Dionysus accuses Pentheus of "hunting after Aphrodite by way of his beauty" (*kallonê*, 459), associated here with the pale skin of women or men who avoid the wrestling grounds and outdoor activities generally (cf. *Ecclesiazuae*, 699, on women's pallor as erotically attractive).

Turning now to comedy, in Aristophanes's *Acharnians*, a character claims that the Thracian king is so truly a lover (*erastês*) of the Athenians that he has inscribed on the city walls, "The Athenians are *kaloí*" (143–144). This is a parody of the practice of lovers, who often commissioned vases for their beloveds, accompanied by the word *kalós*, commonly rendered as "beautiful." But the broad semantic gamut of the word may well have allowed for ambiguity, or what today would be called deniability—that is, claiming that the reference was to the boy's nobility rather than his sexual allure.[35] At *Birds* 1537, Sovereignty, the deity whom the hero, Peisetaerus, must take as his bride to wrest control of the world from Zeus, is described as *kallistê*: it is she who grants Zeus good counsel, good government, moderation—and abuse, since this is comedy, after all, but the emphasis is on her fine qualities. Later, as she enters with Peisetaerus, she is described as possessing ineffable beauty (*kállos*, 1713; cf. 1723) and is compared to the brilliance of the sun. In *Lysistrata*, the heroine praises the *kállos* of

Lampito (79), but the whole point of the women's plot is to drive their husbands wild with desire so that they will end the war (cf. 219–220; 955 *kallistê*, of Myrrhina as she teases her husband).[36]

When we turn again to prose writers of the period, there is nothing much to be found in the orators Antiphon and Andocides. Antiphon uses *kalós* in the usual moral sense. He once observes (in a fragment cited by Athenaeus, 9, 397C) that if you cut away a bird's wings, it loses its *kállos*, since its wings, not its body, are its beauty. Like Antiphon, Andocides once employs the expression, *kalós k'agathos*, a formula used in Athens and elsewhere to identify the upper stratum of society. As Aristotle puts it in the *Politics*, "aristocracy aims to grant preeminence to the best of the citizens, and people say that oligarchies are composed rather of the *kaloí k'agathoi*" (4.8, 1293b40–42).[37] There is confirmation, if it were needed, of the association between a fine form (*eidos kallistos*) and tall stature in the Hippocratic corpus (e.g., *Airs, Waters, and Places*, 12). Many things are labeled "fine," and the adverb occurs frequently, as in all contemporary literature, but the word *kállos* does not appear. In the essay on comely form or comportment (*euskhêmosunê*), however, we read that reflection brings with it "things that tend toward life's beauty [*kallonê*]" (*De decenti habitu* or *On Decency in Dress*, 1). In the Demosthenic corpus, *kállos* is applied several times to splendid works, often of a religious character (cf. *Olynthiac*, 3.25; also *Oration*, 22.76, 24.148), but not to human beauty, save in the exceptional speech called the *Eroticus*, dubiously attributed to Demosthenes and addressed to a youth named Epicrates (see Chapter 3, Section II). The adjectives *kalós* and *kallistos*, however, typically identify noble qualities such as praises and honors, or courage and justice (e.g., *On the Crown*, 80, 215).

There are innumerable instances of forms of *kalós* in Greek literature as a whole, and several thousand of *kállos*, but enough has been said to indicate how the terms function in classical Greek, though many of the most significant passages will come in for discussion in later chapters. Despite the broad range of the adjective, which only sometimes refers to visible phenomena and even where it does may bear other connotations than "beautiful," there is no doubt that in many cases "beautiful" is a reasonable equivalent for *kalós*. The noun *kállos*, on the other hand, principally refers to human attractiveness, very often in erotic contexts, and there is no reason not to render it as "beautiful" in every one of its occurrences. The answer to the question with which we began this chapter, then, is clearly affirmative: there is an ancient Greek word for beauty, clear and unambiguous, although it does not correspond to all the uses of the modern English term (a fact that is significant in itself, as we shall see). Now that we have identified the term, and also the situations in which the adjective may be said to bear a comparable sense, we may proceed to inquire into what the Greeks thought of beauty: what responses it typically elicited, what relation it bore to other values such as virtue, whether and how it might be manifested in abstract entities, and what role (if any) it played in ancient notions of art and aesthetics. These will be among the themes investigated in the following chapters.

3

THE NATURE OF BEAUTY

I. Beauty and Desire 🙟 As the survey of the uses of *kállos* in the previous chapter makes clear, the idea of beauty in classical Greek is closely associated with physical appearance, that is, with the visible, and more especially the human, form. What is more, the adjective *kalós*, when it may plausibly be translated as "beautiful," also tends to refer to human attractiveness. Indeed, one of the advantages of singling out the more narrow sense of the noun *kállos* as the basis for our investigation of the ancient Greek conception of beauty is that it permits a more secure control of those places where the adjective assumes a related sense, and allows us to define more clearly the subset of those uses of the adjective that reasonably come under the heading of "beautiful." As a result of this sharper focus, we can see that the classical Greek notion of beauty is closely related to *erôs*, that is, passionate desire. Indeed, I would say that the fundamental response that is excited by beauty in ancient Greece was understood to be precisely desire (see the frontispiece for an amusing, but not misleading, illustration of beauty's power).

We have already documented the association between beauty and erotic attraction in Homer, in connection with Paris and Helen, as well with Odysseus at the very moment when Athena renders him handsome so as to appeal first to Nausicaa and

then, when he is home, to his own wife: for their reunion is
represented in part as a new courtship, as though Odysseus were
himself one of the suitors. He wins her back in the contest of
the bow that is intended to decide which of the company will be
her future husband. So too, Anchises is said to be beautiful when
Aphrodite takes him as her partner in love, and it is Ganymede's
beauty that attracts the amorous attention of Zeus (also true of
Danae's beauty, Euripides, fr. 1132). Dejanira's beauty makes
her the object of a competition between the river Achelous and
Hercules, and his wife's beauty is the reason why the Lydian king
Candaules treats her as a courtesan—that is, a woman whose
livelihood depends on her allure and ability to inspire passion—
rather than as a proper wife for whom a husband would normally
feel affectionate love or *philia* rather than *erôs*. For the type of
desire that beauty arouses is specifically *erôs*, a word that carries a
particular charge in Greek, in contradistinction to other forms of
fondness, which are represented by *philia* (used for the affection
between friends and family members), *storgê* (used principally for
the affection between parents and children, and in later periods
for a ruler's affection for his subjects), and, in Christian and
later texts, *agapê* (a decidedly non-erotic bond between fellow
believers). The word *love* in English is far broader and can include
all these senses; thus, it is necessary to identify the particular sense
or connotation from the context, just as we have done with the
adjective *kalós* in Greek. As we shall see in Chapter 5, the Latin
amor has the same semantic breadth as the English *love*, and when
comparing Latin usage with Greek it is important to identify the
particular sense of the noun or related verb (*amare*).

We may illustrate the relation between beauty and desire
in some texts that have not been cited so far. Xenophon, in his
continuation of Thucydides's *History* called *Hellenica*, speaks of
a woman whose beauty (she is described as *kallistê*) manages

to corrupt Spartans who visit her, both young and old (3.3.8; cf. 4.1.7). A certain Phillidas, who was in the service of the Spartan polemarchs or military leaders, promises to bring them Theban women who are the most dignified but also *kallistai* to a festival in honor of Aphrodite. The men, we are told, expect to enjoy themselves, but in fact, it is a ruse, and men dressed up as courtesans enter the house and slay the polemarchs (5.4.4–6). But the term *kállos* itself is absent from the relatively sober medium of historiography and turns up rather in Xenophon's *Memorabilia* or *Reminiscences* of conversations with Socrates, where, for example, Xenophon tells of a courtesan named Theodote whose *kállos*— according to one of her admirers—was capable of overpowering reason (*logos*, 3.11.1). Indeed, painters vied to reproduce her beauty. Socrates and his companions straightway set off to see her, and the sight of her, they agree, produces a desire to touch her. When they leave her company, men are afflicted with a passionate longing for her.

In his *Encomium of Helen*, a show piece in the style of Gorgias's similar speech, the orator Isocrates, a contemporary of Plato, affirms that even the virtues must have a share of *kállos* if we are to find them attractive (54). We may want other things, but with respect to what is beautiful (*kalá*) we feel a passionate desire (*erôs*) that overpowers rational planning. Zeus himself was humbled by beauty when he pursued Alcmene, Danae, Nemesis, and Leda. In fact, the beauty of mortals is the most frequent cause of their divinization (59–60): an example is Helen, who was worshipped in Sparta.[1]

The Greeks had their virgin goddesses, of course, most notably Athena and Artemis. These two appear beautiful to us in the many statues that represent them (though Athena in particular, fully armed with spear and helmet, wears a rather formidable look, in contrast to some of the decidedly sexy images of Aphrodite). Yet,

the term *kállos*, though applied to Aphrodite, is rarely attributed
to Artemis or to Athena. When the epigrammatist Rufinus
(*Palatine Anthology*, 5.70) writes to a beloved, *kállos* is specific to
Aphrodite, whereas Athena seems a symbol of strength (most
likely in regard to weaving, but perhaps also in a martial capacity)
and the Muse of singing: "You have the *kállos* of Cypris [i.e.,
Aphrodite], the mouth of Persuasiveness, the body and youth of
the Spring Seasons, the voice of Calliope, the mind and modesty
of Themis, the arms of Athena; the four Graces are with you,
Phile." It would have been unseemly, I expect, to use the term
prettiness in relation to an imposing and mature female figure such
as Athena.[2] Not that Artemis's physical beauty was necessarily
always suppressed: Odysseus compares Nausicaa to the goddess
when he praises her (*Odyssey*, 6.149–152), though he does not
employ the word *kállos*.[3] What is more, certain situations might
evoke the potentially erotic aspect of Artemis or other goddesses
not normally conceived of in this fashion. Thus, Michael Squire
notes that in paintings of Actaeon accidentally spying on the
naked Artemis in her bath, Artemis's pose resembles that of a
particularly lubricious statue of Aphrodite: "The story of Actaeon's
exemplarily transgressive view of the naked Artemis must at some
level *always* have intersected with responses to the Praxitelean
statue [of Aphrodite]."[4] Libanius, in his praise of the city Antioch,
records that Ptolemy was smitten by the beauty of Artemis (*to
kállos tês Artemidos*) and carried her off from Antioch to Egypt
(*Orations*, 11.109). We might ourselves imagine that Ptolemy was
responding to the beauty of the statue, which is what he actually
abducted, but the Greek makes no such distinction between the
goddess and her image. I suspect that *kállos* is applied to Artemis
in order to account for Ptolemy's aberrant desire. We shall return
to the question of beauty as an attribute of works of art versus the
figures represented in the artwork, but we may observe here that

the uses of *kállos* in classical Greek may have obviated the tension between sexual appeal and spiritual beauty that scholars such as Roger Scruton and Javier Moscoso have perceived in respect to images of the Virgin Mary and saints martyred for their chastity (see Chapter 1).

A word is required here on the so-called judgment of Paris, in which Athena and Hera are said to have competed with Aphrodite over which of the three was most beautiful. On the face of it, the story is absurd or at the very least comical. We have already noted that Hecuba, in Euripides's *Trojan Women*, ridiculed the story (see Chapter 2) on the grounds that neither Zeus's wife nor a virgin goddess would have descended to compete with Aphrodite on these terms. But the story is odd in another way as well: we are also told that each of the goddesses offered a bribe to Paris in order to win his vote. According to the *Library* of Apollodorus, Hera offered Paris kingship; Athena, victory in war; and Aphrodite, marriage with Helen. According to this account, the contest would seem to have been over the values that each of the goddesses represented rather than their physical beauty (the elliptical allusion to this episode in the *Iliad* seems to refer to the choice of gifts, 24.30). Indeed, early vase paintings of the scene show only Aphrodite naked, whereas the other two are clothed; that all three were naked is apparently a later conceit even in literature.[5] I have suggested elsewhere that the episode of the beauty contest among the goddesses may have originated in a deliberately comic conflation of two story types, a beauty competition (typically among mortal women) and a choice among ways of life symbolized by the attributes of deities.[6] Certainly, it retained an ironic tone in all subsequent tellings.

The Stoic Chrysippus, sometimes called the second founder of the school, divided causes into several types, one of which he called "procatarctic": this cause provides the initial impulse (*aphormê*) for something to come to pass. The example Chrysippus offers of this kind of cause is *kállos*, the sight of which produces *erôs* in people who are licentious (*akolastoi*).[7] So too, John Stobaeus, who compiled excerpts of classical texts for his son in the fifth century, cites the Stoic definition of *erôs* as "a projection of affection on account of visible *kállos*" (*Eclogae*, 2.91, 10 = *SVF* fr. 395.7), and more particularly in response to the beauty of young boys (*Eclogae*, 2.115, 1 W = *SVF*, 650; cf. the Byzantine lexicon called *Suda*, s.v. alpha 1178, epsilon 2341). An epigram cited by the historian Timaeus (fragment 3b, 566 F.24a.13–16) affirms that "proud Greece, invincible in power, was enslaved by the godlike beauty of Lais," a famous courtesan. The epigram adds that Eros was her sire. The novelists enjoyed emphasizing that *erôs* enters through the eyes, as Achilles Tatius states: "As I looked, I was immediately lost: for beauty [*kállos*] wounds more sharply than arrows and flows through the eyes into the soul; for the eye is the road to the wound of *erôs* [*erôtikôi traumati*]" (1.4.4, cf. 5.13.4, 1.9.4–5). Aristotle too affirms that the beginning of *erôs* (more precisely, *to eran*) is the pleasure that comes through sight (*opsis: Nicomachean Ethics*, 1167a3–4; cf. 1157a6–10, 1171b29–31). The theme is as old as Homer, and perennially popular.[8] The connection between *kállos* and *erôs* is apparent in a number of Hellenistic love epigrams (e.g., *Palatine Anthology*, 5.70, 73, 92, 120, 140, 196, 12.110).

In a lighter vein, we may cite the Aesopian fable ("The Weasel and Aphrodite," #50 in the catalogue by Ben Edwin Perry) in which a female weasel in love with a handsome young man prays to Aphrodite that she may be metamorphosed into a human woman. Aphrodite takes pity on the weasel and turns her into a pretty (*euêdês*) girl. The boy falls in love with her beauty (so the text runs: *erastheis . . . tou kallous autês*), and brings her to his home. The story, sad to say, does not end happily. Aphrodite decides to test whether the physical change was accompanied by a change of character, and sends a mouse into the room. The girl leaps from the bed to chase it in hopes of eating it, and the goddess converts her back to her original form. The point that is relevant here is that the girl's beauty suffices to inspire *erôs* in the lad.

The above fable calls to mind a question raised in a compilation of puzzles known as the *Problems*, a work that survives in the manuscript tradition of Aristotle but is undoubtedly a later product of his school. One of the questions runs as follows:

> Why does a horse enjoy and desire [*epithumei*] a horse, and a human a human, and generally animals of the same kind [enjoy and desire] animals of the same kind and similar to themselves? For not every animal is equally *kalón*, and desire [*epithumia*] is for the *kalón*. So what is *kalón* should be more pleasant. But in actual fact, it is rather the case that not every *kállos* is pleasant . . .[9] nor is the pleasant or the *kalón* pleasant to everyone; for instance, eating or drinking is more pleasant to one person and having sex is more pleasant to another. Therefore, why each mates most of all with the same kind of animal and thereby derives the greatest pleasure from sexual intercourse is another issue [cf. *Problems*, 4.15 and 4.26]: that it is because [the same kind of animal] is most beautiful [*kalliston*] is no longer true. But we think that what pleases us in intercourse is *kalón*, because when we feel desire we enjoy seeing it. Moreover, in the case of other desires the position is similar; for when we are thirsty, seeing the drink is more pleasant. Therefore, what seems to be most pleasant is that which is *kalón* with a view to some need, and for this we also feel a greater desire. (10.52, 896b10–23)

On this account, we might conclude that Aesop's weasel ought not to have felt an erotic passion for a human youth, and indeed I have argued elsewhere that animals typically are not the subjects of *erôs* in the sense of passionate infatuation.[10] Fables, of course, have their own laws, but in any case the Aristotelian text is not concerned with *erôs* but rather sexual desire (*epithumia*). That too is usually taken to be a response to beauty, but if so, why should animals that are not beautiful, at least by human standards, inspire such a desire? To answer this question, the author of the *Problem* reverses the terms and adopts something like Sappho's position. As we saw in Chapter 2, Sappho maintained that people regard as *kalliston* whatever they are passionate for (*eratai*, fr. 16). The Aristotelian text, however, goes on to make clear that something may seem *kalón* to us even though we do not desire it:

> But this is not so in the case of what is so [i.e., *kalón*] in itself.
> And there is a sign of this: for even [grown] men seem to us to be
> *kaloí*, when we look at them without [inserting *ou* with Sylburg]
> a view to intercourse. Are they thus [i.e., *kaloí*] in such a way as
> to give us more pleasure upon seeing them than those [whom we
> typically look at] with a view to intercourse [i.e., boys]? Nothing
> prevents this, if we do not happen to feel desire [at the moment].
> And so may a drink be *kalliôn* [comparative of *kalón*]: if we happen
> to be thirsty, we shall see it as more pleasant. (10.52, 896b23–28,
> trans. Mayhew, modified)

It must be confessed that the text of the *Problem* is challenging to interpret (and may suffer from some corruption), but the core idea seems to be that we can recognize something as *kalós*— whether this consistently means "beautiful" or sometimes simply "good" is unclear—even in the absence of desire, but once desire kicks in, it strongly influences what we regard as fine or beautiful.

The genre in which the relation between beauty and *erôs* is most manifest is the novel. There survive five complete ancient Greek novels, all dedicated to the theme of love and its tribulations. The novelist Longus, writing in the second century, observes in the prologue to *Daphnis and Chloe*: "No one has ever escaped or will escape love, as long as beauty [*kállos*] exists and eyes can see" (1.4). Regarding this passage, Harold Tarrant has remarked on "the traditional connection between love and visual beauty in the ancient Greek tradition." He adds, "The supremacy of visual beauty in the ancient novel is everywhere apparent."[11] The idea that beauty enters through the eyes has roots, as Tarrant observes (177), in the theories of Empedocles and Plato: "It is as if love cannot exist without beauty, a simpler form of the theory well known from Plato's *Symposium*" (e.g., 206C). Longus and the others may have acquired their philosophical information indirectly, perhaps from Plutarch, the biographer and essayist who was closer in time to the novelists (cf., for instance, Plutarch's *Table Talk*, 5.7, 681A–C, which, as Tarrant observes, reflects Plato's *Phaedrus*, 255C–D). "Plutarch has learned from Plato to give priority to the sense of vision when explaining erotic effects in particular" (178, citing Plutarch, *Eroticus*, 766E). Tarrant is aware that Plato distrusts the senses in general, but "in one context sight takes on a role that is different in kind rather than degree, and that is the context of erotic theory" (179, citing *Charmides*, 154A–E); in the *Phaedrus*, it is "sight that triggers our recollection of the beautiful" (181). To be sure, Plato does not maintain that *erôs* is an automatic and inevitable response to the sight of something beautiful (182), but he is nevertheless heir to this tradition.[12]

It should be noted that the ancient Greeks also recognized a kind of attraction that was not inspired by beauty but by its opposite. The paradigmatic example is found in Plato's initial illustration, in the fourth book of the *Republic* (439E–440A), of why the soul is necessarily composed of more than one part. As Socrates tells it:

The story is, that Leontius, the son of Aglaion, coming up one day from the Piraeus, under the north wall on the outside, observed some dead bodies lying on the ground at the place of execution. He felt a desire [*epithumein*] to see them, and also a dread and abhorrence of them; for a time he struggled and covered his eyes, but at length the desire [*epithumia*] got the better of him; and forcing them open, he ran up to the dead bodies, saying, Look, ye wretches, take your fill of the fair [*kalós*] sight. (trans. Benjamin Jowett)

Socrates adds, "The moral of the tale is, that anger at times goes to war with desires [*epithumiai*], as though they were two distinct things" (trans. Jowett, slightly modified). But what is it in the ugly object that causes Leontius's perverse attraction?[13] In the preface to his *Life of Pericles*, Plutarch seems to wrestle with this problem. He writes:

On seeing certain wealthy foreigners in Rome carrying puppies and young monkeys about in their bosoms and fondling them, Caesar asked, we are told, if the women in their country did not bear children, thus in right princely fashion rebuking those who squander on animals that proneness to love [*philêtikon*] and loving affection [*philostorgon*] which is ours by nature, and which is due only to our fellow-men. Since, then, our souls are by nature possessed of great fondness for learning [*philomathes*] and fondness for seeing [*philotheamon*], it is surely reasonable to chide those who abuse this fondness on objects all unworthy either of their eyes or ears, to the neglect of those which are good [*kalá*] and serviceable [*ophelima*]. Our outward sense, since it apprehends the objects which encounter it by virtue of their mere impact upon it, must needs, perhaps, regard everything that presents itself, be it useful or useless; but in the exercise of his mind every man, if he pleases, has the natural power to turn himself away in every case, and to change, without the least difficulty, to that object upon which he himself determines. It is meet, therefore, that he pursue what is best, to the end that he may not merely regard [*theôrein*] it, but also be edified by regarding it. (1.1–3, trans. Perrin 1916)

Although Plutarch does not mention beauty as such in this passage, he seems to be puzzled by the attraction to monkeys and takes it that the eyes, which by nature gaze at everything, find some pleasure in the sight. But, Plutarch says, we ought rather to take as the proper objects of vision acts of virtue, which inspire an ambition [*prothumia*] to imitate them, though we may admire an accomplishment without wishing to practice it ourselves, as in the case of professional dyers, musicians, and even sculptors and poets: "No generous youth, from seeing the Zeus at Pisa, or the Hera at Argos, longs to be Pheidias or Polycleitus; nor to be Anacreon or Philetas or Archilochus out of pleasure [*hêdesthai*, verb related to *hêdonê*] in their poems" (2.1, trans. Perrin). The desire to see things in general is instinctive in us, and the eyes must be trained to take pleasure in appropriate sights.[14]

II. Beauty and Gender: Women, Boys, and Effeminate Men 🪱 Because of its close connection with *erôs*, the idea of *kállos* or beauty is implicated in Greek conceptions of passionate love, which, as many scholars have demonstrated, was constructed along lines different from the reigning pattern today (or at least, until recently). Rather than being organized strictly according to gender, in which the paradigmatic form of love is between a man and a woman, Greek *erôs* from the classical period onward also embraced pederastic passion, that is, the erotic desire an older male might experience for an adolescent lad. Seen this way, the subject of *erôs*—the one who feels it—is characteristically

seen as mature and masculine, whereas the object of the passion is either female (whether a girl or a mature woman) or a pubescent or prepubescent boy.[15] Correspondingly, *kállos* in this period was typically ascribed not only to attractive women but also to male youths. Because erotic passion was conceived of as asymmetrical (a desire on the part of an adult man for a woman or boy but not the reverse), the attribution of beauty to a mature man was fraught, since it implicitly situated him as the receptive or passive partner rather than the dominant or active partner. A grown man who accepted or even cultivated such a role might be perceived as effeminate, and there were even laws in some cities (including Athens) that deprived such individuals of full civic rights (restricted in any case to free adult males), under the charge of prostituting themselves.[16] And indeed, ascriptions of beauty in classical Greek texts do reflect the nonreciprocal nature of *erôs*, in accord with the prevailing (but not absolute) sexual ideology of the time.

As is well known, pederastic love is not represented in the Homeric epics, whether because the custom had not become generalized in Greece in the archaic period or because this particular poetic tradition excluded it, as it excluded many other motifs. This did not prevent later writers, including Aeschylus and Plato (or at least characters in Plato's dialogues), from interpreting the bond between Achilles and Patroclus, for example, as erotic (I deliberately avoid the terms *homosexual* or *homoerotic* because of their misleading implications).

There is, nevertheless a certain skewing in the attribution of *kállos* in the epics and related archaic texts such as the Homeric *Hymns* and the Hesiodic corpus. In the *Iliad*, it is used for certain women—above all Helen (and Aphrodite, of course)—and boys—for example, Ganymede—and it is also applied to Paris, specifically in connection with the seduction of Helen. But Paris is a baffling figure, who does not quite live up to the heroic ideal as it is represented in the poem. In the *Odyssey*, Odysseus is granted *kállos* by Athena at the very moment when it is important that he be attractive to Nausicaa and to Penelope, and it is suggested that he is in some measure rejuvenated as well. But it is only with lyric poetry, and texts of the late archaic and classical eras, that the love for boys becomes a stock theme, and that beauty applied to adult males, as opposed to youths, becomes problematic.

In his *Symposium* (1.9), Xenophon remarks of a handsome young lad that "the *kállos* of Autolycus draws all eyes to him." He adds, "Anyone who saw this would instantly have concluded that beauty is by nature a royal thing, especially if one possessed it in combination with respectfulness and modesty, as Autolycus did then" (1.8; on the sense of "royal" or "kingly" here, see Section IV of this chapter). Isocrates, in his praise of Evagoras (22), affirms that as a boy (*pais*) he had *kállos*, strength, and *sôphrosunê*, and everyone who saw him could testify to his beauty. In the oration called *Eroticus*, attributed to Demosthenes, the speaker praises the qualities of a youth who is outstanding for intelligence and *kállos* (61.1) and advises those who are loved for their beauty not to be puffed up about it (61.3; cf. 61.8, and especially 61.10–11 for the desire that beauty arouses; contrast *kallistos* in 61.6, 61.13, 61.17, 61.24 in the sense of "honorable"). In the dialogue by Lucian called *Erôtes* or *Loves*, in which pederastic love is compared with the love of women, Theomnestus speaks of a boy's *kállos* as "splashing against the eyes" and affirms that sight brings with it the longing to touch (53).[17]

The one adult figure who stands out for his attractiveness in the classical period (roughly the fifth and fourth centuries BC) is Alcibiades, and he is clearly exceptional—not least for his dubious virtues. As Xenophon remarks in the *Memorabilia*,

"Alcibiades was pursued by many dignified women on account of his beauty [*kállos*]" (1.2.24), and he was courted by men as well on account of his allies and abilities. In Plato's *Symposium*, Alcibiades notoriously puts himself in the position of Socrates's *paidika* or "beloved boy," in the hopes of seducing the older man to be his lover (218E): for a mature man, this is an extraordinary posture to adopt, even if he insists it is in hope of moral improvement. Plutarch, in his *Life of Alcibiades*, observes: "Of his beauty, nothing, surely, needs to be said, except that it flourished in each age and season of his body, and rendered him lovely [*erasmios*] and pleasant as a boy, a lad, and a man" (1.4). Plutarch forbears from commenting further, but he records a story about how, as a child, Alcibiades bit the hand of an opponent who was beating him at wrestling. The opponent complained that Alcibiades "fought the way women do," to which Alcibiades replied, "No—like lions, rather" (2.3). Athenaeus quotes a comic poet who dubbed Alcibiades "delicate" or "pretty" (*habron*), and goes on to say that a Lacedaemonian woman (that is, the wife of the Spartan king Agis, who was in love with him) wanted to make an adulterer of him (13.34); we see here, as in the case of Paris, how it is precisely womanly beauty in a man that is attractive to women. His ability to seduce the wives of his compatriots, noted in a fragment of Eupolis, a contemporary of Aristophanes, testifies not to Alcibiades's masculinity but rather to his effeminate looks (Athenaeus 12.48; as Athenaeus remarks in connection with a painting of Alcibiades, his beauty surpassed that of all the women, 12.47). Athenaeus observes that even as a general Alcibiades desired to be *kalós*, sporting a gold and ivory shield emblazoned with an image of Eros, and he adds that Anytus— the accuser of Socrates—was his lover.[18]

Another example of the double-edged nature of beauty is the famous hymn the Athenians sang to Demetrius Poliorcetes upon his triumphant approach to the city. According to Athenaeus:

> Demochares, in the twenty-first book of his *Histories*, says: "And the Athenians received Demetrius when he came from Leucas and Corcyra to Athens, not only with frankincense, and crowns, and libations of wine, but they even went out to meet him with hymns, and choruses, and ithyphallic mummers, and dancing and singing, and they stood in front of him in multitudes, dancing and singing, and saying that he was the only true god, and that all the rest of the gods were either asleep, or gone away to a distance, or were no gods at all. And they called him the son of Poseidon and Aphrodite, for he was eminent for beauty [*kállos*], and affable to all men with a natural courtesy and gentleness of manner. And they fell at his feet and addressed supplications and prayers to him." (6.62, trans. Yonge 1854)

The actual hymn as recorded by Athenaeus, composed by a certain Hermocles, did indeed describe Demetrius as the son of Poseidon and Aphrodite but did not specifically mention his *kállos*, though Plutarch (*Life of Demetrius*, 2.2) insists on his extraordinary beauty (*ideâi kai kállei prosôpou thaumastos kai perittos*).[19] Demetrius was well known for his sexual exploits, which were thought to have distracted him from properly military activities, and it is not impossible that the allusion to Aphrodite concealed a touch of irony, implying a certain resemblance between its honorand and a mythological figure such as Paris. One would not expect a Hercules or a Theseus to be described as "pretty," except perhaps when they were young; thus, Libanius says that Ariadne fell in love with Theseus precisely because of his lovely youth (*hôra: Orations*, 11.81).[20]

One of the crucial documents on ancient Greek pederasty comes from a speech by the orator Aeschines, *Against Timarchus*. Aeschines and Demosthenes had been ambassadors to the Macedonian king Philip in the year 346 BC and had negotiated a peace treaty between Macedon and Athens. Demosthenes was radically opposed to the terms of the deal, and upon the return of the envoys to Athens, he was preparing (with the cooperation of a certain Timarchus) to prosecute Aeschines for treason. To prevent the proceedings, Aeschines sought—successfully, as it turned out—to disqualify Timarchus from speaking on the grounds that he had prostituted himself to another man. Aeschines knew in advance, or pretended to know, that Demosthenes would counter the charge by citing verses composed by Aeschines himself that showed he was a declared lover of male youths (135) and thereby equate his behavior with that of Timarchus. Aeschines defended himself against this allegation by distinguishing between an appropriate passion for a youth and the comportment of Timarchus. Of interest in the present context is the way Aeschines deploys the vocabulary of beauty to make his point. Demosthenes will, according to Aeschines, point to the erotic nature of Achilles's friendship with Patroclus and will praise *kállos*, provided it is joined with restraint or self-control (*sôphrosunê*); for everyone in fact prays for a handsome (*euprepês*) body (133). Indeed, Demosthenes will accuse the Athenians of contradictory behavior, since they all wish that their children be *kaloí kai agathoi* in appearance (*idea*)—an expression that, as we have seen, signifies honorable and good men—and yet, if by their youthful beauty (*kállei kai hôrâi*) they become the objects of rivalry among lovers, they ought (so Aeschines says) to be disenfranchised (134). The equivocation here is clear: parents hope their children will be worthy, not that they will attract the attentions of older men. Aeschines affirms, in reply, that he finds no fault with a just passion (*dikaios erôs*), nor does he claim that those who are outstanding for *kállos* necessarily prostitute themselves (136). His point is that to feel passion for those who are *kaloí* and restrained is the mark of a decent and affectionate spirit, whereas to hire oneself out for money is the sign of a man—note the word *anêr*, an adult male—who is brutal and *apaideutos*, that is, uncultivated in the sense of lacking *paideia* but also carrying an overtone of no longer a child or *pais*. The one kind of love is *kalón*, Aeschines affirms, but selling oneself is shameful (*aiskhron*, 137). Throughout the speech, Aeschines uses the term *kalós* in the sense of good or moral (e.g., of laws, 177; paired with *dikaion*, 121; and cf. *kaloí kai agathoi* several times, e.g., 69, 134), and so it is in the present passage. Later, Aeschines will quote Euripides to the effect that to love in a restrained or temperate way is one of the finest things (*kallista*, 151, quoting Euripides, fr. 672 Nauck = fr. 66* Kannicht, from his *Sthenoboea*). Aeschines is prepared to acknowledge that beauty in boys in not necessarily a sign of perverse character, nor is he averse to the attractions of youths, but speaking in his own voice he prefers to use the more dignified adjective to describe the objects of his amorous fancy.[21]

It is not the case that *kállos* can never be ascribed to a mature male without innuendo of effeminacy or impropriety. Language is not so rigorous in everyday parlance, and in English too one can say that there is a beauty in the elderly in a way that distinguishes it from the allure of youth. It is in this spirit, I believe, that Aristotle affirms that there is a kind of *kállos* appropriate to every age, whether young, at the acme of life, or old—the last characterized by sufficient strength for necessary labor (*Rhetoric*, 1361b7–14).[22] But Plutarch, in his essay *On the Fortune of Alexander* (336B), states what I take to be the more general view: "Fortune often bestows power and rule upon cowardly and thoughtless men, who are uncouth in them, but it adorns and confirms virtue as the only greatness and beauty [*kállos*] in a man" (that is, an *anêr* or adult male). True, in the *Symposium*, Xenophon has Critobulus defend the beauty (*kállos*) on which he prides himself as a good which is not vulnerable to decay. For, he says, if a boy is *kalós*, he will likely remain so as a youth, an adult, and an old man (4.17). His argument, however, is plainly sophistical and depends on the transition from *kalós* in the sense of "physically attractive" to the more abstract sense of "noble" or "virtuous." As we have noted, the transience of boys' beauty was commonplace in discussions of pederasty.[23]

If there was an age, at least for males (and in some respects for women), beyond which it was regarded as unsuitable to be subject to the erotic gaze, we may note too that the Greeks rarely ascribed *kállos* to young children, whether male or female, and generally considered sexual attractiveness to emerge when a girl reached an age at which she might potentially be regarded as marriageable (this could be quite young, as we shall see). Thus, the so-called *Library* of Apollodorus reports that Theseus carried off Helen "when she became outstanding for beauty" (3.128), that is, when she reached the age at which *kállos*, properly speaking, becomes manifest. Xenophon of Ephesus, in his novel *Ephesiaca* or *Ephesian Tale*, relates how the hero, Habrocomes, "was growing daily into beauty" (1.1.2). In Heliodorus's *Aethiopica*, Charicles relates his encounter with a mysterious dark-skinned man who hands over to him the infant Chariclea, the novel's heroine, together with some birth tokens. "He took me to his place and showed me a girl of outstanding and divine beauty; he said she was seven years old, but to me she seemed approaching the age of marriage. Thus does surpassing beauty add something even to the appearance of stature. I stood there with open jaw, in my ignorance of what was happening and my insatiable staring at what was on view" (2.30.6).[24] The man continues to explain to Charicles how he rescued the girl as an infant, having noticed that her eyes had a divine brilliance and that a necklace lay beside her, along with a band woven with letters and images that depicted the child's background. He then observes, "At first she passed unnoticed, but as time went by the girl in her prime was clearly of greater loveliness [*hôra*] than the usual, and her beauty [*kállos*] did not escape notice even if it was buried under the ground" (2.31.3).

Kállos or sexual appeal emerges with adolescence, or rather, we might say, with the approach to pubescence in the case of a very tall and precocious young girl. It is not, however, the infant child's beauty but rather the look in her eyes that captivates the man who rescued her. In *Daphnis and Chloe*, the two foundlings grow up to become exceptionally beautiful adolescents; the newborn Daphnis, however, is more discreetly described as "large and noble-looking" (*mega kai kalón*, 1.2.3); no comparable adjective is applied to the infant Chloe. I have found one example of beauty, that is, *kállos*, ascribed to a small child: in his account of early history, Diodorus Siculus (*Bibliotheca historica*, 2.4.5) describes how the infant Semiramis had been exposed and nourished by doves, until some farmers discovered her, "a baby of outstanding beauty" (*to brephos diapheron tôi kállei*). When she grew up, she proved similarly superior in beauty to all the other maidens (*tôi kállei polu tas allas parthenous diapherousês*, 2.5.1). A noble in the Babylonian court first fell in love with her, and then king Ninus himself, who forced him to surrender her and made her his queen. Clearly, the infant's beauty was not such as to arouse sexual desire in her caretakers, but served as a predictor of her future power of attraction.[25]

III. Beauty and Virtue Beauty, with its connotation of sexual attractiveness, was not only problematic in connection with men; women's beauty could also be a source of arrogance or temptation. For either sex, however, beauty was or could be conceived of as an asset, provided it was accompanied by virtue. We have seen that Theognis (see Chapter 2), writing in the sixth century BC, pairs *kállos* with virtue (*aretê*, 1.933)—that is, the combination of physical and moral excellence—as the joint basis for felicity (*olbos*). In Xenophon's *Memorabilia*, Socrates observes that beauty is included, along with strength, wealth, and reputation, among the ingredients of happiness (4.2.34), though, like the others, it is subject to loss. So too, Xenophon, in his treatise *On Horsemanship* (1.7), praises the combination of *kállos* and strength (*iskhus*) in a horse. In his *Cyropaedia* or "Education of Cyrus," a semi-fictional eulogy of the founder of the Persian Empire, Xenophon reports, "Each person spoke about Cyrus, one mentioning his wisdom, another his endurance, another his kindness, yet another his beauty [*kállos*] and stature." Beauty could figure as one of a list of positive attributes, in which case it need not carry any stigma. Plato, who takes pride of place among philosophers for his analysis of beauty and desire, was especially concerned with elevating *kállos* as a spiritual ideal. Thus, in the *Symposium* (210B), he declares that one must value beauty in souls more highly than beauty in the body (we shall return later to the analogy between corporeal and psychic beauty). Nevertheless, when he is writing in a more popular vein, Plato can have Socrates affirm: "I am leaving out thousands of other things in my comments, such as strength and *kállos* together with health, and in turn many other lovely [*pankala*] things in the soul [*en psukhais*]" (*Philebus*, 26B5–7; Chapter 4 examines the nature of beauty in Plato's dialogues in more detail). Indeed, the archaic poet Tyrtaeus went so far as to affirm, "Few are the people whom virtue and beauty [*kállos*] accompany, and blessed is he who obtains one of these" (1.933–934). Beauty does seem to be granted an independent value, but in the absence of *aretê* it is hard to imagine

Tyrtaeus giving it his undiluted approval. Many writers, however, express a greater nervousness about physical attraction, given the power of *kállos* to inspire passionate love, which was always regarded with a dubious eye.[26] They might protest, for example, that love should take into account not just physical beauty but also character. We noted Isocrates's defense of *erôs*, provided that it was conducted in a temperate way (*sôphrosunôs*); there was always the danger that beauty might turn a man's head (or a woman's) and override any concern for attendant virtues. Thus, in the twenty-third poem in the Theocritean corpus, the opening verses read: "A certain lovesick man [*anêr*] was enamored of an insensitive youth [*ephabos*], of goodly form [*morpha*] but not likewise in character" (23.1–2).[27]

We noted in the previous chapter that beauty and military valor are often contrasted. In the *Iliad*, Hector complains that Paris has "a handsome appearance but there is no force or strength in his spirit" (3.44–45). Paris, for his part, protests that Hector has an unwearying heart in battle, but he must not disparage "the lovely gifts of golden Aphrodite" (3.64). We observed too that a certain Nireus is singled out in the *Iliad* (2.671–275) as "the most beautiful [*kallistos*] man who came beneath Ilium of all the Danaans after the blameless son of Peleus," though he was otherwise weak and undistinguished. Nireus's good looks are thus consistent with his lack of martial prowess. But if beauty is at least implicitly associated with an unmanly nature, more suited to the bedroom than the battlefield, why is Nireus described as most beautiful "after the blameless son of Peleus," that is, Achilles, the hero whose courage and prowess are least in doubt? Clearly, beauty is at least compatible with valor. Nevertheless, I should like to suggest that Phaedrus, in Plato's *Symposium*, might not have read Homer entirely amiss when he relied on this verse, among others, to show that Patroclus must have been Achilles's lover, since Achilles "was more beautiful [*kalliôn*] not just than Patroclus but than all the heroes, and he was still beardless, since he was much younger, as Homer says" (180A). Achilles's beauty is connected, if not with his role as the beloved of Patroclus, at least with his relative youth, as in the case of Telemachus in the *Odyssey* (18.219),[28] and has no special association with bravery or fortitude in this context.[29]

In Euripides's *Andromache*, the title character declares, "It is not *kállos*, woman, but virtues that delight one's bedmate" (207–208). Similarly, a character in a lost play by Euripides (fr. 909) insists that *kállos* is of little help to a woman who would wed well (but virtue does help) (cf. Plutarch, *Conjugal Precepts*, 141D). Needless to say, such affirmations reveal an anxiety over the power of beauty to attract a husband or to steal one away. In Euripides's *Helen*, Helen recalls the judgment of Paris concerning the *kállos* of the three goddesses (23), and her own fatal beauty (27; cf. 261, 304, where *to kállos* is said to have benefitted other women; on Helen's beauty, cf. Isocrates, *Helen,* 16, 58–60). Electra, in Euripides's tragedy by that name, denounces a woman who beautifies herself (*es kállos askei*) as wicked. In a Greek epigram datable to the Roman period, we find the cautionary note sounded in a distich ascribed to a certain Capito, of whom nothing certain is known: "*Kállos* without grace merely delights, but does not grip; it is like bait floating without a hook" (*Palatine Anthology*, 5.67). A pair of verses included in the "Sentences" ascribed to Menander, many of which derive from that poet's comedies, run: "If you see a beautiful [*kalê*] woman, don't be impressed, since much beauty [*kállos*] comes laden with much blame" (fr. 703).[30]

In one highly rhetorical passage, however, Xenophon sums up the nobility of his hero Cyrus and adds that, to see his comrades, you would believe that they "truly lived for the sake of beauty [*eis kállos*]" (8.1.33)—an extraordinary expression intended to capture the grace attaching to their way of life. There is a similar formulation in Xenophon's *Agesilaus*, in which Xenophon contrasts the way the Persian king conceals himself from his people with Agesilaus's openness to the public. According to Agesilaus, rare appearance suits shameful behavior (*aiskhrourgia*), whereas the light lends grace or style (*kosmos*) to a life dedicated to *kállos* (9.1). This sense of *kállos* as defining the quality of a noble and refined life may be especially characteristic of Xenophon; at any rate, I do not find instances of this usage in other writers.

We have seen that *kállos* could on occasion be applied to especially grand actions, as when, according to Herodotus, a flatterer extolled Pausanias for "having performed a deed excelling in greatness and beauty" (9.78). Isocrates too adverts to the *kállos* and *megethos* of deeds performed on behalf of the city (*Antidosis*, 306). The collocation of beauty and magnitude in descriptions of great achievements is not unusual (cf. Isocrates, *Panathenaicus*, 36; Xenophon, *Hellenica*, 4.4.6; Plutarch, *Life of Fabius Maximus*, 26.3; *Life of Pelopidas*, 31.6). The pairing of "beauty" and "size" or "stature" is found often, as we have seen, in connection with personal appearance, whether of men or women (as in the description of Cyrus quoted above), and it has the ring of a formulaic expression. I suspect that, when applied to *erga* or deeds, there was a hint of metaphor, as though the quality of physical beauty were being transferred to an incorporeal entity. However that may be, worthy acts could be imagined as possessing a kind of attractiveness of their own and inviting imitation, thereby allowing for a positive connection between beauty and virtue.

IV. Beauty and the Best: The Role of Class   If beauty was only incidentally associated with virtue in the classical period, as a trait that, when joined with a good character, might complete the image of a person endowed with all good things, one might imagine that such a combination would have been viewed as the particular mark of the aristocracy, which had the leisure and resources to cultivate good looks, rather than of farmers or laborers whose bodies were subject to deformations from their trades. Upper-class Greeks did cultivate a disdain for manual occupations, which they dubbed "banausic," that is, "artisanal" or "craftsman-like" (e.g., Aristotle, *Politics*, 1321a6). In much of modern literature and art, whether learned or popular, the upper classes—especially royalty—are imagined as possessing an inherent beauty that stands out in contrast with peasants or proletarians. I am reminded of the tender sentiments of Edmund Burke for Marie Antoinette, who suffered such indignities under French Revolution (this was before her execution): "It is now sixteen or seventeen years since I saw the queen of France, then the dauphiness, at Versailles, and surely never lighted on this orb, which she hardly seemed to touch, a more delightful vision. I saw her just above the horizon, decorating and cheering the elevated sphere she just began to move in—glittering like the morning star, full of life and splendor and joy . . . I thought ten thousand swords must have leaped from their scabbards to avenge even a look that threatened her with insult. But the age of chivalry is gone" (Burke 2004, 169).[31]

The fairy-tale notion of the natural beauty of the superior classes does in fact find a reflection in a certain branch of classical literature. In the novel *Daphnis and Chloe*, composed, as we have already noted, by a certain Longus sometime in the second century AD, the title characters are foundlings, nursed at first by animals—Daphnis by a nanny goat, Chloe by a ewe—and then raised as foster children by humble herdsmen and their wives. A goatherd, Lamon by name, finds the infant Daphnis, "a male child, large and fine-looking [*kalón*] and amidst birth tokens better than the misfortune of exposure: for there was a purple cloak and a gold buckle and a little sword with an ivory hilt" (1.2.3). Next, the shepherd Dryas comes upon Chloe, "a female child, and alongside her too there lay birth tokens: a golden headband, gilded sandals, and gold anklets" (1.5.3). Their accoutrements suffice to identify them as offspring of wealthy parents. Longus soon skips to the main narrative and the first mention of their beauty: "These children quickly grew up, and their *kállos* appeared greater than country life" (1.7.1). Their attractiveness is mentioned precisely at the point when they are about to fall mutually in love, having reached the ages of fifteen (Daphnis) and thirteen (Chloe). But their beauty is not just a sign of their sexual maturity (see Section II in this chapter) but also of their class status, which distinguishes them from their rustic companions. Since the two children have been raised in the country—Daphnis's foster parents are slaves— their exceptional beauty is an intrinsic sign of superior status, as indeed is the case: they will prove to be the offspring of leading citizens of the town of Mytilene (Daphnis's real father, it turns out, is Dryas's master). Beauty, then, is an indication of upper-class origin: the scions of wealthy urban parents are better looking than country folk and can be recognized as such even when reared in humble circumstances (cf. 4.11.2, where Daphnis's beauty is said to be "such as is not even found in the city"). So too, Lamon says of Chloe that her beauty (*kállos*), as well as her birth tokens, testify to her distance from the class of herdsmen (4.30.4).[32]

And yet, the connection between beauty and class in classical Greek sources is not ubiquitous or even frequent. We have already seen one reason why *kállos* might not have been regularly associated with the upper classes: prettiness in a man might suggest the passive erotic role, which was regarded as shameful in an adult male. Virility, it might be thought, needs no adornment: one thinks of Cromwell's preference to be portrayed "warts

Figure 3.1 Portrait bust (Roman Republic).

and all,"[33] or, closer in time to Greek antiquity, of the veristic sculptural style of the Roman Republic, which exhibited facial features with the fidelity of a wax mask (see Figure 3.1).[34] Even idealized portraits were not necessarily conceived of as beautiful (more on this below).

In the case of women, moreover, beauty might smack of licentiousness and so was unlikely to be singled out as a distinctive quality of citizen wives. In classical Athens, which set the pattern for much of Greek and Roman culture—at least as it is reflected in literature—women were presumed to lead rather sheltered lives, away from the gaze of men who were not near relatives or friends of their husbands. Beauty was the concern of the so-called hetaerae (courtesans), a class of women, generally foreign and not under the tutelage of a local male, who consorted with men for a fee and needed to cultivate a seductive appearance and other attractive traits, such as an ability to sing. In his *Cyropaedia*, Xenophon describes how after gaining a victory, Cyrus's cavalry brings in the spoils from the enemy camp, including "the best [*beltistai*] women, both the wives [*gnêsiai*] and the concubines [*pallakides*] on account of their *kállos*" (4.3.1). Xenophon explains that this is customary in Asia, where they claim that the presence of the women encourages them to fight better, but Xenophon registers his opinion that it may rather be because they prefer to indulge their pleasure (*hêdonê*, 4.3.2). However that may be, it is the courtesans rather than the high-born women who are brought along on their campaigns on account of their beauty. Xenophon is no doubt projecting onto Persian society the attitudes that prevailed in his own, and his language reveals how the existence of an institution or practice such as upper-class prostitution might accentuate the distance between the proper mores characteristic of citizen wives and the sexiness of professional courtesans. Anecdotes testifying to the beauty of hetaerae are too numerous to cite, but we have already seen the case of Theodote, whose looks were enough to deprive men of their reason.

When a man did fall in love with a girl known to be a citizen, at least in New Comedy, he might prefer to emphasize her good qualities, manifested to be sure in her appearance and comportment, rather than her prettiness per se. An example is Menander's *Dyscolus* or "Grouch," the only one among the thousands of plays in this genre that has survived almost entirely intact. The protagonist catches a glimpse of the old misanthrope's daughter when she has emerged, quite exceptionally, from her house (this itself is the cause of some scandal to her relatives), but though he is struck by her *kállos* (193), what he most praises is her good character: she is somehow urbane or liberal in character, even though she was raised in the countryside (*eleutheriôs agroikos*, 201–202). Indeed, it is an advantage that she has been raised by the old curmudgeon, since she has been sheltered from the silly gossip of nurses (381–389). Perhaps the English word *beautiful* is capacious enough to include the kind of looks that bespeak a decent upbringing, but such women are no competition for an experienced hetaera when it comes to *kállos*, and it would be unseemly for a married woman to cultivate such an appearance. In Menander's *Epitrepontes*, Smicrines, the father of Pamphile, whose husband appears to have taken up with a hetaera, observes, "He'll set up house now with the lovely [*kalê*] lady he's engaged" (695–696, trans. Furley 2009). Again, a little later:

> It's hard, Pamphile,
> for a freeborn woman to compete with a whore.
> She knows more tricks, has more experience, shrinks
> from nothing, out-flatters, stoops to sordid things. (793–796,
> trans. Furley 2009)

It is the more unlikely, then, that such glamour would be considered characteristic of upper-class women. To be sure, the conventions that governed New Comedy were not a faithful reflection of everyday Athenian life, but they were part of, or helped to construct, an ideology according to which hetaerae, who were sexually alluring as a condition of their profession, were invariably foreign, that is, not of Athenian citizen families and hence ineligible for marriage. Men might fall in love with citizen girls and seek their hand, but what made such women attractive was their modesty and refined comportment rather than their sexual allure.[35]

We noted Xenophon's remark in his *Symposium* to the effect that anyone who looked at the handsome young Autolycus "would instantly have concluded that beauty is by nature a royal thing, especially if one possessed it in combination with respectfulness and modesty, as Autolycus did then" (1.8). But *royal* (*basilikon*) here refers to Autolycus's power to attract all eyes; there is no implication that princes are naturally more beautiful than other mortals. A fragment of Menander makes it clear that royal power and beauty are two of several sources of worldly pride, all of which are evanescent: "When you wish to know who you really are, look at the tombs as you travel; here are the bones and light dust of men who were kings and tyrants and wise and proud of their birth and money and fame and the beauty of their bodies" (fr. 538).[36]

Aristophanes's *Clouds* provides a description of what a decent young man should look like. In a contest between personifications of traditional morality and hedonistic self-indulgence, the former seeks to persuade young Phidippides of the advantages of a virtuous life:

> if you carry out these things I mention,
> if you concentrate your mind on them,
> you'll always have a gleaming chest, bright skin,
> broad shoulders, tiny tongue, strong buttocks,
> and a little prick. But if you take up
> what's in fashion nowadays, you'll have,
> for starters, feeble shoulders, a pale skin,
> a narrow chest, huge tongue, a tiny bum,
> and a large skill in framing long decrees.[37]

The physical ideal that is sketched out here may be seen in classical sculpture and vase paintings, and represents a model type. But there is no mention of *kállos* in the passage, and the reason is clear enough: Aristophanes wishes to avoid any hint that boys such as these are appealing to would-be lovers. We may, of course, suppose that they are handsome rather than pretty or sexy, which is what the word *kállos* typically suggests. Like many other languages, English employs—or at least used to employ—distinct terms to represent the ideal appearance of men and women (cf. Chapter 1, n. 24). More likely, ancient Greeks would have applied to such lads a term taken from the moral sphere, such as *kaloí kai agathoi* (cf. *Clouds*, 797). At all events, the physique praised here is attained by exercise and sound living, and is not conceived of as a natural attribute of the upper classes.[38]

There is a character in Homer's *Iliad* who is described as ugly and deformed; what is more, he is an obstreperous fellow and something of a thorn in the side of the Greek leaders. His name is Thersites and, despite his brief appearance in the epic, he is legendary for his harsh tongue:

> Thersites alone kept chattering on, unmeasured in speech, whose mind was full of a great store of disorderly [*akosma*] words, to criticize the kings, idly, and in no order [*kata kosmon*], but whatsoever he deemed would raise a laugh among the Argives. Evil-favoured was he beyond all men that came to Ilium: he was bandy-legged and lame in the one foot, and his two shoulders were rounded, stooping together over his chest, and above them his head was warped, and a scant stubble grew thereon." (2.212–219, trans. Murray 1924, modified)

Thersites is not one of the royal figures or *basileis* (cf. 2.214, 247, 250), but neither can he be taken to be representative of the ordinary soldiers at Troy. His deformities are symptomatic of his ill temper rather than of his class status as such, though his behavior is particularly obnoxious in that he berates his betters.[39] His ugliness does not imply that the highest echelons of the warrior caste were especially handsome.

If Thersites's misshapenness is not necessarily a sign of his lower class status, what shall we make of the figurines, so popular in the Hellenistic period, of disheveled, often drunken old women? A well-known example of the type is a statuette now in the Munich Glyptothek (see Figure 3.2; a similar but not identical reproduction is in the Capitoline Museum).

But her appearance, especially to the untrained eye, may be misleading. In an essay on how emotions are manifested in sculpted figures of drunken women, Jane Masséglia appeals to the fourth *Mime* of Herodas, in which two women comment on votive statues in a sanctuary, to show that the feature most likely

Figure 3.2 Drunken old woman (Hellenistic period).

to have impressed ordinary viewers of a work of art was the lifelikeness of the representations.[40] Masséglia pays close attention to details that ancient viewers would have noticed, such as the expensive chiton the woman is wearing that has slipped from one shoulder, her many rings, her posture, her seated position, and her manner of clutching the jug in her hands almost as if it were a child. As Masséglia notes, "Coroplastic evidence from the Greek world presents drinking and childcare as the only two narrative possibilities for old women in classical antiquity" (420). She concludes that "the reason for her sitting position and head thrown back . . . is an emotional one. It is enjoyment" (423) resulting from her pleasure over the wine. Viewers might have felt repugnance at the transgressive behavior of the old woman, just as Homer's audience would, I expect, have found Thersites's outburst distasteful. Indeed, Masséglia suggests that they might have disapproved of her just because of her finery and jewelry, discouraged at religious festivals in many places, though in others the reverse seems to have been the case. Masséglia concludes that the figure might have evoked disgust and admiration in equal measure, at least for the technical quality of its execution. What is most pertinent here, however, is that there is no sign that the woman is of the lower classes; she is physically unappealing in part because she is old (the ancient prejudice concerning the unattractiveness of old women amounts to an obsession)[41] and in part because she is inebriated; her social status is irrelevant, unless it is all the more disagreeable for a wealthy woman to be violating norms of comportment in this way.

To return, after this detour, to *Daphnis and Chloe*, what explains the change in the social conception of beauty between the classical period and the time, several centuries later, in which Longus's novel was composed—if indeed the difference is real and not a function of the paucity of our sources? We may remark, for one thing, that even in this genre so given to the celebration of physical attractiveness, the greatest beauty may be diminished or lost as a result of harsh circumstances—above all, falling into slavery. In Xenophon of Ephesus's tale, the hero and heroine have been so deformed by their hardships as to be unrecognizable by their faithful slaves, after a separation of little more than a year (5.10.10–11, 5.12.3–4).[42] The protagonist of Achilles Tatius's novel, in turn, fails to recognize his own beloved, so altered is her appearance as a consequence of her enslavement (5.17.3–9). In these cases, beauty does not miraculously abide under the brutal regime of servitude.[43] Conceivably, the ancient romances were meant at some level to expose the contingency of middle- or upper-class life in a world where people were vulnerable to kidnapping and enslavement.[44]

The heroes and heroines of the romantic Greek novels are invariably children of respectable, well-to-do families, but they are not distinguished from their peers in respect to class. *Daphnis and Chloe* is the exception rather than the rule, and the reason may be that it is the only novel that can be characterized as pastoral, that is, narrating the lives of the rural herdsmen. The distinction, then, is between rustic and urban life rather than between the ruling stratum and a subject population. The Athenian democracy tended to deemphasize natural differences between rich and poor, and one would not expect to find a sharp distinction in the physical appearance of ordinary citizens compared to the aristocracy, even assuming that physical beauty was perceived as a noble and desirable trait. When independent, agriculture-based city states gave way to the Hellenistic monarchies, with their cultivated courtiers, there emerged a genre that featured precisely herders as opposed to farmers, and regarded the former with a supercilious gaze and ironic detachment: this was the bucolic or pastoral genre, best represented today by the idylls of Theocritus. If slaves were deformed by their condition, herdsmen could be seen as members of a naturally inferior class, subject to the kind of patronizing representation from which ordinary farmers were protected by the traditionally high esteem accorded to agriculture as opposed to trade and the crafts.[45]

The noun *kállos* is not particularly common in the pastorals, though its occurrence in the second idyll may be worth noting. Simaetha recalls the moment she fell in love with Delphis: "As soon as I saw him, I went mad, my heart was inflamed with fire, poor me, and my beauty withered" (2.82–83). The use of *kállos* here marks Simaetha as something other than a proper citizen girl, as we would infer also from the fact that she lives alone and is available for an affair with a handsome young man. The herdsmen themselves are not especially ugly, though they imagine that their beloveds are beautiful. But perhaps the two remarkable poems concerning the Cyclops Polyphemus, in which the huge brute is helplessly enamored of the sea nymph Galatea, hint indirectly at the social distance between the rustic world and urban society's upper strata. It may be that Longus found inspiration in the bucolic tradition not only for the setting of his story but also for the motif of beauty as a mark and privilege of the upper classes.[46]

We have seen that physical beauty is closely associated with erotic desire, and that the assignment of beauty is conditioned by the prevailing conception of erotic roles. It bears, accordingly, a tense and equivocal relation to virtue and to social class, as both a positive attribute and a suspect trait, characteristic of courtesans and pretty boys rather than adult males and respectable characters generally. But *kállos* also had wider applications, which we have so far only discussed in passing; these are the subject of the following chapter.

4

BEAUTY TRANSFIGURED

Although the Greek word *kállos* primarily signifies erotic attractiveness when ascribed to the human form and characteristically elicits desire in the beholder, the term did have a wider application, and beauty might be attributed to various objects and even to abstract ideas. In this chapter, I discuss two principal extensions of the idea of beauty: to art and to the realm of abstract concepts.

I. Aesthetic Beauty 🙠 We have already observed that in Homer, *kállos* is once ascribed to a handsome cup (*Iliad*, 23.740–743), which Achilles offers as a prize to the swiftest runner in the funeral games for Patroclus. As a reward, it is a desirable item, and perhaps *kállos* suggests not just its appearance or the quality of its craftsmanship but also the kind of attractiveness that arouses a wish to possess it. In the classical period—but above all, in Hellenistic and later texts—the term is applied to particularly handsome animals as well as to flourishing or otherwise noteworthy landscapes; it is also a common enough attribute of cities, often as seen from outside or as one approaches them.[1] Indeed, Menander the Rhetor compares the attraction of a beautiful city directly to the passion experienced by a lover (*On Epideictic*, 428.7–25 Spengel; cf. Menander Rhetor, *On the Division of Epideictic Oratory*, 339.11–18, 352.6–25 Spengel).[2] But the principal association is still with the sense of sight. Plato, in his discussion of art as imitation in the tenth book of the *Republic*, applies the word to such things as furniture or implements (*skeuos*): whoever makes the thing will have a correct opinion concerning its beauty and defectiveness (*ponêria*), provided that he associates with and heeds the one who uses it. It is the latter who has actual knowledge (601E). By "beauty" here, Plato seems to mean something like functionality, which would best be judged by the person who employs the item, but he presumably has in mind also its correct proportions or dimensions. Thus he speaks of the "virtue and beauty and correctness" (*aretê kai kállos kai orthotês*) of a utensil or animal or action (601D), the three abstract terms being roughly synonymous (a few lines later he contrasts *ponêros* rather with *khrêstos*, "useful," 602B). In these uses too, beauty continues to be associated with vision.

But *kállos* is also attributed to things that are not seen. For example, Aristotle, in observing that physical beauty is not necessarily a sign of excellent character, notes that it is "not equally easy to perceive the *kállos* of the soul and that of the body" (*Politics*, 1254b38–39). The metaphorical extension of the term to the psychological realm is motivated here, I expect, by the comparison with corporeal beauty.[3] Plato makes a similar move in the *Symposium* (210B), when he declares that one must value beauty in souls more highly than beauty in body: it is the desire to relate the two ideals that induces Plato to speak of beauty residing in the psyche (cf. Plato, *Philebus*, 65E, where Socrates affirms that the mind, or *nous*, has a greater share of *kállos* than does pleasure; Plutarch, *Amatorius*, 757E, speaks of "*kállos* simultaneously of body and soul"). In the *Republic*, Socrates defines virtue or *aretê* as "a kind of health and beauty and well-being of the soul," whereas vice is the reverse (444E); clearly, he is offering these terms by way of analogy with physical fitness and flourishing. So too, the doxographer Arius Didymus says, "By way of analogy, if bodily beauty is choiceworthy in and of itself, beauty of the soul would be choiceworthy in and of itself as well; but the beauty of the soul is justice, which causes us not to do wrong and to be noble [*kaloí*]" (89.1; cf. 65.2). And Origen says that "health and beauty somehow [*pôs*] arise in the soul" (*Scholia on the Song of Songs*, 17.284.12 Migne).[4] Most often, the contrast between corporeal and spiritual excellence is clear, as in Plato's *Philebus* (26B5–7), where Socrates affirms (quoted also in Chapter 3), "I am leaving out thousands of other things in my comments, such as strength and *kállos* together with health, and in turn many other lovely [*pankala*] things in the soul [*en psukhais*]."[5] To be sure, Socrates waxes more metaphysical later in the dialogue, when he speaks of beauty not only in connection with perceptible shapes—which is, he acknowledges, how ordinary people (*hoi polloi*) speak (a crucial concession)—but also in respect to purely geometrical figures of the sort produced by carpenters' instruments (for the universal fire as beautiful, cf. 29C1–3). Even here, though, the term continues to refer to visible forms.

The Platonic conception of beauty had a great impact on Christian thinking, and the Church Fathers carried on the tradition of analogizing the beauty of the soul to that of the body. Thus, John Chrysostom affirms, "Just as those who are in love with splendid bodies, when they are absent, carry with them the vision of the one they miss [*tên pothoumenên . . . opsin*], so we who are in love with the beauty [*kállos*] of your soul carry with us always the shapeliness [*eumorphia*] of your mind [*dianoia*]" (*De paenitentia*, 49.277.4–9). In his treatise *What Kinds of Women One Ought to Marry*, Chrysostom writes: "Why do you speak to me of the shapeliness [*eumorphia*] of the body? Take note of an abundance of moderation [*sôphrosunê*], take note of the *kállos* in the soul" (51.235.41–43). One passage in which the beauty of the body and the virtue of the soul are clearly distinguished is in Gregory of Nyssa's tract *On the Annunciation*, where he says of the Virgin Mary: "Of all peoples, she alone was deemed worthy to give birth to God; she alone bore the one who bears all things by means of his word. We may wonder not only at the *kállos* of the Mother of God, but also at the virtue [*to enareton*] of her soul" (60–62). Gregory does not seek to interpret Mary's physical beauty as an expression of her virtue; the two attributes are distinct, and there is no reason to suppose that he is concerned about the kind of ambiguity in the nature of beauty that troubled Roger Scruton and Javier Moscoso (see Chapter 1).

Nevertheless, the extension of the noun *kállos* goes beyond physical or visible appearance, and the term is found also in connection with language in the classical period. In Plato's *Symposium* (198B4–5), Socrates responds to Agathon's eloquent speech in praise of Eros, in which he dwells on the beauty of the god (cf. 196B4–5) by declaring, "Who could hear the beauty [*kállos*] of your final words and phrases without being thunderstruck?" To be sure, beauty is here ascribed to speech, but I suspect that Socrates is being gently ironic, transferring to Agathon's rhetoric the attribute that he had insistently applied to Eros himself. Shortly afterward (210A), Socrates refers to words (*logoi*) as *kaloí* but describes bodies as possessing *kállos*. Aristotle, in the *Rhetoric* (1405b5–8), says that the beauty (*kállos*) of a word (*onoma*) lies "in the sounds or the sense [*en tois psophois ê tôi sêmainomenôi*]." Aristotle's successor Theophrastus, in a fragment (95.1 Wimmer = 687 Fortenbaugh et al. 1992) likely derived from his essay *On Style*,[6] reportedly defined *to kállos* as follows: "*Kállos* of a word [*onomatos*] is what is pleasing to hearing or to sight or noble in significance [*to têi dianoiâi entimon*]." The source for this information is the treatise *On Interpretation* or *On Style* (*Peri hermeneias*, 173), attributed to the Peripatetic thinker and

politician Demetrius of Phalerum (ca. 350–280 BC). The date of
this treatise is much debated, and the modern consensus seems to
be that it may well be as late as the second century AD.[7] The essay
indicates that a river may have *kállos* (6), and mentions Sappho's
poems about beauty (166), but there is reference also to the
beauty of an epistle. Such beauty results from friendly sentiments
and a liberal use of adages (232). We are also told that periods
containing multiple clauses produce *kállos* rather than forcefulness
(*deinotês*, 252; for the same contrast, cf. 274).

Dionysius of Halicarnassus (first century BC), in his essay *On the
Composition of Words* (3), cites a passage from the *Odyssey* (16.1–16)
and notes that it is not the diction that renders it so persuasive,
for the words themselves are ordinary enough; nor does it contain
remarkable metaphors or other tropes: "What remains, then,"
he asks, "except to hold the composition [*sunthesis*, that is, of
the words] responsible for the beauty of the style [*tou kállous tês
hermêneias*]?" He goes on to quote a passage from Herodotus (1.8),
and concludes once again that the persuasive force of the style (*hê
peithô tês hermêneias*) resides not in the beauty of the words but in
their arrangement (*suzugia*).[8] Of course, Dionysius too uses the
term *kállos* for physical beauty, as when he notes (16) that Homer,
in describing the kind of handsome sight that induces pleasure,
chooses words that have appropriate sounds. Longinus, for his
part, applies the word *kállos* in the plural to the beautiful qualities
of objects such as honeycombs or buildings, but also to style or
hermêneia (*On the Sublime*, 5.1). Pollux (second century AD), in his
Lexicon (1.2), explains that he aimed to select his entries not with
a view to quantity but rather to *kállos*, though when it comes to
giving synonyms for *kállos*, he selects terms such as *hôra* (youthful
prime), *anthos* (flower), *anthêsis* (flowering), *lamprotês* (brightness),
stilpnotês (glistening), and *aiglê* (sunbeam), which plainly refer to
visible qualities (3.72), and he takes the trouble to explain that

the comic poets were fond of calling purple-dyed clothing *kállê*,
the plural of *kállos* (7.63, citing Eupolis), as though this were an
exceptional usage (but cf. Aeschylus, *Agamemnon*, 923, cited in
Chapter 2).

But it is with Hermogenes's treatise *On Style* (second century
AD) that *kállos* comes into its own as a technical term and a
stylistic category; it is the subject (along with *epimeleia* or "care" in
composition) of the twelfth chapter of Book 1. For Hermogenes,
beauty is above all a matter of harmony and proportion. As he
puts it:

> In general, beauty is a symmetry of limbs and parts [*summetria
> melôn kai merôn*], along with a good complexion [*eukhroia*], and it
> is through these that a speech [*logos*] becomes [beautiful], whether
> entire types [of style] are combined into the same [speech] or they
> [i.e., the elements] make up each type individually, for these are,
> as it were, their limbs and parts. It is necessary, then, if a speech
> is to be beautiful [*kalós*], whether it is variegated or uniform, that
> it have symmetry among these, that is, harmony [*euarmostia*], and
> that a kind of good complexion bloom upon it, which takes the
> form of a single quality of character throughout, and which some
> indeed naturally call the color [*khrôma*] of a speech.[9]

Hermogenes locates the source of the analogy between
the beauty of the body and that of discourse in a famous
passage in Plato's *Phaedrus* (264C), in which Plato compares
a well-organized speech to the human form. As Hermogenes
puts it, "This is what Plato means, I think, when he says a
speech should have a head and extremities and mid-parts
that are suited to one another and to the body as a whole,
but should not be each one tossed together confusedly, even
if they are individually beautiful [*kalá*]; for a beautiful [*kalós*]

speech can never be produced in this way" (Plato himself does
not invoke the idea of beauty in this passage). Hermogenes
goes on to indicate the kinds of stylistic devices that produce
such beautiful effects, all of which involve diction (*lexis*), for
example, figures of speech, clauses, combinations of words,
and the like. Thoughts or ideas (*ennoiai*) are not part of beauty,
strictly speaking. Hermogenes particularly stresses balanced
clauses (*parisôsis*), though one should avoid rigorous parallelism.
Anaphora can contribute to beauty, as can the opposite of
anaphora, that is, similar endings of a phrase (Hermogenes
calls this rhetorical figure antistrophe). Variation of case in the
same word (polyptoton); avoidance of hiatus; rhythm (provided
it does not slip over into verse), especially the rhythm of
clausulae, that is, the cadences at the end of phrases—all are
productive of *kállos*. It is clear that for Hermogenes beauty is
closely connected with symmetry and balance, features that
apply naturally to visible objects.

Thus, it would appear that even when the term *kállos* is applied
to nonhuman objects, it does not entirely lose its connection
with the visible and continues to bear, however lightly, overtones
of attractiveness and perhaps a quasi-erotic, or at least sensual,
appeal. Speeches, after all, were thought to exercise a kind of
magical power over their audiences, an ability to overcome reason
not by the strict logic of their arguments but by their sonorousness
and related stylistic effects: as early as Homer, the Sirens were
imagined to exert a fatal attraction over anyone who listened to
their songs. These resonant devices were what made a speech
"pretty." Such prettiness was not the same thing as effectiveness or
persuasiveness, both of which were prized more greatly. A forceful
style, like that of Demosthenes, was incompatible with an excess
of such charm. Rather, *kállos* was simply one element—and not
the most important one—in a panoply of stylistic resources.

We may see an example of the kind of attractiveness the Greeks found in balance and order in a remarkable story in Xenophon's *Oeconomicus*. Socrates recounts how the Spartan admiral Lysander admired Cyrus of Persia's orchard, in which the trees were planted so precisely as to arouse wonder at the order and symmetry of their rows; impressed as he is by their beauty (*kállos*), Lysander is the more amazed at whoever it was who measured them out and organized them in this way. When he learns that Cyrus himself did so, he is astounded, and upon observing the *kállos* of Cyrus's clothing, perfume, and jewelry, he expresses his surprise all the more. Cyrus assures Lysander that he never sits down to dinner without first engaging in some warlike or agricultural activity, upon which Lysander felicitates him as a truly good and happy man (4.20–25). Nevertheless, there is perhaps an undertone of criticism in this praise. Lysander frankly approves of beauty in a stand of trees, but he only takes notice of Cyrus's care with his personal appearance after hearing that Cyrus did the planting. He seems genuinely taken aback: "What are you saying, Cyrus? Did you really plant some of these with your own hands?" My suspicion is that Lysander regarded Cyrus's elaborate attire as effeminate and had to be reassured about Cyrus's military and agricultural competence before venturing to shake his hand (a sign of friendship) and bestow the compliment. Be that as it may, *kállos* could, as we have seen, be ascribed to things that are remarkable to behold, like the carpet on which Agamemnon feared to tread in Aeschylus's tragedy and the awe-inspiring monuments mentioned by Demosthenes (*Olynthiac*, 3.25, cited in Chapter 2).[10] Such attractive objects do not inspire *erôs* in the usual sense, but they are perceived, I think, as being desirable.

There is, however, a passage in Aristotle's *Eudemian Ethics* that would appear to endorse precisely a way of appreciating beauty that is removed from desire. Aristotle is discussing the virtue of temperance or *sôphrosunê*, and he observes, "Since a temperate person is so in regard to pleasures, it is necessary that he be so in regard to some desires." Aristotle goes on to specify that the desires or appetites (*epithumiai*) in question are principally those of touch and taste, or more simply touch, and he remarks that a person is not temperate "with regard to pleasure, through sight, in fine things [*kalá*], apart from a desire for sex, and in regard to distress at ugly things [*aiskhra*]," nor again in regard to the pleasure taken in harmonious or unharmonious music by way of the sense of hearing, nor in that deriving from good or foul smells; for no one is considered to be intemperate for feeling or not feeling pleasure in such things. The provision, "apart from a desire for sex," indicates that Aristotle is thinking of pleasure as distinct from the ordinary response to beauty. He goes on to say, "If, in fact, someone who is contemplating a fine [*kalós*] statue or horse or human being, or is listening to someone singing, does not wish [*bouloito*] to eat or drink or have sex but rather to contemplate the fine things [*ta kalá*] or listen to the singers, he would not seem to be intemperate." Aristotle notes further that animals, in contrast to human beings, are by nature more or less insensitive to pleasures other than touch and taste, such as the pleasures of harmony or *kállos*, for they seem to feel nothing in the contemplation of fine things (*ta kalá*) or in listening to what is harmonious. Thus, though many animals have a keen sense of smell, the pleasure they take in odors is incidental to their association with food; unlike human beings, they are incapable of enjoying aroma in and of itself (3.2, 1230b21–1231a12). Although I have translated the adjective *kalós* as "fine," it is clear that Aristotle has in mind the response to beauty, at least in regard to visual pleasure, as indicated unambiguously by the noun *kállos*; thus, the Bollingen translation of Aristotle's complete works gives: "Temperance is shown not in regard to visual pleasure in the beautiful (so long as it is unaccompanied by sexual appetite) or visual pain in the ugly" (Solomon 1984, 1949).

James Porter says the following of this passage: "What we find in Aristotle is in fact an interesting claim about pure aesthetic pleasure, and one comparable in ways to Kant's. It is a claim that wants to isolate the simple, unadorned act of aesthetic contemplation by itself, abstracted from all other impinging wants and desires" (Porter 2010, 53). Porter goes on to say that Kant's idea of lingering in the contemplation of the beautiful "is a partial calque, though no doubt an unintentional one, on Aristotle" (54). We must, however, take the context into account. Aristotle is here discussing temperance or moderation, as part of an analysis of the several virtues. His point is that, whereas an excessive delight in sex, which is inspired by physical beauty, is the mark of the profligate, not all pleasures that result from seeing or hearing are to be judged in this way: there is nothing intemperate about the wish—Aristotle does not say "desire"—to look at a fine statue or listen to pleasing music when the appetites are not thereby aroused. These pleasures resemble the pure or unmixed pleasures that Plato describes. They do not satiate desires (and hence relieve a painful state) but are pleasant in themselves. Perfect geometrical shapes elicit such a pleasure and possess beauty (*kállos*), Plato says, though not of the sort people usually suppose when they think of living creatures or paintings. Rather, the pleasure they produce is characteristically their own (*oikeia, Philebus*, 51C). Certain odors, sounds (Plato calls them "smooth and bright"), and colors such as pure white have this capacity, and so does learning (51D, 53A–B, 52A–B). Aristotle is making a similar claim (adapted to his argument about temperance) about two kinds of pleasure. Those pleasures that do not satisfy appetites (*epithumiai*) are aesthetic in the Greek sense of the term; that is, they are perceived by senses (*aisthêseis*). Though Aristotle speaks of statues and songs, he is not isolating a response specific to art or even to beauty in its several manifestations (the term *kállos* is applied only to visual objects) but to naturally pleasing stimuli from statues to horses to the fragrance of blossoms. All this seems to me to be far removed from Kant's concerns. Thus, the kind of dilemma or confusion that besets the English term *beauty*, with the peculiar sense it has acquired in modern aesthetic discourse, was less likely to arise.

That symmetry or proportion is somehow constitutive of beauty may be an elementary intuition, but the Greeks soon developed theories to explain why certain forms, and more particularly human appearance, might seem beautiful. Proportion seems to have been identified early on as the principal factor in determining beauty. Sometime in the latter half of the fifth century BC, the sculptor Polyclitus, a native of Argos, produced a treatise that he called *Canon*, in which he set forth his artistic principles.[11] *Canon* in Greek means a measuring rod or yardstick, and measure was the basic thesis. Polyclitus is said to have illustrated his theoretical principles in the statue called the Spearbearer (*Doryphoros*), of which there survive only copies that betray some variation on the original work (see Figure 4.1).

Although Polyclitus' treatise, like the original statue, is lost, we know from numerous later citations that he emphasized symmetry and harmony among the body's parts as essential to beauty, a view that was dominant among classical thinkers—we have seen one example of its application to rhetoric, in the citation from Hermogenes—and has remained so down to today.

According to Galen, the Stoic philosopher Chrysippus maintained that human beauty (*kállos*) resides

> not in the symmetry of elements [*stoikheia*] but in that of parts [or portions, *moria*], that is, of finger to finger, and of these collectively to the palm and wrist, and of these in turn to the forearm, and of the forearm to the upper arm, and of all these to

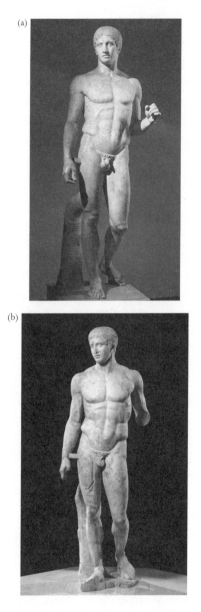

Figure 4.1 Polyclitus's Spearbearer (*Canon*). Top: Album/Art Resource, NY. Bottom: The *Doryphoros*, Roman, (second century BC)/Minneapolis Institute of Arts, MN, USA/The Bridgeman Art Library.

everything else, as is written in the *Canon* of Polyclitus. For having taught us in that treatise all the symmetries of the body, Polyclitus confirmed his argument with a work: he made a statue in accord with the principles of his argument, and called the statue itself, like the treatise, the *Canon*. That the beauty of the body lies in the symmetry of its parts is in accord with the views of all physicians and philosophers. (*On the Views of Plato and Hippocrates* 5)

It is possible that Polyclitus was influenced by Pythagorean doctrines of harmonics, and that his ratios were in some fashion based on these, but this is not entirely certain. Polyclitus's tract was enormously influential, and we may suppose that it encouraged, to some extent, the transfer of the idea of beauty from the human form to other less-tangible objects, such as music or verbal compositions, or indeed the soul itself, in which a harmony of elements could be discerned.[12] Thus, the fifth-century excerptor John Stobaeus cites a fragment ascribed to the Stoic Chrysippus: "Just as the *kállos* of the body is a symmetry of limbs [*melôn*] as they are arranged in it with respect to one another and to the whole, so too the *kállos* of the soul is a symmetry of reason [*logos*] and its parts [*merôn*] with respect to the whole of the soul and one another" (Stobaeus, *Ecl.*, 2.62, 15 W = *SVF*, 278.10).[13] Much later, Saint Basil of Caesarea (fourth century) would explain that "the true *kalón* is a symmetry in the soul that is disposed in accord with reason, since virtue is a kind of midpoint [*mesotês*] and symmetry.... Hence, what is symmetrical in respect to virtue is beauty [*kállos*] of the soul" (*Enarratio in prophetam Isaiam*, 5.174.12–21). Vice, on the contrary, is a lack of proportion or mean.

II. Ecphrasis or Pictures into Words   If we turn to the realm of art, specifically the visual arts as we understand the term today, we may illustrate how *kállos* was applied by way of some texts that purport to describe works of this kind, and which constitute a type of subgenre modern scholars have named "ecphrasis" (in classical Greek, the term had a rather wider range and covered verbal descriptions of various sorts).[14] The satirist Lucian (second century) composed a monologue called *Zeuxis and Antiochus*, in which the speaker explains that he, like the great painter Zeuxis, is indifferent to praise based on the novelty of his compositions. Zeuxis and the speaker prefer that their art be judged by those capable of recognizing their technical skill (2.5), such as precise lines, good mixture of colors, and satisfactory proportions, the criteria by which experts evaluate craftsmanship (more on this aspect in Chapter 6). Beauty is mentioned only connection with the upper part of the female centaur depicted in the painting, which is described as *pankalon* (except for the ears, 6). The ignorant masses that look only to innovation, says Zeuxis, "praise only the dross, but take little account of whether it is well made (*kalôs ekhei*) and in accord with art in relation to light" (7).[15] In Lucian's dialogue called *Images* (*Eikones*), Lycinus describes to Polystratus an extraordinarily beautiful (*pankalê*, 1) woman he has just seen. Polystratus exclaims, "That's some marvellous beauty [*terastion ti kállos*] you're sketching" (2). To capture her appearance, Lycinus appeals to specific features of a variety of famous statues, reversing the process by which Zeuxis is said to have composed his portrait of Helen of Troy: selecting the most perfect features of five different women.[16] On this basis, Polystratus succeeds in identifying the woman as Panthea, the mistress of the Roman emperor Lucius Verus. But he proceeds at once to insist that her spiritual beauty is even greater than her physical. As he puts it, "You seem to praise her superficial qualities, that is, her body and form [*morphê*], but you have not seen the virtues of her soul, nor do you know how great its beauty [*kállos*] is, far better and more divine than that of the body" (11). Lucian here exploits the conventional trope, noted above, by which *kállos* is transferred from the body, to which it is most typically ascribed, to the soul. But he easily slips back into ordinary usage a sentence later, when he affirms that he praises her mildness, humaneness, high-mindedness, modesty, and cultivation ahead of her *kállos*, "since these are held to be worth more than the body." A moment later he is willing to assert that perfect *kállos* resides in the combination of the soul's virtue and the body's shapeliness (*eumorphia*).[17] But the beauty of the soul is also attractive and inspires *erôs*. As Polystratus says, the soul's beauty is *erasmiôtera* ("more loveable") than the body's (21). He concludes with the flourish that, as Homer puts it, Panthea can compete with Aphrodite for *kállos* and with Athena for deeds (22). In the end, beauty refers primarily to physical appeal, and Athena stands for other qualities.

Philostratus, called the Elder, composed two books of ecphrases (*Eikones*), and in these, as in Lucian's work of the same name, beauty is ascribed not to works of art but to the figures they represent. The fourth of the series describes how the young Menoeceus sacrificed his life for the welfare of his city, Thebes. As his soul departs his body, Philostratus seems to hear its complaint and remarks, "Souls too experience desire [*erôs*] for beautiful things [*kalá*]" (1.4.3). The sense of *kalón* here is suggested by the reference to passion, though one might equally well render it as "noble things."[18] There is an apparent reference to beauty also in the sixth ecphrasis, which is of a painting of Cupids (*Erôtes*). Four of these are said to be *kallistoi* (1.6.3), which perhaps means not that they are the loveliest (are some Cupids prettier than others?) but rather that they are the most finely wrought. Immediately afterward, Philostratus says that the entire scene is a *kalón ainigma*, "a fine riddle," using the term *kalón* here in a broader sense. As we have seen in other contexts, there are usually signs to indicate when the adjective *kalós* bears the sense of "beautiful." Thus, a boy and a girl are said to be beautiful (*kalô*, dual) and to have been on fire for one another (1.12.3); elsewhere, Philostratus remarks that it is easy to paint Ariadne and Theseus as beautiful (*kalê, kalós*, 1.15.2; conceivably the adjective here suggests valor in the case of Theseus).[19] Narcissus, upon looking into the pool, is "thirsting for beauty" (*kállos*, 1.23.5; cf. 2.5.3, where *kállos* is used of the beauty of the Amazon Rhodogune; 2.9.5, of Panthea even as she is dying). Philostratus observes that jewelry embellishes the looks of women of middling beauty (*kállos*) but does not favor either ugly or very lovely women (*agan hôraiai*, 2.8.5). At one point, horses that are sweaty and dust covered are said to be less handsome (*káloi*) but more true to life (*alêthesteroi*, 1.27.2). A fine-looking animal might indeed be described as *kalós*, or even as possessing *kállos*, and Philostratus applies the adjective also to olive trees (2.6.1), seas (2.16.4), a city (2.17.13), and even grapevines (2.34.2). But it is the contrast between *kalós* and truth that stands out here: most often, *kalós* refers precisely to mimetic quality. Thus, at 2.28.3, the painter's work is called *kalá*, but the reference is not to beauty but precisely to accuracy of technique in drawing a spider in accord with nature (*kata tên phusin*), right down to its awful fuzz; this is the mark, says Philostratus, of a good craftsman and one who is tremendous with regard to the truth (*deinou tên alêtheian*). As Plutarch neatly puts it in his essay, *How a Youth Should Listen to Poems*, "imitating something excellent [the term is *kalós*] is not the same as doing it excellently [adverb, *kalôs*]" (18D). So too, Philostratus can speak of a tiara that has been represented accurately (*kalôs memimêtai* at 2.31.1), with no implication that it is beautiful (cf. 2.9.4, of grave offerings). Olympus, the inventor (by some accounts) of the flute, is described as exploring *kállos* (1.21.1); the sense here, however, is not a beautiful song as such so much as pretty musical effects, a usage familiar, as we have seen, from treatises on style.

The younger Philostratus (grandson of the Elder), who also composed a book of ecphrases, is particularly alert to the gendered nature of beauty, as in his description of nymphs as possessing an "unbeatable *kállos*," though they incline, as he puts it, to "feminine loveliness" (*thêleian hôran*, 1). Of Hesione, chained to a rock, like Andromeda, and exposed to a sea monster, Philostratus writes: "The circumstances do not allow me to represent the beauty [*kállos*] of the girl accurately, since her fear for her life and her anxiety over what she sees dim the bloom of her youthful attractiveness [*hôra*]" (12 = 884.8–12). Again, of Atalanta, who fought the Calydonian boar and is dressed in hunting gear, he says: "Her beauty, which is naturally masculine in appearance [*arrenôpon*], the occasion makes still more so: she casts no alluring glance [*ephimeron*], but strains the beams of her eyes for a sense of the action" (15). Meleager's face, in turn, is so tense that nothing can be said about its beauty (*kállos*, 15). Nor can Philostratus say anything, he affirms, about the beauty of the generals, Eurypylus and Pyrrhus, because they are covered in armor, though he notes that they are both tall, young, and energetic (10 = 875.31–876.3). The term *kalós*, in turn, is broader in significance. After recounting the celestial images on the shield of Achilles, now carried by his son Pyrrhus, Philostratus turns to what he calls the finest thing (*kalliston*) on earth, namely the two cities depicted there (10 = 876.33–35).

In the third or fourth century, one Callistratus tried his hand at describing not paintings but statues. He too notes that soft skin and tender limbs are suitable for a beautiful girl (*kalê*, 1.4) as opposed to a satyr. Narcissus, who is described as being about the same age as the Erôtes or Cupids, seems to radiate lightning from the beauty (*kállos*) of his body (5.1), and the spring into which he gazes is also lovely (*pankalos*). There might seem to be a reference to the beauty of a work of art as such, rather than to the figure represented in it, in Callistratus's account of Lysippus's statue of the personified *Kairos*, that is, "Timeliness." According to the Loeb Library translation, Callistratus calls it "the most beautiful of statues which the artist wrought [*hoper agalmatôn kalliston ho dêmiourgos tekhnêsamenos*]" (6.1, trans. Fairbanks 1931). But "most *kalón*" might better be rendered as "finest" or even "most true to life." Callistratus goes on to specify that in this statue, "technique competed with nature [*pros tên phusin hamillômenês tês tekhnês*]" in producing an exact or true image. *Kairos* was modeled on a youth's attractiveness (*hôraios*), which was evident as well on his ruddy cheeks.[20] Callistratus explains that "all that is youthful [*hôraion*] is timely [*eukairon*], and Timeliness is the only craftsman of beauty [*kállos*]" (6.4). The reference is clearly to the beauty of the figure, not that of the artwork. Of a statue of Orpheus Callistratus affirms that "it is *kalliston* to see, for bronze, jointly with art [*tekhnê*], engendered beauty [*kállos*]" italicize (7.1), and it signaled the musical nature of Orpheus's soul by way of the splendor of his body.[21] I suspect that the superlative adjective *kalliston* is employed here as the term of art to refer to a successful representation (it might be rendered as "excellent"), whereas the noun *kállos* refers specifically to the physical beauty of the subject. Upon entering a temple which housed "the finest semblance [*tên kallistên eikasian*]" (12.1), Callistratus saw a statue of a centaur as centaurs ought to look, as he puts it, "the stone most accurately [*kallista*] representing the mane and everything striving for a true image [*alêthês tupos*]" (12.3). So too, when Callistratus speaks of a contest in fine works of painting (*tôn tês graphês kalôn*, 14.1), it is likely that he has in mind not so much beauty as mimetic achievement.

Callistratus waxes more metaphysical in his description of the statue of Paean, identified either with Asclepius or

Apollo.[22] He affirms, "What we are seeing seems to me to be, not an image [*tupos*], but a fashioning of the truth [*tês alêtheias plasma*]."[23] Callistratus goes on to remark that "the face enthralls the senses of the viewer, for it has not been shaped for a superficial beauty [*kállos epitheton*] but it lifts its holy [*panagnon*] and propitious eyes and flashes forth an unutterable depth of majesty blended with modesty" (10.2). Beauty is on the surface and corporeal; the more profound truth is not describable in physical terms.

In the above accounts of works of art, there are no sure instances in which beauty is ascribed to the work as such, as an aesthetic object, irrespective of the people or objects represented in the work. Even in the case of Polyclitus's *Canon*, it is not at all clear that he is describing the ideal dimensions and proportions of a sculpture as opposed to the human figure represented in the sculpture, or indeed that Polyclitus would necessarily have seen a difference between the two. He might well have replied that a work of art is beautiful when, and just because, it captures the figure of a beautiful subject, thereby sidestepping the issue that has proved so contentious in modern aesthetic theory, namely whether an artwork can be called beautiful even though it depicts a person or scene that we should be inclined to call ugly in itself (see Chapter 1). To the best of my knowledge, this question was not raised in the literature of classical antiquity.

What is more, although the figure represented in Polyclitus's statue is that of a young male, there is no apparent reason to assume that his beauty is in some way an indication of his virtue or other spiritual qualities. As we know, male youths in classical Greece were considered to be sexually attractive, and the statue of the nude, beardless, spear-bearing lad might well have been viewed as sexually alluring, not as an image of an immature child or a divinity sheltered from male desire. Modern critics have rightly praised the dynamic quality of the contrapposto posture, with the hips and shoulders at uneven heights and the tension in legs' position creating a sense of energy and movement. But the figure is undeniably attractive, and this may well be an aspect of the beauty that the ancients, and Polyclitus himself, saw in it. There is no necessary rupture here between beauty and desire.

The ancient Greek idea of beauty is not limited to the attractiveness of a desirable body or, more widely, of a visible object that is somehow splendid and eye-catching.[24] Beauty came to be associated particularly with the notion of symmetry and proportion in things like music or rhetorical style, and even in more abstract entities, such as the soul, though it seems to have retained a sense of charm or appeal. This is true even at the idealized level of Platonic forms, as we shall see. It is here that there arose an unexpected challenge to the theory that beauty consists in symmetry and the ratio among parts.

III. Transcendent Beauty   In his anthology of quotations from classical sources, John Stobaeus cites this from Hermes Trismegistus: "All those human beings who are lovers of the body can never behold the sight of the *kalón* and the good; for, my son, *kállos* is the kind of thing that possesses neither form nor color nor body" (*Anthologium*, 1.21.9). The hermetic writings that survive and are ascribed to this mysterious figure, the Thrice-Greatest Hermes, date to the Christian era, but the conception of beauty recorded here has its roots in Plato's theory of ideal forms, existing in a purely intellectual or noumenal dimension and free of all corporeal attributes.

There is a dialogue by Plato (though some scholars prefer to ascribe it to a disciple of his) that is often said to have as its topic the nature of beauty, just as Plato's *Euthyphro* is on the subject of piety or holiness and his *Charmides* deals with temperance and his *Laches* seeks to define courage. These are instances of what are sometimes labeled "What is X?" dialogues, which revolve around the characterization of one or another concept, usually related to ethics. The dialogue in question is the *Greater Hippias* or *Hippias Major*, which features the well-known Sophist Hippias as Socrates's interlocutor (the "Major" in the title serves to distinguish it from another dialogue involving Hippias, called the *Hippias Minor*). This dialogue certainly belongs to the "what is" type. Socrates pretends that he himself was asked, in the course of a conversation in which he was faulting some things as shameful or repulsive (*aiskhra*) and praising others as *kalá*: "How do you know, Socrates, what kinds of things are *kalá* and *aiskhra*? Come then, can you tell me what the *kalón* is [*ti esti to kalón*]?" (286C8–D1). Our question is how to understand the expression *to kalón*: does it mean beauty, as Drew Hyland has argued (as we saw in Chapter 2), or rather something like "excellence" generally, with no particular implication of attractiveness, physical or otherwise?

The discussion takes its point of departure when Socrates professes to be impressed by how much Sophists earn, to which Hippias replies, "You know nothing about the *kalá* in this; for if you knew how much money I have made, you would be amazed" (282D6–7). Some translators render *kalá* here as "beauties," but if so, the term is being used very loosely, a bit the way we say "it's a beauty" in English slang. Hippias is more concerned, however, with demonstrating how fine his art is, and this is surely the sense of *kalón* here. Socrates acknowledges as much when he replies, "What you're saying is *kalón*, Hippias, and a great proof of your wisdom" (282E9).[25] Again, Hippias applies the adjective to the noun *epitêdeuma* (286A3, B2), "habitual practices" or "behavior." The initial context sets up the expectation that the idea in question will be something like honor or even virtue. Thus, when Socrates comes round to asking Hippias what the *kalón* is (and he has just remarked that Hippias has arrived *eis kalón*, that is, at just the right moment or opportunely), it is hardly clear that the subject about which Socrates is inquiring is beauty.[26]

It is true that when Socrates specifies shortly afterward that what he wants to know is not "what is *kalón*" but rather "what is the *kalón*," Hippias replies, rather fatuously, "a *kalê* maiden is *kalón*" (287E4), which presumably means something like "a pretty girl is a fine thing." This response completely misses the point of Socrates's question. Hippias's reply certainly shows that the notion of beauty could be triggered by the term *kalós*, but at the same time makes it clear that beauty is at best one example of excellence. In this, his answer resembles the Theocritean verse cited in Chapter 2, "A boy's *kállos* is *kalón*" (23.32), that is, a good thing, though it is transient. Socrates shows the flaw in Hippias's definition by observing that a *kalê* mare or lyre or pot would also be a fine thing (*kalón*), so Hippias's attempt is not very helpful. Backed into a corner, Hippias says that a pot too can be *kalón* if it is made *kalôs* (adverb), that is, well, but it nevertheless does not compare with a fine horse or maiden or other such things that are *kalá* (288E6–9; Hippias seems to have forgotten the beautiful bowl that Homer mentioned in the *Iliad*). Socrates upsets this argument by pointing out that the most beautiful maiden will be ugly when compared to a divinity, citing Heraclitus to the effect that the wisest human being appears a mere monkey when matched with a god in respect to wisdom or beauty (*kállos*) or anything else (289B2–5). This is one of only two passages in the dialogue in which the noun *kállos* occurs (the other being at 292D3, to which we will return in a moment), and it appears to be only one fine thing among many. In any case, when Socrates presses Hippias to explain what it is by virtue of which a maiden or horse or lyre is *kalós*, Hippias declares that it is gold (289E3).

It is clear that the argument is not progressing very well, and Socrates gives short shrift to Hippias's reply by pointing out that a gold pot or ladle will hardly be more suitable for preparing lentils than one made of wood, and if less suitable, then less *kalê* (290D6–291B6). Here it is clear that for Socrates a fine item is one that performs its function, and looks good or right for that reason; this may be a sound account of why we like the appearance of a thing, but it is not about beauty as such. Perhaps taking his cue from Socrates, Hippias next offers that the finest thing for a man is to be rich, healthy, and honored through to old age and to be buried nobly (*kalôs*) by his descendants (291D9–E2), an ideal modeled on Solon's description of the most prosperous (*olbios*) life in Herodotus's tale of his encounter with Croesus (1.30). Again, this fails to isolate what it is that renders all things worthy of the name *kalós*.

Socrates here represents his imagined interlocutor as irritably demanding an answer to the question, "What is *kállos* in and of itself [*auto*]?" (292D3–4), resorting here (with what I take to be exasperation) to the noun as a way of short-circuiting the kind of adjectival response that has been offered so far (such and such is *kalón*). Certainly, Socrates is not discouraged from pursuing the question of whether it is *kalón* for everyone to die old (not to mention the gods), a sense of the word that hardly corresponds to "beautiful." We need not follow the various other definitions proposed for the *kalón*—such as what is fitting, or useful, or advantageous, or good—but may turn directly to Socrates's suggestion that the *kalón* is just what provides pleasure through hearing or sight (297E5–7). Thus, we call behavior or laws fine if they either look or sound fine to us (298B2–4). Pleasures that derive from the other senses are not particularly noble, so they may be dismissed, but even so, Socrates desires to know what the pleasures deriving from sight and sound have in common. The answer to this proves elusive as well. The argument is intricate and the reasoning perhaps dubious,[27] but Socrates's final option seems to have brought the discussion closer to the idea of beauty as it was commonly understood, in reference to visual (and by extension, auditory) attractiveness. The aporetic conclusion may serve as a prelude to the more metaphysical discussion of beauty in other dialogues,[28] and in this respect the second formulation of the central "what is . . . ?" question by Socrates's imagined interrogator, in which he substitutes *kállos* for *to kalón*, may point forward to a narrowing of the focal concept. If so, there is nevertheless a long delay till the discussion comes round to something like beauty in the ordinary sense, and in the meantime *kalós* retains its wide semantic range. It is thus misleading to take the subject of the dialogue as beauty *tout court*.[29]

Plato did, however, recognize a special place for beauty in his metaphysical doctrine of "forms," or in Greek, *ideai* or "ideas." Above all in his *Symposium, Phaedrus*, and *Republic*—often regarded as constituting the core of his so-called middle dialogues (though the chronology is based largely on inference from the texts)—Plato introduces a transcendent interpretation of beauty, placing it alongside such idealized abstractions as the good, justice, and the one. Given that the subject of the *Symposium* is erotic passion (the dialogue takes the form of a series of eulogies of the god Eros), it is no surprise that beauty should play a role. Socrates is described as having dressed up for the party at Agathon's house, celebrating his victory in the tragic performances and looking especially *kalós* (174A). This sets the scene for a discussion of appearance, but the term is applied also to wisdom (175E). In the first speech, Phaedrus affirms that the *erôs* of a lover for his young beloved is a uniquely powerful stimulus to great and fine (*kalá*) deeds (178D, cf. 179C), though he also argues that Patroclus must have been the lover of Achilles rather than the other way around (as Aeschylus

had represented it), since Achilles was handsomer (*kalliôn*) than
all the other Greeks (180A; cf. Chapter 2). The next speaker,
Pausanias, observes that an action (*praxis*) is neither *kalê* nor the
reverse (that is, *aiskhra*), but a deed is *kalón* if it is performed
well (*kalôs*). That is why not every kind of *erôs* is necessarily
kalós (180E–181A). The doctor Eryximachus, who comes next,
represents *erôs* as a universal force of attraction that is not directed
only toward those who are *kaloí* (186A). He too divides *erôs* into
a noble and a shameful sort (186D, 187D). Agathon is the first
to use the term *kállos* in the *Symposium* (196A; Aristophanes uses
neither the adjective nor the noun in his discourse); he refers
to Eros as *kallistos* and *aristos* ("best," 195A), and he explains the
former term by observing that the god is youngest and most
tender (*hapalos*, 195D), has a supple and symmetrical form
(194A), and has a beautiful complexion (196A), all of which
amply confirm his *kállos* (196B; cf. 197B–C, E; Agathon goes on to
demonstrate the god's *aretê*).

Socrates, in turn, professes to be flabbergasted by Agathon's
speech, which he deems *kalós*, especially for the beauty (*kállos*) of
the words and phrases in the peroration (198B). He nevertheless
maintains that praise should not be simply pretty (*kallista*) but
true (198D–E), and he immediately turns the tables on Agathon
by observing that if the gods made the world as they did out of
erôs for things that are *kalá*, as Agathon had affirmed, then Eros
the god is nothing other than *erôs* (passion) for *kállos* (beauty,
201A). And since one can desire only what one lacks, Eros must
lack *kállos*, and what lacks *kállos* cannot be *kalós* (201B). Socrates
makes the further move of identifying *kalós* with *agathos* or "good"
(201C), which involves a certain sleight of hand, since it depends
on the moral significance of the adjective. On this note, Socrates
introduces the discourse of Diotima (201E), who explains that
just because Eros is not *kalós*, it does not follow that he is *aiskhros*

("ugly" or "shameful"), since there is a middle term, which is neither (202B). What is more, since the gods are *kalói*, Eros must be something other than a god, namely a *daimôn* or intermediate spirit. Because he desires what is *kalós*, he is associated with Aphrodite (203C): here, the idea of beauty is uppermost. Diotima concludes that those who are lovers of wisdom are likewise in an intermediate state, neither wise nor wholly ignorant (204A), and so Eros, always desiring what is most *kalón*, must himself be a philosopher. Diotima next says that what is really *kalón* is also lovable or desirable (*eraston*, 204C) and then, in a complex and much-discussed argument that we need not explore here, concludes that *erôs* is a desire for immortality along with the good, since one wants to possess the good forever (206E–207A), and seeks to give birth to this in bodies and still more souls that are *kalós* (209B; we have noted previously this shift from corporeal to spiritual beauty). But one who loves beauty in any given body will then seek the beauty that all bodies have in common, and from there will proceed to love beauty in souls, and beyond that, will come to see (*theasasthai*) the *kalón* that resides in behavior and laws and then behold the beauty (*kállos*) of all kinds of knowledge, until perceiving that single knowledge which is the knowledge of the *kalón* itself (210B–E), which is invariably the same and the cause of beauty in all things that participate in it (in the rest of her lesson, Diotima employs only *kalón*). Reference to the noun *kállos* returns in the exchange that Alcibiades reports with Socrates, in which he professes to believe that Socrates can improve him: "You see an incredible beauty [*kállos*] in me," Socrates says, "one that is far superior to your own comeliness [*eumorphia*]" (218E). He adds that if Alcibiades is planning to exchange beauty for beauty, he is getting the better bargain, for instead of an appearance (*doxa*) of *kalá* he will obtain the truth. Throughout the dialogue, beauty remains an object of vision, though it may be beheld not

just by ordinary sight but by the mind; indeed, it may have been
Plato who coined the expression, "the mind's eye" (cf. *Symposium*,
219A, *tês dianoias opsis; Republic*, 533D, *to tês psukhês omma; Sophist*,
254A, *tês psukhês ommata*). For all its elevation to the level of a
transcendent idea, beauty remains the object of *erôs* or desire
and is the source of human aspiration to higher things—that is,
to all that is *kalón*. According to Plato, we seek the good because
the good is beautiful, a conceptual synthesis that continues to
influence aesthetic theories to this day, as we saw in Chapter 1
in connection with the views of Alexander Nehamas and Elaine
Scarry.

Plato developed his conception of the beautiful in the *Phaedrus*
and the *Republic*. In his first speech in the *Phaedrus*, Socrates
describes a youth who was very handsome (*kalós*, 237B) and for
this reason had many lovers, among whom one who was in fact
in love with him tried to persuade him that he was not. This lover
affirms that love is a kind of desire (*epithumia*), although even those
who are not in love desire things that are *kalá* (237D). Clearly,
he means to convince the lad that he himself has a noble interest
in him. Love, in any case, is a desire that is drawn to beauty
(238B–C). In his second speech, in which he retracts the earlier
one, Socrates praises a kind of *mania* or madness like that of the
prophetesses, who achieve fine things (*kalá*, 244B1; cf. *kalá erga*,
245B2). But *erôs* too is a fine madness, for the sight of beauty here
below evokes the memory of true beauty (*kállos*); a lover is one
who, under the influence of such madness, loves things that are
kalá (249D–E). Now, there are lots of fine things that are images
of the ideal world, such as justice and moderation, but beauty
(*kállos*) by its nature is brighter and thus more easily recollected
(250B; cf. 250C–D). Of all the ideal forms, beauty is perceived by
the eyes, which are its special instruments (250D; cf. 251B, 251E,
252A; at 251C and 254B it is the beauty of a boy that is specified,

and this is clearly presupposed throughout). Indeed, Plato speaks of the "flow of beauty [*kállos*] going back toward the beautiful one [*kalós*] by way of the eyes" (255C). Of all things on earth, it is beauty—physical, bodily beauty, particularly that of boys—that is most capable of drawing us upward to the dimly recollected world of pure ideas.[30] In the *Republic*, Socrates takes it for granted that a god is in no way lacking in beauty or virtue (381C), and he later defines virtue as a kind of health, beauty, and well-being of the soul (444D); the "kind of" (*tis*) presumably signals the transfer to the psyche of terms usually employed in reference to the body. Plato again distinguishes between seeing things that are *kalá* and the mind's beholding the *kalón* itself (476B), and he immediately thereafter rephrases the contrast as one between things that are *kalá* and the beautiful (*kállos*) itself (476C; cf. 479A; contrast 491C, where bodily beauty is a potentially negative trait, like wealth or strength, since it draws one away from virtue; cf. 591B, 618A, for ordinary corporeal beauty). Ideal beauty exceeds all other things, even transcendent ideals, precisely in beauty (509A; cf. 615A).

Platonic beauty, then, retains a close connection with the visible, evident in the very term *idea*, which derives from the verb meaning "see." In Plato's system, the self-subsisting, objective idea of beauty serves two purposes. First, it inspires the desire that attracts us toward the transcendent (we feel the inadequacy of our body-bound lives and senses). Second, it accounts for why certain things in this world are beautiful: it is by virtue of participation in the ideal form, a process that Plato never quite explains satisfactorily but which relates sensible phenomena to the noumenal universe.[31]

Plato's theory was to have enormous influence on later thought (Alfred North Whitehead characterized the entire European philosophical tradition as "a series of footnotes to Plato"),[32] and his most prominent disciple, sometimes regarded as the founder of Neoplatonism (a modern coinage), was Plotinus (third century AD), the author of a set of tracts preserved in six books, each containing nine sections or mini-treatises and hence called *Enneads* (i.e., groups of nine; they were organized in this fashion by Plotinus's pupil Porphyry). The first essay, chronologically speaking, in the *Enneads* (1.6.1) is devoted to the theme of beauty. Plotinus begins by observing that "*to kalón* is principally in sight," but he immediately adds that "it is also in hearing in respect to the composition of words, and in every kind of music as well; for melodies and rhythms are fine [*kaloí*]. And, as we proceed higher and away from sensation [*aisthêsis*], there are habits that are fine [*kalá*], and actions, and characters, and kinds of knowledge [*epistêmai*], and there is a beauty of virtues [*to tôn aretôn kállos*]." The debt to Plato is manifest, as is the easy slippage between the terms *kállos* and *kalós* that smoothes the transition from visible to more abstract entities, since *kalós* is the appropriate adjective for fine or noble actions and traits. Thus, there is something of a surprise effect when Plotinus concludes his climactic sequence by referring to the *kállos* of the virtues, since this suggests a perceptible kind of beauty. But for Plotinus, as for Plato, the apprehension of these more abstract ideas is analogous to vision (see *Enneads*, 3.9.5: "the soul itself must be like vision"; cf. 4.4.24–25). Plotinus is moved shortly afterward to inquire whether all things are beautiful by virtue of one and the same beauty (or "fineness": *heni kai tôi autôi kalôi*), or whether there is one kind of *kállos* in the body, and another in other things—in other words, the very dilemma, it would seem, that exercised Roger Scruton (see Chapter 1). But Plotinus's concern is in fact rather different. If beauty resides, he reasons, in the harmony and symmetry among the parts of an object, then it cannot be an attribute of intellectual things, since they are partless. Platonism thus posed a fundamental challenge to the theory associated with Polyclitus, according to which beauty consists precisely in proportion, for on these terms the idea of beauty could not itself be beautiful.[33] Rejecting the explanation according to proportion, then, Plotinus argues that ideal beauty, which is simple, imparts to compound things a semblance of true beauty by molding as far as possible their diverse parts into a unified whole. As we shall see, this conception was to find a profound echo in the emergence of the modern discipline of aesthetics in the eighteenth century, beginning with the treatise by Alexander Gottlieb Baumgarten, who is credited with inventing the term in his treatise, *Aesthetica* (1750–1758).[34]

Like Plato, Plotinus understood beauty—above all, the idea of beauty—to exercise a profound attraction on the soul, which he likened to *erôs*. Thus, he waxes lyrical on the experience of perceiving the true cause and nature of beauty: "And one that shall know this vision—with what passion of love shall he not be seized, with what pang of desire, what longing to be molten into one with This, what wondering delight . . . ! He loves with a veritable love, with sharp desire; all other loves than this he must despise, and disdain all that once seemed fair" (trans. MacKenna 1969). The language is that of erotic desire, with which ideal beauty preserved an intimate relation.[35]

The Christian appropriation of Neoplatonic thought was complex, especially in relation to the ascription of beauty to God. It was an article of faith, of course, that human beings were created in God's image, but any analogy between a beautiful person (as beauty is ordinarily conceived) and the appearance of God carried the danger of a kind of trivial anthropomorphism, the more threatening in Christianity because God was understood to have assumed a human form with the birth of Jesus Christ (who was considered by some Church Fathers to be in fact beautiful), and also because God, although entirely transcendent, was nevertheless represented in the pictorial arts. We can see the tension clearly in the discussion of this problem by Gregory of Nyssa, in his treatise *On the Creation of Man* (*De opificio hominis*, chapter 5):

> It is true, indeed, that the Divine beauty [*kállos*] is not adorned
> with any shape or endowment of form, by any beauty of colour,
> but is contemplated as excellence in unspeakable bliss. As then
> painters transfer human forms [*morphai*] to their pictures by
> the means of certain colours, laying on their copy the proper
> and corresponding tints, so that the beauty of the original may
> be accurately transferred to the likeness, so I would have you
> understand that our Maker also, painting the portrait to resemble
> His own beauty, by the addition of virtues, as it were with colours,
> shows in us His own sovereignty. Manifold and varied are the
> tints, so to say, by which His true form is portrayed: not red, or
> white, or the blending of these, whatever it may be called, nor a
> touch of black that paints the eyebrow and the eye, and shades, by
> some combination, the depressions in the figure, and all such arts
> which the hands of painters contrive, but instead of these, purity,
> freedom from passion, blessedness, alienation from all evil, and
> all those attributes of the like kind which help to form in men the
> likeness of God. With such hues as these did the Maker of His own
> image mark our nature. . . . The Godhead is mind and word: for "in
> the beginning was the Word" and the followers of Paul "have the
> mind of Christ" which "speaks" in them. Humanity too is not far
> removed from these: you see in yourself word and understanding,
> an imitation of the very Mind and Word. Again, God is love, and
> the fount of love: for this the great John declares, that "love is of
> God," and "God is love": the Fashioner of our nature has made

this to be our feature too, for "hereby," He says, "shall all men know that ye are my disciples, if ye love one another. (trans. H.A. Wilson, slightly modified)

Divine beauty has been so transformed, in relation to any conception of physical beauty in human beings, as to constitute little other than moral and intellectual excellence; only the term *kállos*, and its relationship to love, connect this account with Plato's own vision.[36] Two centuries earlier, Clement of Alexandria denounced pagan representations of the gods in these terms: "An image [*agalma*] is truly dead matter shaped by the hand of an artist; but for us it is not a perceptible [*aisthêton*] image of perceptible matter, but an intelligible [*noêton*] one. God, the only real God, is not perceptible but intelligible" (*Protrepticus*, 4.51.6). There is no mention of beauty in this connection. A hundred years or so before Clement (late first early second century AD), the Stoicizing orator Dio Chrysostom, in his defense of images of the gods (which he puts in the mouth of the sculptor Phidias), conceded that "no sculptor or painter is capable of representing mind and intelligence in themselves" (*Oration*, 12.59), but certain attributes such as majesty and power or gentleness and concern can be indicated, for "their similarity of shape manifests the kinship of human beings and gods, somehow, in the form of a symbol [*en eidei sumbolou*]" (12.77).[37] It is notable that Dio does not list beauty among the divine attributes that are represented in this way, perhaps just because it would be difficult to discriminate divine beauty, which is in some sense intellectual, from the beauty of the image.[38] We can see here the seeds of the dilemma concerning the representation of spiritual beauty that was to exercise Roger Scruton and Javier Moscoso in our time (see Chapter 1).

IV. Back to Beauty: Themistius's Oration to Gratian

In the year 376 or early in 377 (in all likelihood), shortly before the fatal battle at Hadrianopolis in which the Roman co-emperor Valens suffered a drastic defeat at the hands of the Goths, Themistius pronounced an oration in honor of Gratian, Valens's nephew, who had been appointed Augustus or junior ruler at the age of eight by his father Valentinian. At the death of Valentinian, the nephew had risen effectively to the status of sole ruler of the Empire.[39] The speech, which was delivered before the Senate in Rome and in the absence of Gratian himself, is remarkable for its praise not just of the young emperor's virtues but also of his physical beauty. Indeed it bears the title *Erôtikos* in the only manuscript in which this oration survives, along with the subtitle or alternative title, *On Royal Beauty (Peri kállous basilikou)*.[40]

The titles are well chosen: Themistius presents himself in this discourse as nothing short of Gratian's lover. He compares his journey westward to Rome to the hardships a lover endures, such as camping out before the door of his beloved.[41] Until then, he complains, he had never been aware of experiencing so difficult a trip, spending a night in the open air, or, to sum it up, "the devices entailed in the pursuit of beauty [*kállos*]" (163B), although he considers himself to be no mean enthusiast for amorous exercise, even if still far from an accomplished athlete or champion. Now, however, he has experienced all the trials of lovers, and more: "a run along a route almost equal to that of the sun from the Tigris to the Atlantic Ocean, a scarcity of resources, a difficult passage . . . , sleepless days upon sleepless nights" (163C). Themistius insists that he slept outdoors and on the road, barefoot and uncovered, without the wherewithal to sustain life, but he never gave up. In other words, he was in the grip of pure Eros, and he did not "know if the nature of this *daimôn* has ever appeared or shone so brightly

in any other human being" (163D). Themistius goes on to affirm
that his hair had already begun to turn white, and yet he never
before had expected to experience love. The reason, he explains,
was not so much torpor or want of passion (*anerastia*) on his part
but rather the fact that he had never encountered the initial access
that a lover (*erastês*) requires, namely, "a fine soul in a fine body"
(*kalê psukhê en kalôi sômati*, 164A), a soul young and flowering in a
body similarly so, a soul already aglow but with the promise that
it will develop still further with time. Themistius declares that he
had sought this kind of boyfriend (*paidika*) and had haunted the
gymnasia and wrestling arenas, in search especially of poor and
humble youths, since he had heard that poverty is more likely to
result in wisdom whereas satiety breeds arrogance (*hubris*). But
these youths turned out to be "camping out far from the true
beauty [*kállos*] that is worthy of a lover" (164C). Thus, Themistius
suffered for a long while and "endured pangs over the passion for
that beauty [*kállos*] which philosophy had portrayed for him, for
a youth noble [*kalós*] and attractive [*erasmios*], who blended both
beauties [*kallê*], those of the soul and the body." His vain aspirations
for such a love led Themistius to conclude, he avows, that such an
ideal was exclusively in the sphere of the mind and "impossible to
grasp with the senses" (165A), like the perfect circle or triangle,
which cannot be reproduced in materials such as wood or stone or
drawn as figures.

Unable to free himself from the desire for such an ideal love,
Themistius is suddenly reminded of the passage in Plato's *Phaedrus*
(the manuscript of the speech erroneously reads *Phaedo*) in which
Socrates affirms that there are different kinds of beauty (*kállos*),
and he realizes that for intellectuals (*philologoi*) the object that
attracts them is that pertaining to Zeus, namely royal beauty.
He therefore abandoned the palaestras and betook himself to
the imperial court, and there indeed he found suitably virtuous

and Zeus-like men in Constantius II and Julian, the son and brother (*adelphos*, but more loosely here signifying "relative") of Constantine, but their beauty [*kállos*] was already overripe (165C) and no longer at a suitable age to inspire *erôs.* Clearly, Themistius has in mind not the bond of friendship or *philia* between adult males but rather the one-sided passion of an adult male for an adolescent boy. What he needed, he realizes, was a "mystagogue" to initiate him into the mysteries of *erôs* (165C), someone not far from the age of youth (*paidika*). And this he found in Gratian, as he drops all indirection and addresses himself directly to his young king, "the blessed object of his hunt" (165D): "For I am not able to have before my eyes that beauty [*kállos*] for the sake of which I travelled from one end of the earth to the other . . . , without directing and fixing my eyes upon you" (165D). Once found, Themistius adhered to his beloved prince and traveled the world to see him, the unique example of a combination of king and philosopher. His beauty, moreover, is so outstanding as to render the barbarian virtuous (that is, *kalós*, 166C), the Gete tame, the Persian humane, the Armenian Roman, the Spaniard Greek, and the nomad sedentary, "metamorphosing each from its previous ugliness [*aiskhos*] into the contrary beauty [*kállos*]" (166C).

Themistius goes on to insist that even if he is a lover of royal waistlines (*zônê*, 166C), he really prefers the head and eyes as the seat of intelligence and the place from which Athena sprang. Themistius portrays Athena as filling the heavens with beauty (*kállos*: a rare association of the goddess with beauty) and rendering all things "fine and lovely [*kalá kai erasta*] thanks to good order" (167A). Good kings do the same within their own sphere, and whatever they touch they render fine and lovely. Themistius announces, however, that this is not the occasion on which to speak about those other beauties (*kallê*, 167B), those cities and villages, their buildings and bays and the bridges that cross their rivers, so that the cities have cast off their age and are now rejuvenated (the connection between youth and beauty is subtly suggested here as well).[42] Themistius goes on to describe the beautification of Constantinople, and in particular the more useful construction of its aqueduct, before entering on a fulsome tribute to Gratian's virtues, which are comparable to those of Alexander the Great and Hercules—both sons of gods—though Gratian surpasses them in youth, power, and self-control. Gratian is disposed to heed the counsels of philosophers, is clement and generous, and his victories are achieved by the beauty and harmony of his soul (*têi tês psukhê kallonêi kai eumousiâi*, 176B) rather than by force of arms: "not only philosophers, it seems, but even barbarians are now in love with [*erôsi*] Gratian's brilliance and willingly yield and submit to him, bested by his judgment [*gnômê*]." Themistius insists that "Gratian's beauty [*kállos*] and the comeliness [*eumorphia*] of his soul" (176C) were what prevailed against the barbarians. The message that love conquers all is indeed inscribed in a bronze representation of the Gigantomachy, in which only the Giant who stands opposed to Eros is represented as having let his weapons fall and submitting joyfully to his opponent.

Themistius has gone some way toward shifting the focus from Gratian's physical beauty to his moral character as the basis for the erotic attraction he exerts on the orator and others, but there is no question that Gratian's appearance is a major element in his charm, as Themistius chooses to represent it. It is true that Themistius begins the speech by recollecting that Socrates himself declared, according to Plato's *Symposium*, that the only subject in which he considered himself an expert was that of erotic love. He continues by rehearsing the myth that Socrates recounts in the *read Symposium* concerning the origin of Eros as the offspring of Poverty and Provision (hence, his condition of permanent lack and desire). But Themistius's attitude toward Gratian scarcely conforms to the vision of Diotima in the Platonic dialogue. As we have seen, physical beauty in the *Symposium* is construed as a worldly manifestation of higher beauty, and its purpose is to draw the soul upward, so that it transcends attachment to any single beautiful individual and indeed to all perceptible or material things: one must leave behind the false attractions of this world and gaze fixedly on the noetic ideal, which is absolute and unchanging. Themistius has no wish to rise above the sensible attractions of Gratian; as he explicitly affirms, he was wrong to have supposed—before he met the juvenile emperor— that ideal beauty was accessible only to the intellect and "impossible to grasp with the senses." Gratian unites perceptible and moral beauty; neither is sacrificed to the other.

It is remarkable that the word *kállos* occurs some twenty-two times in this speech, along with the nearly synonymous *kallonê*, which appears three times. This represents a very high concentration for a word that is relatively sparse in its distribution compared to the adjective *kalós*. We have seen that *kállos* refers generally, though not exclusively, to physical beauty, particularly that of human beings, and carries a connotation of sexual attractiveness.[43] Themistius himself indicates the distinct senses of the substantive and the adjective when he affirms that Gratian's beauty (*kállos*) was so outstanding that it could render even a barbarian *kalós*, a contrast reminiscent of the Theocritean verse, cited above, in which a boy's beauty is declared to be a fine thing (23.32). We have also observed that grown men who, like Paris in the *Iliad* or the Athenian Alcibiades, are described as possessing *kállos* are also often of dubious moral standing (see Chapter 3). Themistius, reflecting this sensibility, is careful to emphasize Gratian's youth and state that such a passion as he professes would have been entirely out of place with respect to an older man, such as Constantius or Julian.

Themistius, then, was writing within a tradition in which beauty, which was unambiguously identified by the word *kállos*, was associated first and foremost with the human form and its ability to arouse sexual desire. The extensive use of this term confirms Themistius's intention to represent himself as the lover of the young Gratian, and Gratian, who at the time the speech was delivered would have been about seventeen years old (he is believed to have been born in or around 359), as his beloved (*erômenos* or *paidika*). This rhetorical strategy may strike the modern reader as bold or presumptuous on the part of Themistius, and conceivably insulting to the young emperor. There is a risk here, of course, of projecting our own values and expectations onto a different culture. Yet even by classical standards, Themistius's representation of his relationship to Gratian seems unusual. It may reflect a genuine intimacy between the wise rhetorician and the youthful ruler, which might naturally find expression in terms of the classical model of love for boys. Amy Richlin has argued forcefully that the letters exchanged between the young Marcus Aurelius and his tutor, Marcus Cornelius Fronto, are cast in the language of pederasty.[44] Indeed, Fronto several times refers to the *kállos* of the young emperor. Though this was a private correspondence, the fact that the letters survive (in a palimpsest, to be sure) to this day indicates that they must have circulated beyond the writers themselves. Still, Themistius's public assumption of the role of *erastês* in a speech delivered to the Roman Senate seems to be a step beyond Fronto's pretentions.[45]

Themistius may have wished to cast himself as Gratian's philosophical adviser, a posture that philosophers such as Plato took to be the noble purpose behind the love of boys. He praises Gratian for his willingness to heed the advice of others, and of philosophers in particular, and he may have conceived of himself as offering a kind of mirror for princes. Beyond the effort to define and defend his personal status as royal counselor,

Themistius may also have wished to promote the ideal of leadership through love rather than conquest and force of arms. Themistius was an enthusiastic exponent of cosmopolitanism under the aegis of Rome. Thus, in one speech (34.25), he expatiates upon the gentleness of the Romans, who do not hate their enemies but "deem them worthy of being spared, as human beings." He goes on to affirm that "he who proceeds to the utmost against arrogant barbarians makes himself king of the Romans alone, but he who conquers and yet spares knows himself to be king of all human beings, and one might justly call this man truly humane [*philanthrôpos*]." Playing on the root sense of *philanthrôpos* as "lover of mankind," Themistius states that Cyrus was a lover of Persians (*philopersês*) not of humanity, Alexander a lover of Macedonians, Agesilaus of Greeks, Augustus himself a lover of Romans. A true lover of mankind and a king in the unqualified sense (*haplôs*) is the one who inquires simply whether a person begging for clemency is a human being, irrespective of nationality (it is worth noting that Themistius, unlike his contemporary Libanius, was in favor of integrating barbarians into the empire, a policy followed by Theodosius).[46]

Themistius's exploitation of the topos of lover and beloved to define his relationship to Gratian was a daring move, I believe, and may have served several purposes at once. I wish to call attention here to the fact that the language of lover and beloved is fully erotic, and is not denatured or watered down by the appeals to Plato's *Symposium* or the high-minded references to Gratian's spiritual qualities. There is, no doubt, an element of metaphor involved, but Themistius has gone out of his way to represent his passion for the beautiful young emperor as authentically erotic. Among other things, the use of the term *kállos* is a sign of his intentions.

5

BEAUTY ACROSS CULTURES: ISRAEL AND ROME

We have seen that the ancient Greek terminology for beauty and the values associated with the idea do not map precisely onto the lexicon of modern English, nor does ancient Greek *kállos* correspond exactly to the way beauty is understood in modern aesthetic theory (we shall return to this matter in Chapter 6). Classical Greek usage might be expected to differ from that of other ancient tongues as well, and this is in fact the case. Nevertheless, a comparative study yields some surprises. As I was seeking a first approximation to a comparison between the Greek and Latin vocabularies for beauty, it seemed best to examine two versions of the same text, one in each language. As it happens, the most extensive bilingual work that survives from antiquity is the Bible, or more precisely, the Hebrew Bible (or Old Testament) in its Greek translation known as the Septuagint, which was prepared sometime between the third and first centuries BC, and the Latin Vulgate translated by Saint Jerome from Hebrew with the Greek version at hand. But the choice of the Hebrew Scripture as the text brought with it a further opportunity, since it would now be possible to compare Greek usage with the Hebrew. In this chapter, we begin by triangulating Hebrew, Greek, and Latin terminology for "beauty" by way of the three surviving ancient versions of the Hebrew Bible, with a special focus on the Hebrew and Greek equivalents, and then turn to some Roman texts to see how Latin terms stand in relation to the Greek.

I. Beauty in the Bible ✿ We have noted in Chapter 2 that the term most commonly taken to mean "beautiful" in classical Greek is the adjective *kalós*, although it has in fact a much wider semantic range and can also signify "honorable," "noble," and "good." If one adds the definite article to the adjective, producing the phrase "the *kalón*," the sense is equally broad and may indicate not just "the beautiful" or "beauty" but also, and more frequently, "virtue," "honor," and the like. Now, classical Greek did, as we saw, have a noun, *kállos*, that is closer to the modern sense of beauty. We have mentioned more than once the Theocritean verse that neatly illustrates the contrast between the narrow reference of [*Kállos*] and the wider use of the adjective *kalós*: "A boy's beauty *kállos* is a *kalón* thing," even though it is fleeting (23.32). We have seen too that there is a similar contrast in the Greek text of 1 Esdras 4:18. The Revised Standard Version (RSV) of the Bible translates:

> If men gather gold and silver or any other beautiful [*horaion*] thing, and then see a woman lovely [*kalê*] in appearance [*eidos*] and beauty [*kállos*].[1]

"Lovely in beauty" seems as redundant as affirming that "beauty is beautiful"; it appears preferable, accordingly, to take *kalê* (feminine of *kalós*) in the sense of "outstanding" or the like and render the phrase "excellent in stature [or appearance] and in beauty." A failure to distinguish between the noun *kállos* and the adjective *kalós* has led, as we have observed, to some confusion in the scholarly literature. It is thus particularly interesting to see that ancient Hebrew presents an analogous conundrum to the student of the history of beauty.

In his book, *Disability in the Hebrew Bible*, Saul Olyan devotes the first chapter to "Constructions of Beauty and Ugliness," and the first subsection is entitled "Male and Female Beauty" (Olyan 2008, 15–19). Olyan begins by analyzing "the qualities of the beautiful male in texts that describe the physical appearance and behavior of heroic leaders," and he observes that Saul "is described as 'a handsome young man' (*baḥur waṭôb*), an expression drawing together the notions of youth and physical attractiveness. In fact, the text goes on to state that 'there was no man of the children of Israel more handsome (*ṭôb*) than he; from his shoulder upward he was taller than all the people'" (15, 16; the biblical quotation is from 1 Samuel 9:2). Olyan goes on to note, "Other texts suggest qualities associated with the beautiful male in addition to noteworthy height and youth, e.g. 1 Sam 16:12, where David is described as 'ruddy, with beautiful eyes, and handsome with respect to appearance' (*'admônî 'im yepeh 'ênayim weṭôb ro'î*)," and he compares as well 1 Samuel 17:42, where "we are told that Goliath despised David because 'he was a youth, and ruddy, with a handsome appearance'" (16). So too, "agility, and speed in movement" are "associated with male attractiveness." Olyan adds, "Characteristics such as exceptional height; youth; ruddy, clear skin; beautiful eyes; plumpness; thick hair on the head; a beard in the case of a mature man; rapid, agile movement; and physical strength are constructed as emblematic of male beauty in biblical texts. These are the qualities that define technical expressions such as 'handsome' (*ṭôb*) and 'beautiful' (*yapeh*)" (17).

The problem is that the word (*ṭôb*), which is most often translated as "good," has at least as wide an application as the Greek *kalós*, and there is some doubt as to its precise sense even where the term modifies a human being and the context suggests physical attractiveness (hence, perhaps, Olyan's decision to render it as "handsome" rather than "beautiful"). To take a case—one of any number—where a possible ambiguity might arise, Isaiah 5:9 reads, according to the RSV:

> The LORD of hosts has sworn in my hearing:
> "Surely many houses shall be desolate,
> large and beautiful houses, without inhabitant."

At least one version (the Darby translation), however, offers a slightly different sense:

> In mine ears Jehovah of hosts [hath said],
> "Many houses shall assuredly become a desolation,
> great and excellent ones, without inhabitant."[2]

Are the houses beautiful or are they excellent? The word for "large" or "great" (גדולים) in the original Hebrew is perhaps unproblematic, but the term for "good" (טובים) is the plural of *ṭôb*. Should we understand that the houses have an aesthetically pleasing appearance, thus justifying the rendering "beautiful," or ought we to stay with something closer to the basic sense of "good" and opt instead for the more neutral "excellent," "fine," or the like?

It is instructive, in this connection, to look at how the Septuagint renders the passage. The feminine plural adjectives *megalai kai kalaí* correspond respectively to the Hebrew words for "great" or "large" (גדולים) and "excellent" or "beautiful" (טובים). But the latter is unhelpful in making the sense of the Hebrew more precise, since *kalós* has, as we know, a breadth of meanings comparable (though not identical) to that of the Hebrew *ṭôb*. Though neither term excludes the sense of beauty, they both leave open the possibility that the sense is something more like "well wrought" or "fine," or perhaps even "noble."[3]

If we turn to the Latin Vulgate translation, we may be tempted to suppose that the translator, Jerome, opted clearly for the aesthetic sense, whether or not he was in this instance rendering the original strictly:

> in auribus meis sunt haec Domini exercituum
> nisi domus multae desertae fuerint
> grandes et pulchrae absque habitatore.

The Latin word *pulcher* can indeed mean beautiful, but as we shall see, it too has other connotations, and once again we may harbor some reservations about just what meaning Jerome intended.

Now, just as there is a term in Greek that refers primarily to physical beauty in human beings, although it may also be applied more widely, so in Hebrew there is a root that signifies beauty in this more restricted sense and, in contrast to the Greek, has both nominal and adjectival forms. The root in question is *yapeh*, and Olyan renders its adjectival form as "beautiful" in the passage cited previously.[4] Forms of the root *yapeh* occur much less frequently than forms of the root *ṭôb*, as one might expect from its relatively narrower semantic range. Like *ṭôb*, adjectival *yapeh* may be rendered as *kalós*, but it is noteworthy that it seems never to be translated as *agathos* or "good," whereas this is a very common (indeed, the most frequent) rendering of *ṭôb* (e.g., Genesis 50:20). What is more, *ṭôb* is also translated as *asteios* ("clever," Exodus 2:2), *orthôs* ("rightly," Exodus 18:17), *eu* ("well," the adverb of *agathos*, Numbers 10:29), *sumpherôn* ("advantageous," Deuteronomy 23:7), *alêthinos* ("true," Isaiah 75:2), *khrêstos* ("worthy," Jeremiah 24:2, several times), *eklekton* ("choice," Ezra 31:16), *katharos* ("pure," 2 Chronicles 3:5, of gold), and by periphrastic phrases such as *dokei* ("it seems right," Esther 1:19), *areskei* ("is pleasing," Numbers 36:6), and the like.

When *ṭôb* is rendered as *kalós*, moreover, there is frequently a defining phrase such as "in appearance," both in the Hebrew and in the Greek, that specifies the physical sense of the term. For example, in Esther 2:2, the Septuagint gives: "Let beautiful [*kalá tôi eidei*] young virgins be sought out for the king" (RSV).[5] When *ṭôb* is rendered as *hôraios* (1 Kings 1:6), a term that basically means "young" ("in season") and hence beautiful, it is again modified by *têi opsei*, "in appearance."

Occasionally, *ṭôb* or *kalós* is used for physical beauty without any modifier, as at Esther 1:11, in describing the beauty of Vashti, where the Hebrew has "in appearance" but the Septuagint gives simply "she was *kalê*." A noteworthy exception is Genesis 6:2, on the women sought out by the angels or sons of God; here we have just the feminine plural form of *ṭôb* in the Hebrew and "they [the angels] saw that they were *kalaí*" in the Greek (cf. the Vulgate *quod essent pulchrae*). Doubtless the women were beautiful, but I wonder whether some moral quality may also be intended here (at Nahum 3:4, the bare adjectives are applied to a prostitute, which perhaps suggests physical beauty). When *ṭôb* is applied to ears of corn, as at Genesis 41:5, it may be rendered as *kalós*,[6] but again the sense of "fine" or "excellent" would seem to be just as appropriate as "beautiful."[7] At 1 Samuel 9:2, where *ṭôb* modifies Saul, the Septuagint has *anêr agathos*, that is, "a good man" (cf. the Vulgate *electus et bonus*).[8] Here is how David is described in the Septuagint version of 1 Samuel 16:12: "Now he was ruddy, and had beautiful eyes, and was handsome" (RSV), or in a more literal rendering, "With *kállos* of eyes and good [*agathos*] to see [*horasei*]," but here the Hebrew term that is rendered by the noun *kállos* is precisely *yapeh*.[9]

It is true that forms deriving from the root *yapeh* may also be qualified with the expression "in appearance" or the like,[10] but as

I have indicated, it is most often used for human beauty.[11] Indeed, *yapeh* and its cognates are frequently rendered by the Greek *kállos*.[12] Where *yapeh* and its relatives are translated by the adjective *kalós*, the Greek may add an intensifying particle signifying "very" or the like.[13] At 1 Kings 1:3, *kalê* is used without qualifier for a young woman (*neanida kalên*, Vulgate *adulescentulam speciosam*, as again at 1:4); the association with youth perhaps helps to define the sense of *kalós*, but the Greek may have avoided the noun *kállos* here for its too close association with erotic attraction (cf. Amos 8:13, where beautiful virgins are *kalaí*).[14] The Greek version of the Song of Songs shows a preference, however, for the bare *kalê* (feminine);[15] it may be that the patently amorous context helps to determine the sense of *kalós* in this work.

Sometimes *yapeh* is ascribed to such items as especially handsome animals or trees, in this resembling the transferred use of the Greek *kállos*.[16] A reference to the king's beauty at Isaiah 33:17 seems to have been interpreted broadly by the Septuagint translators, who give *meta doxês*, "high esteem" (the Vulgate has *in decore suo*).[17] At Jeremiah 4:30, on the vanity of Israel's adornment, the Septuagint employs the term *hôraïsmos*; here, the reference to lovers (*erastai*, Latin *amatores*) leaves no doubt as to the meaning.

Sometimes, the Greek will use *kállos* although the original Hebrew has some other term expressing "high quality." An example is Isaiah 37:24. The Greek speaks of the beauty [*kállos*] of the cypress, whereas the Hebrew has מבחר or "choice" (the RSV has "choicest"). In this case, the Latin sticks more closely to the Hebrew and reads *excelsa cedrorum* or "the highest, most outstanding of the cypresses."[18] At Ezekiel 28:17, there is a double occurrence of *kállos* in the Greek:

> Your heart was proud because of your beauty [*kállos*];
> you corrupted your wisdom for the sake of your splendor [*kállos*].
> (RSV)

The RSV eliminates the redundancy, but the Latin preserves the repetition in the Greek:

elevatum est cor tuum in decore tuo perdidisti sapientiam tuam in decore tuo.

It is possible that the Latin version is exploiting a certain confusion, specific to the oblique cases (apart from the accusative), between *decor* and *decus* (the Latin ablative *decore* can correspond either to the nominative *decor*, which most commonly represents physical beauty, or to the nominative *decus*, which more often signifies honor, glory, or other moral qualities). The Hebrew clearly distinguishes the two terms, with only the first (*yapeh*) meaning "beauty" in the strict sense, whereas the second (יפעתך) more properly means "brightness" or "splendor."

The Greek *kalós*, in turn, may render Hebrew terms other than *ṭôb*. Thus, at Isaiah 22:18, in the phrase *harma kalón* (*harma* = "chariot"), the latter term represents the Hebrew כבודך, "honor" or "glory," and is so rendered by the Vulgate (*currus gloriae*) and the RSV ("splendid chariots"). *Kalós*, then, is in general best taken to mean "excellent" or "fine" in the Septuagint.

We may see something of the distinction between the key terms, *ṭôb* and *yapeh*, *kalós* and *kállos*, in a passage in the book of Esther (1:11), noted briefly above. The RSV reads:

to bring Queen Vashti before the king with her royal crown, in order to show the peoples and the princes her beauty [*kállos*]; for she was fair [*kalê*] to behold.

The Septuagint text is somewhat fuller here, but we may note in particular the juxtaposition of *kállos* (corresponding to "beauty") and *kalós* (corresponding to "fair"). The Greek is, in fact, faithful to the Hebrew, where *yapeh* corresponds precisely to *kállos*, whereas *kalê* renders *ṭôb*, that is, "good" or "fine." However, the Greek fails to render the phrase "in appearance" that qualifies the latter term in the Hebrew (cf. the English "to behold"). The Latin Vulgate, taking the two terms to be more or less synonymous in this context, introduces a pleonasm:

> to show the peoples and the princes her beauty [*pulchritudo*]; for she was very beautiful [*pulchra*].

Perhaps it was with a view to avoiding the sense of mere repetition that Jerome added the adverb *valde* ("very").

We may conclude our survey with an example from Ecclesiasticus. The original Hebrew text has been partly recovered from the Geniza deposits and Masada, and there is also some evidence for the Vetus Latina (that is, the early and now mostly lost version of the Hebrew Bible made from the Greek version and supplanted all but entirely by Jerome's Vulgate),[19] but the comparisons that follow involve just the Septuagint and the Vulgate. At Ecclesiasticus 9:8, we read:

> Turn away your eyes from a shapely [*eumorphos*] woman, and do not look intently at beauty [*kállos*] belonging to another; many have been misled by a woman's beauty [*kállos*], and by it passion [*philia*] is kindled like a fire. (RSV)

The connection between beauty and passion is clear, although the Greek text here uses the word *philia*, a term that signifies love generally, including that between husband and wife, rather than *erôs*, which one might have expected. The Latin version uses *species* for *kállos*, which is a good fit (as we shall see) and *compta* ("elegant, neat") for *eumorphos* (in the English version, "shapely").

It is worth noting that *philia* is rendered as *concupiscentia* in the Vulgate, a term that fits the context of erotic desire better than *amor*, which can stand in for *erôs* but is more general in its application and (like *philia*) does not of itself necessarily indicate sexual passion.[20]

We may now take stock of the results of this survey of ancient Hebrew, Greek, and Latin terms for beauty. Concerning the Greek of the Septuagint, we may affirm, I think, that Aryeh Kosman's "urge . . . to say that the Greeks had no concept of beauty" (see Chapter 2) may properly be resisted; once again, if we turn our attention to the noun *kállos* rather than the adjective *kalós*, the sense of "beauty" seems perfectly clear. What is more, *kállos* corresponds very well to the meaning of the Hebrew root *yapeh* and its derivatives, which both supports the interpretation of *kállos* that has been offered so far and confirms that the Greek translators recognized this specific sense in the Hebrew term. As for the Latin translators—whether the Vetus, where we can identify traces of it, or the Vulgate—*bonus* most commonly renders the Hebrew *ṭôb* and the Greek *kalós*. For *yapeh* and *kállos* the usage is less clear: *pulchritudo* has a fairly broad semantic range that to a certain extent parallels that of *kalós*, as we shall see, but it very commonly is used for physical beauty; the noun *species* and the adjectives *speciosus* and *formonsus* (or *formosus*) tend to refer more narrowly to physical appearance. We may observe too that the Hebrew, Greek, and Latin terms for beauty retain a primary connection with the visual, and in particular with the beauty of the human form. This in turn brings the words into the erotic sphere, and so the idea of beauty in all three languages is associated with attractiveness and desire.

The various tales and episodes recounted in the Bible do not reveal an entirely clear stance on the moral implications of beauty. For example, in relation to the books of Samuel and Kings, where references to beauty are most frequent, Michael Avioz concludes, "In all the stories it appears that the beautiful women are presented as good in the story, or at least not as bad women. There is no explicit negative assessment of any of them, or a hint that they exploited their beauty in order to achieve certain aims, such as Helen of Troy, for example" (Avioz 2009, 358–359).[21] With respect to male beauty, however, Avioz maintains, "Regarding Saul, Eliab and Absalom, focusing on the attribute of beauty emphasizes their spiritual vacuity. Only regarding David is the attribute of beauty a positive trait without reservation" (359). Yet one might rather point to the association in the Bible between male beauty and youth. Although there is nothing resembling the ideology of pederasty in the Hebrew Bible, young men are represented as particularly attractive, and their beauty stirs at least the admiration of others, whether men or women.[22] In Psalm 45, Stuart Macwilliam observes that "in the context of male-to-male gaze, it is indeed the physical beauty of the king that strikes the psalmist, but given the demands of gender performativity male beauty is there not to be desired but to evoke respect for the manly virtues that it symbolizes—virtues centring around power (military prowess, regal authority)." Macwilliam argues that the queen, on the contrary, "is defined entirely in terms of her physical beauty and the desire that it evokes in the male gaze" (Macwilliam 2009, 268). Macwilliam recognizes in the Song of Songs (e.g., 1:15 and 4:7) that *yapeh* presents "a picture of beauty desired, without explicit assumptions of male ownership." However, he regards this as an exceptional instance and cites the example of Queen Vashti in the book of Esther, "whose beauty is required by the king to promote his prestige before his courtiers and people (Esth. 1:11)." So too, "Abishag, twice and emphatically described as *yapeh* in 1 Kgs 1:3–4, is there simply to act as a bedfellow for David" (268). But if the Bible presents a skewed image of beauty in respect to gender, Macwilliam nevertheless finds that interpreters and commentators have contributed to this imbalance:

> In the rare cases where male beauty does show itself, it is my contention that we should view with suspicion the analysis of its function offered by generations of (male) commentators. My suspicion is that their various attempts to explain away the sexual desirability of the male body are (unconsciously) driven by an ideologically masculinist agenda, which leads them to overlook some plausible alternative exegetical insights. (271)

In particular, Macwilliam finds that "Joseph's beauty . . . is ambiguous. On the one hand, the narrator may well intend us to understand by it a sign of divine favour; on the other, both by its narrative consequences and by its identification with Rachel's female beauty, it also signifies vulnerability and danger, just as female beauty often does" (275).[23]

In a recent series of articles, James Alfred Loader has explored the notion of beauty in the Hebrew Bible, touching on such topics as beauty and awe, the darker side of beauty, and beauty as an attribute of the products of human labor (see Loader 2011, 2012a, 2012b). These are valuable contributions because they reveal a sensitivity among the authors of the Bible to the things that we regard as beautiful, but they run the risk of lumping together qualities and responses of different kinds, at least in respect to what we may call the folk taxonomy implicit in the Hebrew vocabulary. Erotic attractiveness had a terminology of its own, which did not spill over into all the other categories that we ourselves might include under the heading of the beautiful. Although the focus of my argument here has been the comparison of Hebrew usage with that of classical Greek, the results may shed some light on attitudes toward beauty in the Hebrew Bible, precisely by exhibiting how Hebrew, like Greek, distinguished erotic attractiveness from other pleasing or appealing attributes. Thus, when the terms in question—*kállos* and *yapeh*—were applied beyond their usual sphere, they carried a particular resonance, just as the limits of their semantic range, the domains to which they were rarely or never ascribed, are also worth noting. In particular, they do not seem to have signified anything like a strictly aesthetic property in the modern sense of the term.

Today, as we have noted in Chapter 1 and elsewhere, the conception of beauty extends widely, and it is often treated as an aesthetic category that rises above mundane desire and is an object of pure, transcendental contemplation.[24] This notion, which has roots in a de-eroticized version of Platonic metaphysics as well as in modern notions of the aesthetic going back to Kant, finds application to religious art in particular (as we saw in Chapter 1) but may also be applied to the experience we have upon reading holy texts. Thus, Krzysztof Sonek, in a recent book entitled *Truth, Beauty, and Goodness in Biblical Narratives*, argues that there is a difference between a beautiful work of art, which is fleeting, and the beauty of a work of art, which is eternal. A given passage in the Bible may not be beautiful in itself but points to a beauty beyond. As Sonek puts it, we feel that "there must exist a reality, a realm of beauty, which goes beyond the literary text itself" (Sonek 2009, 198). Sonek quotes Władyslaw Stróżewski, a disciple of Roman Ingarden, who explains:

> Our language is able to distinguish between two different things: "a beautiful work of art" and "the beauty of a work of art . . . " We take the greatest delight in the beauty to which the work leads us and in which this work participates.[25]

Sonek affirms: "When we read biblical narratives as literature, we discover that the beauty they communicate is not simply equal to the sum of their particular aesthetic features. Those features comprise various ideas, stylistic figures, and structures, but we would not say that they *are* beauty. They are *beautiful* because they *reveal beauty*." I do not wish to quarrel with Sonek over the nature of our own experience upon reading biblical stories: some of us may well react in just the way he describes, a response which, as Stróżewski observes, our own language facilitates. But in this respect our language would seem to differ from ancient Hebrew, Greek, and Latin, in which the concrete or corporeal sense of beauty prevailed, and it may be well, when reading the Bible or other ancient texts, to keep in mind the things that their languages did and did not distinguish.[26]

II. Beauty and Desire between Greece and Rome

Latin is rich in words meaning "beautiful": in addition to *pulcher* and *pulchritudo*, which we will examine in detail, there are *formosus, speciosus, decorus*, and *bellus*, along with the nouns *formositas* (rare in the Republican period, but found once in Cicero and thereafter in Apuleius and other writers) and *decor*. In his detailed study of the Latin terminology, Pierre Monteil argues that *formosus* applies primarily to visible shape (*forma*), above all to the human form. Monteil points out that in archaic texts the term is commonly applied to men (only once to a woman in comedy: Terence, *Eunuch*, 730), and signifies a healthy or strong body. From the time of Cicero onward, it acquires the more general sense of good proportion, even in connection with abstract entities, and comes to be applied especially to women (occasionally to men or boys) in amorous contexts, where *formosa* alone may indicate "la belle," that is, "a beauty" (Monteil 1964, 58–60). Thus, the speaker in Cicero's dialogue, *Tusculan Disputations*, asks why no one falls in love either with an ugly (*deformis*) youth or with a handsome (*formosus*) old man (4.70); the implication is that age is not attractive in an erotic way.

Bellus is relatively rare in classical Latin, even though it is the term that gave rise to words for beauty in the romance languages (Italian *bello*, French *beau*, Spanish *bello*, etc.). The word perhaps had a colloquial ring and tends to mean "glib" or "slick," often of someone who cultivates appearance rather than quality; as a result, it is often employed ironically. One finds the word, for example, in Plautus's *Bacchides* (345, 725) and *Captivi* (956), where it is amusingly contrasted with *bonus* ("good") and suggests a debonair quality (it is paired with *lepidus* or "charming"; cf. *Menaechmi*, 626; *Truculentus*, 934, where it is paired with *scitus*, "clever"). Catullus 23.9 associates the word with *urbanus*, and at 24.7 allows that the lover of Juventius (of whom Catullus is enamored) is *bellus* but utterly impoverished (cf. 78.83, 81.2). The term is relatively rare in Cicero and is used most often in his letters, which are more informal than his other works (*To His Friends*, 7.16.2, 16.18.1; *To Atticus*, 14.3.1, applied to an architect); interestingly, it modifies the word *ironia* in Cicero's history of Roman oratory (*Brutus*, 293; cf. *On the Orator*, 2.239, where Cicero speaks of *bella* material for witticisms). Some epigrams by Martial capture the flavor of the word:

> You declaim nicely [*belle*, adverb]; you plead causes, Atticus, nicely; you write nice [*bellas*] histories, nice poems. You compose nicely mimes, epigrams nicely; you are a nice [*bellus*] litterateur, a nice astronomer, and you sing nicely [*belle*] and dance nicely, Atticus; you are a nice [*bellus*] performer on the lyre, you are a nice player at ball. Seeing that you do nothing well [*bene*], yet do everything nicely [*belle*], would you have me describe you? You are a great dabbler. (2.7, trans. Ker 1919)

> Cotilus, you are "a pretty fellow" [*bellus homo*]: many call you so, Cotilus; I hear them. But, tell me, what is a pretty fellow? "A pretty fellow is one who arranges neatly his curled locks, who continually smells of balsam, continually of cinnamon; who hums catches

from the Nile and Gades; who waves his depilated arms in time to
varied measures; who all the day lolls amid the women's chairs,
and is ever whispering in some ear; who reads billets sent from one
quarter or another, and writes them; who shrinks from contact
with the cloak on his neighbour's elbow; who knows who is the
lover of whom; who hurries from one party to another; who has at
his fingers' ends the long pedigree of Hirpinus." What do you say?
Is this thing, Cotilus, this thing a pretty fellow? A very trumpery
thing, Cotilus, is your pretty fellow. (3.63, trans. Ker 1919)

Pierre Monteil, in his study of terms for beautiful and ugly in
classical Latin, takes *bellus* to be a diminutive of *bonus*, and hence
to suggest "un bon petit" (233), and to lie at the opposite extreme
to *pulcher*, always connoting an insufficient development of beauty,
a lack of maturity (like "cute").[27] But *pulcher* too could, as we shall
see, be employed ironically, and the contrast is perhaps overly neat
(or *bellus*).

Speciosus, deriving from the noun *species* or "image," is absent in
early Republican literature and occurs only three times in Cicero:
once of a gladiatorial troop in a plainly ironic context (*Pro Sestio*,
134), once of a fine orator with no trace of satire, and once in a
letter to Atticus, of a just case or cause (16.7.6). It is also found
three times in the continuators of Caesar's war commentaries,
and a few times in Columella's treatise on agriculture, where it
is used straightforwardly to mean "handsome" or "fine" (in
reference to trees and the like). In Quintus Curtius Rufus's
history of Alexander the Great (5.1.8, 7.5.20), it begins to
approximate the sense of "specious," as again in Horace, where it
connotes a false or merely external splendor, as at *Epistles*,
1.16.44–45: "But his whole household and neighborhood see
him as foul [*turpis*] inside, though he is *speciosus* in his handsome
[*decorus*] hide" (cf. *Epistles*, 1.18.52, for the adverb in a gently

mocking sense; *Epistles*, 2.2.116, of fine old words once used by Cato but now needing a dusting off if they are to be used by poets). Livy employs the term fairly often, and again, there is frequently a suggestion of superficial attractiveness as opposed to genuine value. For example, it is used of a peace that is sure [*certa*] even if it is not *speciosa*, that is, glamorous or impressive in appearance (39.54.7). It is a favorite word of Quintilian, who often employs it in a positive sense, but can also lend it a derisive twist: "Yet many people, anxious to win a reputation for eloquence, are content with passages which are merely showy [*speciosis*] or contribute nothing to the proof" (7.1.41, trans. Russell 2002, 173).

The adjective *decorus* is defined by Cicero as equivalent to the Greek *prepon* (*Orator*, 70), that is, "fitting" or "suitable," and although this sense does not exhaust the word's full range of meanings (it sometimes seems to mean "attractive" with no special implication of decorum), it is not the primary term used in amorous contexts. There are two nouns deriving from this same root in Latin, *decus* and *decor* (in most oblique cases, they are indistinguishable: thus *decoris* is the genitive of both). Isidore of Seville, who composed a manual of Latin usage called *Etymologies* in the early seventh century, affirms in his brief treatise *On the Differences between Words* that *decus ad animum refertur, decor ad corporis speciem* ("*decus* refers to the mind, *decor* to the beauty [*species*] of the body," 1.163). However, the distinction is not strictly observed by classical writers, and Saint Augustine, as Jean-Michel Fontanier observes, "treats the two words as interchangeable."[28]

It is the word *pulcher*, however, that offers the widest range of meanings and is the most common term for "beautiful" in all respects. Pierre Monteil traces the original meaning to an augural context, where it is said to bear the sense of "favorable" when applied to omens (e.g., Ennius, *Annales*, 91, *et simul ex alto pulcherrima praepes / laeva volavit avis*, cited in Cicero, *On Divination*, 1.107). Monteil comments, "Without a doubt, *pulchritudo* expresses the idea of beauty; but it is not so much physical and anatomical (*forma*) as supernatural and symbolic of prosperity" (76).[29] There are, however, difficulties with this interpretation, which is not recognized, incidentally, in the *Oxford Latin Dictionary*. Thus, when Ennius (*Annales*, 18) applies the term *pulchra* to Venus, in a context in which she grants Anchises the power of prophecy, there is not sufficient reason, I think, to construe the adjective as signifying "beneficent" rather than "beautiful" (77). There are many instances, to be sure, in which *pulcher* carries the sense of flourishing or excellent of its kind, or simply pleasant (the adverb *pulchre* is often used like the colloquial English *beautifully*); in this respect, it has something of the breadth of the Greek *kalós*, though without the more narrow connotations of high status (the members of the aristocracy identified themselves as *boni*, the usual equivalent for *kalós*, not as *pulchri*). But when a character in Plautus's *Poenulus* exclaims, "O lovely [*pulcrum*] day, and festive and full of Venus' charm, worthy of Venus, by god, whose holiday, the Aphrodisia, is today,"[30] the connection with Venus is surely relevant to the choice of the word *pulcher*, and there is no need to take *diem pulcrum* in the broad sense of "day blessed by the gods" ("Jour béni des dieux," 83).

Plautus, along with Cicero, stands out among the Latin authors whom Monteil surveys (down to Apuleius) for instances of *pulcher*, and among his comedies, the *Miles Gloriosus* leads the pack with nine occurrences (omitting the adverb from the reckoning).[31] But if Monteil is happy to render *pulchra mulier nuda erit quam purpurata pulchrior* (*Mostellaria*, 289) as "Une femme belle sera sans atours plus belle que sous la pourpre" ("A beautiful woman will be more beautiful naked than dressed in royal purple," 95), noting that, "already at the level of the most ancient texts, *pulcher* seems often to express beauty in general,"[32] he rather unaccountably (in my view) opts for the sacral interpretation in connection with Pyrgopolynices in the *Miles*. Thus, he renders the line *serva illam pulchram pulcher* (v. 1054) as "you whom heaven blesses, save this perfect woman,"[33] and comments, "Pyrgopolynices' *pulchritudo* is, as we have seen, a kind of divine favor, of which physical beauty (*forma*) is only one aspect" (95).[34] And when a courtesan addresses the soldier with the words, *pulcher, salve* (v. 1037), Monteil translates, "Greetings, O Propitious One" ("Salut, ô Propice," 78). Again, when the soldier declares of himself, *nimiast miseria nimis pulchrum esse hominem* (v. 68), Monteil renders, "An excess of divine favor is a great nuisance," and he explains, "Pyrgopolynices does not find himself too handsome at all, rather he is proud of his physique (*formast ferox*, 1390), but he laments his too frequent good luck."[35] Monteil misses the irony that this ostensibly tough warrior prides himself precisely on his ability to attract women by his beauty, which, in the conventional construction of gender roles in Greece and Rome, casts him as comically effeminate (he will be threatened with castration at the end of the play).

Like *kalós*, then, *pulcher* has a wide range of connotations. When it modifies human subjects, it regularly signifies "beautiful," and the emotional response that it evokes is erotic desire or *amor*. Thus, in Virgil it is often an attribute of women (in the *Aeneid*, of Scylla's feminine breast, 3.426; of Dido, 4.192; of Proserpina, 6.142, where the notion "propitious" might be relevant), or of attractive young men, above all Euryalus (5.344, 9.179, 9.433), but also Mezentius's son Lausus (7.649) and Aventinus, the son of Hercules. Hercules himself is also described as *pulcher* (*satus Hercule pulchro / pulcher Auentinus*, 7.656–667; cf. also *pulchra prole*, 1.75). Aventinus presents a fearsome enough appearance, dressed in his father's lion skin (7.669), but as a youth he is nevertheless handsome, whereas his bravado gives the impression of being rather a self-conscious imitation of his sire's strength, depending more on costume than on his own *virtus*. Monteil renders this verse, "the son of the divine (or auspicious) Hercules, the divine Aventinus," 77 ("le fils du divin (ou favorable) Hercule, le divin Aventinus"), but there seems no reason to see Aventinus as a particularly propitious figure. The application of the adjective to Hercules is unusual (beauty is more often an attribute of goddesses, as at Ovid, *Metamorphoses*, 8.780, of Ceres; Petronius, 133, of Dione; Apuleius, *Met.*, 10.32, of the Horae). As Donatus, the fourth-century commentator on Virgil, remarks (on v. 4.149), "*Pulchritudo* is rather inappropritate to Hercules" (*Herculi satis est incongrua pulchritudo*; it may be worth noting that some manuscripts of the *Aeneid* have *Hercule forti*, "brave Hercules"). Some therefore prefer to take *pulcher* here as a synonym for *fortis* or the like.[36] I expect Virgil may have meant to suggest rather that Aventinus's good looks were what he principally inherited from his father, at least as Hercules would have appeared in his younger days. But the adjective is also applied to a noble death (*Georgics*, 4.218; *Aeneid*, 2.317, 9.401, 11.647), to cities or regions (*Aeneid*, 4.266, 4.432, 11.270), to a river (*Aeneid*, 7.43), and to the abstract idea of freedom (*Aeneid*, 6.821), as well as to a fine work of handicraft (*pulchros tapetas, Aeneid*, 9.358).[37] These uses correspond to those of *kalós*, and indeed for most of them (especially cities and rivers) one can readily find parallels with the attribution of the noun *kállos* as well.

A handy source for illustrating the semantic range of *pulcher* is Pliny the Elder's *Natural History*, which surveys a wide variety of items, including works of art. Pliny modestly avers that even attempting a great task, without fully achieving it, is *pulchrum*, that is, grand or noble (*praef.*, 15). In conformity with Greek usage, he describes Europe as the most *pulchra* of regions (3.5); so too, he describes Italy as *pulcherrima*, specifying as its outstanding qualities the nature of its people, its climate, and its geographical location, and so the sense of the adjective may be something like "ideal" (37.201; cf. 4.44, 6.75, 6.93 of cities; 5.132 of the island Rhodes). Pliny affirms that a water snake known as the hydra is *pulcherrimum*, though it yields to none when it comes to poison (29.72). But he applies the term also to wine (14.92, citing verses of Fabius Dossennus); wood or trees (16.42, 16.77); a knot of some sort that grows on maple trees (*bruscum*, 16.68, though Pliny says that *molluscum* is *excellentius*, that is, "even better" for furniture and the like); perfume (20.19); women's clothes (19.8); a type of silver ore found in Spain (33.96); and gold, which is said to be *pulchrius* than silver insofar as it is softer (33.98; cf. 37.129 and 37.193, of gemstones). In these latter cases, the sense is something like "fine" or "good of its kind," sometimes with respect to a specific use. Pliny says that the house of Crassus was *magnifica*, though that of Quintus Catulus was a bit *praestantior* ("more impressive," perhaps), but Gaius Aquilius's house was by all accounts *pulcherrima* (17.2), the handsomest of all (cf. 35.138, 36.109; 36.102, of temples). Occasionally Pliny uses *pulcher* for human beings, as in his account of a potion that, when imbibed by parents to be, is said to make their children *pulchros bonosque*; Pliny specifies the meaning in the following sentence, when he says that the children will turn out to be *excellentes animi et formae*, that is, outstanding in mind (*bonos*) and looks (*pulchros*, 24.166).[38]

Pliny also applies the term *pulcher* to art, and here it is necessary to take account of nuances. To fashion a work *pulchre* (adverb) signifies doing it "well," usually in the sense of mimetic fidelity, corresponding to the Greek *kalôs*. Thus, Virgil is said to have described most excellently (*pulcherrime*) the appearance (*forma*) of horses that one ought to choose (8.162). Of a colossal statue of Apollo, Pliny wonders whether it is more marvelous for its bronze or its *pulchritudo* (34.43); the term may express the beauty of the god or the fine quality of the workmanship. He states that Phidias's Minerva (not the famous one in the Parthenon) was of such outstanding *pulchritudo* that it acquired the nickname "beauty" (*tam eximiae pulchritudinis, ut formae cognomen acceperit*, 34.54); it would appear that in this case he rendered the goddess in a particularly attractive way. It is no surprise to learn that Phidias's Venus too was "of outstanding beauty" (*eximiae pulchritudinis*, 36.15; cf. 36.18, on the *pulchritudo* of Phidias's statue of Jupiter at Olympia). Lysistratus of Sicyon, the brother of Lysippus, made casts directly from the face and instituted the practice of producing likenesses (*similitudines*); until then, Pliny says, sculptors sought to make images *quam pulcherrimas*, that is, as beautiful as possible. Here, attractiveness is clearly contrasted with mimetic fidelity, in much the way the elder Philostratus affirmed that sweaty and dusty horses were less fine (*kaloí*) but truer to life (*alêthesteroi*, 1.27.2). Lysistratus's predecessors made the subjects of their sculptures more attractive than they really were. But when Pliny affirms that Praxiteles, though most famous for his marble sculptures, nevertheless also "produced *pulcherrima* works in bronze [*fecit tamen et ex aere pulcherrima opera*]," the reference is clearly to the quality of the statues as opposed to their subjects, since he lists as examples, along with the abduction of Proserpina and an image of Venus, Dionysus, the personified Drunkenness, and a satyr (34.69). It would be odd to characterize a satyr as beautiful (see frontispiece). Pliny may mean here that the statues are of fine workmanship, rather than that they are beautiful (cf. 35.19, on the *pulcherrima opera* of a knight named Turpilius), but it is clear that the sense of *pulcher* is broad enough to be applied, if only occasionally, to works of art as such.[39]

The association between *pulcher* and *kalós* in a literary context emerges clearly in Horace's *Ars poetica* (99–100), where he affirms, "It is not enough for poems to be *pulchra*; they must also be *dulcia* ["sweet" or "pleasing"], and lead the listener's mind whither they will." This distinction is paralleled in Dionysius of Halicarnassus's treatise, *On the Arrangement of Words*, and goes back at least as far as Aristotle, who writes rather dismissively, "To subdivide style [*lexis*] further, e.g., that it should be pleasing and magnificent [*hêdeia kai megaloprepês*], is superfluous" (*Rhetoric*, 3.12, 1414a18–20). According to Dionysius, who claims a certain originality for his account of what renders a composition "pleasant and fine" (*hêdeia kai kalê*, 4.128), artistic prose has two goals: pleasure, afforded by the *glaphuros* or smooth style, and persuasiveness and power (*peithô kai kratos*), which pertain to the austere style (2.30). As he insists, "Let no one suppose that it is odd if I posit two goals and separate *to kalón* from pleasure [*hêdonê*], nor think it strange if I think that a style [*lexis*] may be pleasing but not *kalón*, or again *kalón* but not at all pleasing" (10.11–26; cf. *On Demosthenes*, 47.11–19).[40] *Kalós* here has the sense of "powerful" or "dignified."[41] In Horace, then, as Niall Rudd observes, "*pulcher* means 'formally correct,' 'well made,' even 'noble'" (Rudd 1989, ad loc.). It emphasizes the craftsmanship that enters into the composition of poetry, not the ostensible beauty of the work.

Writing in a Platonic frame of mind, Cicero declares in his rhetorical treatise *The Orator* that "there is nothing so *pulchrum* in any genre that there is not something even *pulchrius* [that is, more so] whence that came . . . ; for what cannot be perceived by eyes or ears or any other sense we can nevertheless comprehend by thought and the mind" (8; cf. 101). When Phidias made his images of Zeus and Athena, he had in view not some mortal as a model; rather, he beheld "a kind of outstanding image [*species*] of *pulchritudo* itself" (9). So too, "we see the image of perfect eloquence in our mind." Later, Cicero remarks, "Just as some women are said to be the more *pulchrae* when they are unadorned, since this very thing is more becoming [*decet*] to them, so this subtle kind of speech delights even when it is unkempt" (78); the analogy between erotic allure and the charm of a certain style of oratory is clear. But to speak *pulchre*, Cicero states, is nothing other than "to speak with the finest thoughts [*sententiae*] and the choicest words" (227). In *On the Orator*, Crassus makes clear how the harmonious order of words and sounds contributes to the finest form of speech:

> But as in most things, so in language, Nature herself has wonderfully contrived, that what carries in it the greatest utility, should have at the same time either the most dignity, or, as it often happens, the most charm [*venustas*]. We perceive the very system of the universe and of nature to be constituted with a view to the safety and preservation of the whole; so that the firmament should be round, and the earth in the middle, and that it should be held in its place by its own nature and tendency.... This order of things has such force, that, if there were the least alteration in it, they could not possibly subsist together; and such beauty [*pulchritudo*], that no fairer appearance [*species*] of nature could even be imagined. Turn your thoughts now to the shape [*forma*] and figure of man, or even that of other animals; you will find no part of the body fashioned without some necessary use, and the whole frame perfected as it were by art, not by chance. How is it with regard to trees, of which neither the trunk, nor the boughs, nor even the leaves, are formed otherwise than to maintain and preserve their own nature, yet in which there is no part that is not attractive [*venusta*]? Or let us turn from natural objects, and cast our eyes on those of artifice; what is so necessary in a ship as the sides, the hold, the prow, the stern, the yards, the sails, the masts? which yet have so much charm in

their appearance [*in specie venustatem*], that they seem to have been
invented not for safety only, but also for pleasure [*voluptas*]. ...
It happens likewise in all parts of language, that a certain
agreeableness and grace [*suavitas et lepos*] are attendant on utility,
and, I may say, on necessity; for the stoppage of the breath,
and the confined play of the lungs, introduced periods and the
pointing of words. (3.178–181, trans. Watson 1860, modified)

Beauty is achieved by the balance among parts, in language as in
the visual arts and the human form or even the entire cosmos,
which contribute collectively to the integrity of the whole.[42] A
Greek writer might have characterized all these items as *kalós*, in
the sense of "well made" or "impressive," and might indeed have
ascribed *kállos* to any one of them; nevertheless, the generalized
application of *pulcher* and *pulchritudo* seems to stand apart from
treatments of *kállos* in the Greek tradition.

We can appreciate the continuity of classical thinking about
beauty and style by turning to Augustine's reflections on Christian
discourse. Writing four centuries after Cicero, Augustine
characterizes as *pulchrum* a style in which sentences are marked by
clauses in anaphora, but it is still more *pulchrum*, he says, to attach
to each clause two subordinate members (*On Christian Teaching*,
4.7.54). Nevertheless, a speech "derives its beauty [*pulchritudo*] of
expression, if indeed this emerges, from the power of its subject
matter, and not from a concern for elegance [*decus*]" (4.20.118,
trans. Green 1997, 129, slightly modified). Indeed, a fine style
that masks corrupt thought is all the more offensive: "Just as it
is more lamentable if someone's body is *pulchrum* but his mind is
ugly [*deformis*] than if he had an ugly body as well, so too those who
eloquently say things that are false are more to be pitied than if
they say such things in an ugly way" (4.28.157). The comparison

between the attractiveness of speech and that of the human body remains a constant in Latin rhetorical discourse.

Jean-Michel Fontanier, in his analysis of beauty in Saint Augustine, observes that "Augustine never treats artistic beauty as an independent problem," nor does he acknowledge a contrast between natural and artistic beauty, as Hegel does, for example.[43] Augustine approached the question of beauty directly in his *Confessions*:

> These things I then knew not, and I loved beautiful things [*pulchra*] that were inferior. I was sinking to the very depths, and to my friends I said, "Do we love anything but what is beautiful [*pulchrum*]? What then is beautiful [*pulchrum*]? And what is beauty [*pulchritudo*]? What is it that attracts and wins us to the things we love? For unless there were in them a grace and beauty [*decus et species*], they could by no means draw us to them." And I marked and perceived that in bodies themselves, there was one thing that was a kind of whole, and for that reason beautiful [*pulchrum*], and another thing which was attractive [*decere*] because it was fittingly [*apte*] accorded with something else, as a part of the body to its whole, or a shoe to a foot, and the like. And this consideration sprang up in my mind, out of my inmost heart, and I wrote *On the Beautiful and Fitting* [*De pulchro et apto*] in, I think, two or three books. You know, O Lord, for it is gone from me; for I have them not, but they have strayed from me, I know not how. (4.13.20, trans. Pusey 1838, much modified)

Augustine never returned to the question of beauty in any detail, though he mentions it in passing in various writings. Fontanier doubts that Augustine's question, "What is *pulchrum*?," is an echo of Plato's *Hippias Major* (22–24; cf. Chapter 4 in this book), and I am inclined to agree. Augustine makes it clear elsewhere that

what is fitting (*aptum*) is subordinate to what is *pulchrum*, for
pulchrum is praised in itself, whereas *aptum* is judged in relation to
something else (Augustine, *Epistle*, 138.1.5, quoted by Fontanier,
23). So too, in his *Confessions* (4.15.24), Augustine describes what
is *pulchrum* as "that which is attractive in and of itself" (*quod per
se ipsum deceret*) as opposed to "what is fitting, which is attractive
when it is adapted to something else" (*aptum, quod ad aliquid
adcommodatum deceret*). There is a Platonic ring to this formulation,
and indeed Varro, one of the interlocutors in Cicero's *Academica
Posteriora* (1.5.19), says that Plato located "health, strength, and
beauty in the whole" (*in toto*), whereas other qualities reside in
the parts, for example, swiftness in the feet and sonorousness
in the voice (Fontanier compares Horace's dictum in the *Art
of Poetry, componere totum*, 24).[44] Of course, the harmony of
the parts is manifest only in the whole, but Augustine may be
thinking also of the self-subsisting idea of the beautiful, which, as
Plotinus had argued, is simple and therefore cannot consist in the
symmetry or proportion of its component parts (see Chapter 4,
Section III). As James O'Donnell observes in his commentary on
Augustine's *Confessions* (1992, ad 4.13.20), "The place of beauty
in A[ugustine's] works is affected by his reading of Plotinus 1.6."[45]
But whether Augustine was alluding to Plotinus in the present
context must remain moot.

III. Beauty and Art   When it comes to the pictorial
and plastic arts, however, the richest sources for the use of *pulcher*
and *pulchritudo* are Cicero's speeches against Verres. Of the ninety-
one occurrences of *pulcher* in Cicero's speeches (according to
Monteil's count), forty-two (by my count) appear in this set of
orations alone, not counting eight additional instances of the adverb
(e.g., *pulcherrime factum*, 2.1.49) and ten of the noun *pulchritudo*.
This is not surprising, perhaps: the speeches deal with Verres's

depredations during his administration of the province of Sicily, when he plundered the island's finest works of art. Cicero signals the aesthetic value of these objects precisely by the term *pulcher*. To take but a few examples, he refers to the statues stolen by Verres from the temple of Apollo in Delos as "most *pulchra* and ancient" (*signa pulcherrima atque antiquissima*, 2.1.46); so too those plundered from Chios, Erythrae, and Halicarnassus. The statue of Tenes, the founder of Tenedos, is described as *pulcherrime factum* (2.1.49).[46] Corinth, which had been destroyed by Mummius in the previous century, is described as *urbem pulcherrimam atque ornatissimam* and *plenissimam rerum omnium* (2.1.55); there is nothing unusual in applying the term *pulcher* to a town (the same is true for the Greek *kállos*, as we have seen), but the reference here is clearly to the multitude of artworks that adorned the city (cf. 2.2.4, 2.4.115, 2.4.117, and 2.5.95, of Syracuse; 2.5.127, of Rome). By contrast, when he speaks of an attractive woman or boy, Cicero uses *formosus* instead (five instances: 2.1.91 and 2.1.92, of *homines*; 2.4.136, of *mulieres*; 2.5.63, *erat ea navis plena iuventutis formosissimae*; 2.5.73, *formosi homines et adulescentes et artifices domum abducti*).[47] However, when it comes to a particularly chaste woman, Cicero employs the term *pulchritudo* (*mulierem eximia pulchritudine; sed eam summa integritate pudicitiaque existimari*, 2.1.64); it is her reputation for chastity that ignites the lust of Verres, who has never even set eyes on the lady (there is evidently an implicit allusion to Tarquin's passion for Lucretia), but it is worth noting that here too, Verres is aroused by pulchritude (cf. 2.2.87, of Himera sculpted in the form of a beautiful woman).

What Cicero finds (or pretends to find) most appalling, and indeed incomprehensible, is Verres's passion to own these artworks, that is, to keep them for himself rather than dedicate them to the embellishment of Rome. Thus, he intones:

Why should I speak of Marcus Marcellus, who conquered Syracuse, that highly adorned city? Why of Lucius Scipio, who waged war in Asia, and conquered Antiochus, a most powerful monarch? Why of Flamininus, who subdued Philip the king and Macedonia? Why of Lucius Paullus, who with his might and valor conquered king Perses? Why of Lucius Mummius, who overthrew that most beautiful and highly adorned city, Corinth, full of all sorts of riches, and brought many cities of Achaea and Boeotia under the empire and dominion of the Roman people? Their houses, though they were rich in virtue and honor, were empty of statues and paintings. But we see the whole city, the temples of the gods, and all parts of Italy, adorned with their gifts, and with memorials of them. (2.1.55, trans. Yonge 1856, slightly modified)

Again, he observes of the treasures of Himera, which, after its destruction, had been moved to Thermae:

These, and other works of art, Scipio had not thrown away carelessly, in order that Verres, that brilliant man, might carry them off, but he had restored them to the people of Thermae; not that he himself had not gardens, or a suburban villa, or some place or other where he could put them, but because, if he had taken them home, they would not long have been called Scipio's, but theirs to whom they come by his death. Now they are placed in such places that it seems to me they will always seem to be Scipio's, and so they are called. (2.2.87, trans. Yonge 1856, modified)

Cicero complains that Verres stripped bare a temple of Cybele at Enguinum, where Publius Scipio had deposited very some fine wares, and asks him:

Are you, indeed, the only man who delights in Corinthian vases? Are you the wisest at perceiving the mixture of that celebrated bronze, and of the tracery of those works? Did not the great Scipio, that most learned and accomplished man, understand it too? But do you, a man without one single virtue, without education, without natural ability, and without any information, understand them and value them . . . ? It was because he thoroughly understood how *pulchra* they were, that he thought that they were made, not for the luxury of men, but for the ornamenting of temples and cities, in order that they might appear to our posterity to be holy and sacred monuments. (2.4.97, trans. Yonge 1856, much modified)

According to Cicero, Verres was not only a pillager, he was also ignorant of what the fine objects that he craved were really worth—not in economic terms, but for their larger civic and religious functions. Verres stands accused not just of greed but of irreverence for robbing an ancient statue of Ceres (2.4.99): "Listen, also, O judges, to the man's singular covetousness, audacity and madness, especially in polluting those sacred things, which not only may not be touched with the hands, but which may not be violated even in thought." Cicero invites the judges to compare the rapaciousness of Verres with the benign conduct of Marcellus, when he conquered Syracuse:

With respect to the decorations of the city, he had a regard to his own victory, and a regard to humanity; he thought it was owed to his victory to transport many things to Rome which might be an ornament to this city, and owed to humanity not utterly to strip the city, especially as it was one which he was anxious to preserve. . . . The things which were transported to Rome we see before the temples of Honor and of Virtue, and also in other places. He put nothing in his own house, nothing in his gardens, nothing in his suburban villa; he thought that his house could only be an ornament to the city if he abstained from carrying the ornaments, which belonged to the city,

to his own house. But he left many extraordinary things [*permulta
atque egregia*] at Syracuse; he violated not the respect due to any god;
he laid hands on none. (2.4.120–121)[48]

For all the violent denunciation of Verres's depredations,
Cicero is also addressing a larger question, namely what is it about
fine works of art that inspires such a lust for possessing them? They
bring no honor to the owner, such as derives from endowing or
bestowing public monuments. They are stripped of their original
religious and social contexts and meanings, and are desired for
reasons that appear almost abstract.[49] Even their monetary worth
does not wholly explain the covetous need for such objects, which
are not acquired simply to be put up for sale (though they can
serve this purpose as well). Cicero seems to be wrestling with the
nature of the collector's passion and inquiring what motivates such
a strange desire. Other scholars have noted with some wonder the
intense competition in Rome to decorate private mansions with
Greek and other foreign art.[50] But what do the various objects—
the statues, vases, tables, bowls, candelabra, and the rest—have in
common, that they can all be the objects of the collector's desire?
Cicero impugns Verres's taste, but he believes there is such a thing
as taste, a recognition of artistic worth. I suggest that Cicero
appropriated the term *pulcher* and its cognates to identify that
aesthetic quality and the mysterious attraction that it exercises on
the beholder.[51]

It is for that reason that I am inclined to believe that *pulcher*, as
Cicero employs it in relation to works of art and craftsmanship,
is not limited to the sense of "well made," as *kalós* is in Greek.
It was natural to see beauty as the property that inspired such
a powerful drive to possess, since beauty was closely associated
with erotic attraction, which has an analogous effect on the
viewer. Cicero compares Verres's passion for a woman of whose

pulchritudo he had merely heard to a woman's fanatical desire
for a special piece of jewelry: "We have heard in mythology of
Eriphyla being so covetous that when she had seen a necklace,
made, I suppose, of gold and jewels, she was so excited by its
beauty [*pulchritudo*], that she betrayed her husband for the sake
of it. His covetousness [*cupiditas*] was similar; but in one respect
more violent and more senseless, because she was desiring
[*cupiebat*] a thing which she had seen, while his passions [*libidines*]
were excited not only by his eyes, but even by his ears" (2.4.39,
trans. Yonge). There does seem to be something erotic about the
collector's desire for works of art.

In his study of beauty in art, Alexander Nehamas observes,
"Our reaction to beautiful things is the urge to make them
our own, which is why Plato called *erôs* the desire to possess
beauty—a sour note to contemporary ears, to which it sounds
as if he is condoning a wish to dominate, exploit, and manipulate
that we have learned officially to disparage" (Nehamas 2007,
55). In Chapter 1, I cited Nehamas's puzzlement about this
proprietary urge: "If beauty inspires the desire to possess and
own its object . . . , it might seem reasonable to believe that those
who value art for its beauty are either philistines or perverts"
(11). I noted that Elaine Scarry too is suspicious of the impulse
to own: "Beauty is sometimes disparaged because it gives rise to
material cupidity and possessiveness." She adds, "If someone wishes
all the Gallé vases of the world to sit on his own windowsills"—
Verres may come to mind—then "it is just a miseducated version"
of the desire to keep a beautiful object in view (Scarry 1999,
7). Cicero seems to have been wrestling with just this problem
concerning the nature of beauty, but rather than attempt to define
a purely aesthetic response to beauty that would be independent
of desire, he set against the possessive passion a different sense of
what art was for: the adornment of public spaces that conferred

reputation on the benefactor and symbolized the power and glory of the state. Since the idea of nobility or moral excellence was embraced by the notion of *pulchritudo* in a way that differs from the normal semantic range of "beauty" in English, Cicero could contrast the public spirit of a Scipio and the selfish passion of Verres by exploiting the nuances of a single Latin term.

In his philosophical works, Cicero, in line with Greek ideas, defines *pulchritudo* in terms of symmetry and proportion and sees it particularly as an attribute of the universe, a sign of its divine order. Thus, in *On the Nature of the Gods* (2.98), Cicero's Stoic spokesman declares, "For, leaving aside oversubtle arguments, the beauty [*pulchritudo*] of those things which we say have been established by divine providence can be seen directly by the eyes."[52] On earth, correspondingly, the most beautiful shape is that of human beings (1.47): "For as it seems fitting that the most excellent nature, whether because it is blessed or eternal, should also be the most beautiful [*pulcherrima*], what composition of limbs, what arrangement of features, what form, what appearance, can be more beautiful [*pulchrior*] than the human?" Again like the Greek philosophers, Cicero extends the idea of physical beauty to that of the soul. Cato, Cicero's Stoic interlocutor in *On Ends*, puts it this way: "The features of the soul are more beautiful than those of the body" (*animi enim liniamenta sunt pulchriora quam corporis*, 3.75). Cicero elaborates in the *Tusculan Disputations* (4.31): "And just as, with the body, there is a certain appropriate configuration [*figura*] of the limbs with an agreeable kind of color and that is said to be beauty [*pulchritudo*], so too in the mind an evenness of beliefs and judgments and consistency together with a certain firmness and stability in accord with virtue or that possesses the power itself of virtue is called beauty [*pulchritudo*]."[53] Correspondingly, the virtues themselves, or virtuous deeds, may be labeled beautiful (e.g., *De officiis*, 1.18, 3.19). In the *Brutus* (70), Cicero provides a thumbnail sketch of the evolution of sculpture and painting, which finally attain near perfect beauty in the works of Polyclitus and artists like Apelles; here, then, is the idea of beauty in connection with a work of art. Once again, however, it is not entirely clear whether Polyclitus's achievement, according to Cicero, lay in recognizing and reproducing the most beautiful human form or in producing a work of art whose beauty was independent of that of the object imitated.[54]

The temple of Athena in Syracuse was notable in antiquity for the workmanship of its doors. As Cicero tells it:

> It is incredible how many Greeks have left written accounts of the beauty of these doors: they, perhaps, may admire and extol them too much; be it so, still it is more honorable for our republic, O judges, that our general, in a time of war, should have left those things which appeared to them *pulchra*, than that our praetor should have carried them off in a time of peace. On the folding-doors were some subjects most minutely executed in ivory; all these he caused to be taken out; he tore off and took away a very beautiful head of the Gorgon circled with snakes; and he betrayed, too, that he was influenced not only by the workmanship [*artificio*] but also the price and profit; for he did not hesitate to take away also all the golden knobs from these folding-doors, which were numerous and heavy; and it was not the workmanship [*opere*] of these, but the weight which pleased him. (*Verrine Orations*, 2.4.124, trans. Yonge 1856).

Cicero recognizes that tastes differ and that what appeals to the Syracusans, or to Greeks generally, may not be equally attractive to Romans. But Cicero seems to agree that the Gorgon's head or face was especially *pulcher* (*Gorgonis os pulcherrimum*). We imagine Gorgons, with their serpentine locks, to be paradigms of ugliness. Perhaps the face of this one was pretty, despite the snakes that encircled it.[55] Or *pulcher* in this context may convey divine favor, as Monteil argued, thus sidestepping the aesthetic aspect altogether. Again, we may suppose that Cicero is referring to the craftsmanship, which he mentions immediately afterward: whatever one might say of the Gorgon's physical attractiveness, it was well made, and might even be assumed to represent faithfully the image that people entertained of such a creature. But I should like to suggest that we just possibly see here an intimation of the issue raised for modern aesthetics by works like Matisse's *Blue Nude*, that is, the tension between the beauty we ascribe to a work of art, which is what makes us wish to possess it or at least have it in sight as much as possible, and the physical beauty—the prettiness, if you wish—of an attractive human figure, which inspires a sexual desire. Cicero would not, I feel certain, have described the Gorgon as *formosa*, which would have unambiguously signified good looks.[56] But the constant application of *pulcher* to a wide variety of artworks encouraged an extension of the word's ordinary sense to cover something like what we would regard as aesthetic appeal—with all the paradoxical consequences that this entailed. Verres's passionate, if perverse, response to such beauty may well be an early instance, however exaggerated, of a strictly aesthetic response.

6

GREEK BEAUTY TODAY

I. The Varieties of Aesthetic Experience   In the preceding chapters, I have argued that the ancient Greek vocabulary distinguished between a type of beauty that was closely associated with erotic attraction and denoted by the noun *kállos*, and a more general notion of excellence signified by the adjective *kalós*, which might denote beauty when the distinction in question had to do with the human form but also meant "noble," "good," "well done," or even "virtuous" when applied to objects animate or inanimate, or to more abstract items such as moral conduct, laws, and the like. *Kállos* might also be ascribed to particularly attractive creatures other than humans; to certain features of landscapes or cities; and to such immaterial things as music, literary style, and even—in Platonic metaphysics—to purely intellectual concepts or forms. Yet it never entirely lost a connection with the kind of appeal that inspires desire. Moreover, it was not generally applied to artworks as such but rather, in the case of the plastic arts, to the figure represented in the work, and with literary artifacts to a specific kind of prettiness achieved through balanced clauses or verbal sonorities. In this sense, *kállos* never rose to the level of a strictly aesthetic idea, as that feature that is characteristic of art as such. The elevation of beauty to the status of the aesthetic property per se would have to await the

Renaissance, and on a theoretical level, the eighteenth-century invention of aesthetics.

But although beauty and the desire it produced in the beholder were not the unique determinants of art, they did constitute one among an array of qualities and responses to literary, plastic, and musical creations, as well as to certain natural features. It is often taken for granted today that art should yield pleasure, and ancient critics too recognized pleasure as one of the sentiments that art might arouse. But the pleasure that works of art yield was typically understood to derive from their technical excellence, above all in regard to fidelity to the object depicted; this is what in Greek was called *mimêsis*, that is, "imitation" or, as some prefer to render it, "representation."[1] The word is familiar today in literary theory largely on the basis of Aristotle's *Poetics* (4, 1448b4–27). Aristotle explains that there are two reasons why poetry came into being. First, imitating is innate to human beings, and everyone enjoys simulations; that is why we enjoy watching an exact likenesses of things that are in real life painful to see, "for example the figures of the most contemptible animals and of corpses." Now, we must recall that Aristotle is discussing tragedy, which one might think is not in itself very pleasant to watch. It is worth remarking that he nowhere says that tragedy is beautiful, save perhaps in the suggestion that plays should have a reasonable length, neither too long nor too short, in the same way that bodies are not fine (*kalós*) if they are too small to make out their individual parts (hence one has no sense of their proportions, as in the case of tiny insects) or too large to take in at a single look, for example a mile-high giant (1450b34–51a15). So why do we enjoy tragedy? Because we enjoy seeing good representations, irrespective of whether the object represented is pretty or ugly. Aristotle's second reason is that it is pleasurable to learn, and when people see likenesses they recognize the connection with the real thing.[2] Aristotle is explaining why poetry came into existence, not why people enjoy representations of repugnant things, but his account illuminates the source of tragic pleasure. What is more, his theory presupposes that art does not deceive in the way Clement was to argue (see Chapter 4): to enjoy a work of art, one must precisely recognize that it is a representation and not the real thing.

Some centuries later, Plutarch, in his essay *How a Youth should Listen to Poems*, observes that poetry, like painting, is imitative, and that the pleasure poetry provides is due not to the beauty of the thing represented but rather to the faithfulness of the reproduction (18A). This is why, he says, we enjoy imitations of sounds that are by nature unpleasant, such as a pig's squeal, a squeaky wheel, the rustle of the wind, or the beating of the sea (18C). As Plutarch puts it, "Imitating something fine [*kalón*] is not the same as doing it well [or "finely," *kalôs*]" (18D, cited in Chapter 4).[3] Plutarch is seeking here to prevent young people from imagining that the satisfaction they derive from a good imitation is a sign that the person or thing represented is good. But he explains incidentally why it is that people derive pleasure from images of things repulsive in themselves. Once again, pleasure is associated with imitation rather than with beauty.[4]

There are other explanations for why tragedy is pleasurable. A comic poet named Timocles, a slightly later contemporary of Aristotle's, has a character in one of his plays affirm (*Dionysiazousae*, fr. 6 Kassel-Austin = Athenaeus 6.2) that tragedy takes our minds off our own troubles and we enjoy seeing that others are suffering more than we are. Others maintain that our pleasure derives from the knowledge that the actor is not really being harmed: again, this view depends on an awareness that what we are seeing is a representation. Pleasure is also said to result simply from novelty. As Telemachus says to his mother Penelope in the *Odyssey*, "People praise whatever song circulates newest among the listeners" (1.351–352). But none of these accounts mentions beauty, the source of which is most commonly ascribed to the appreciation of fine technique.[5]

Apart from pleasure, a work of art may also elicit various emotions (pleasure was usually conceived of as a sensation rather than an emotion in the strict sense). As is well known, Aristotle affirmed that the emotions proper to tragedy were pity and fear, and he presumably held that different emotions were characteristic of other genres, such as invective or comedy (he may well have mentioned these in the lost second book of the *Poetics*, which was devoted to comedy). Aristotle seems to have meant that these emotions are a response to the entire work, that is, the plot or story as a whole, and not to individual events or moments in the action. That is why he maintained that we should be able to experience pity and fear even upon reading a summary of a good tragic plot, and he disparaged vivid special effects, like costumes or scenery, that might serve to produce a shock or sense of horror but not genuine emotions, which involve rational appraisal and are not simply instinctive reactions to offensive sights or sounds.[6] It is worth emphasizing that the emotions that Aristotle mentions in connection with tragedy are not responses to art as such—they are not analogous to the aesthetic emotion that some modern philosophers have posited (see Section 2 in this chapter)—but are specific to stories of a certain kind. What is more, they are the same emotions that people experience in response to events in real life. Aristotle nowhere distinguishes the pity we may feel for characters on stage from the emotion we might have upon hearing a true story of undeserved misfortune, though people of course know that the events they are witnessing in the theater or reading in a book are fictional: no one leaps onto the stage to help the suffering hero.[7]

Ancient thinkers, from the fourth-century BC orator Isocrates to Saint Augustine, puzzled over why we sometimes react more sensitively to purely fictitious events than to real-life catastrophes. Isocrates wrote, for example, that "people consider it right to weep over the misfortunes composed by poets, while ignoring the many true and terrible sufferings that happen on account of war" (4.168). And Augustine asked in his *Confessions*, "What kind of pity is there in fictional stories and dramas? For the listener is not moved to offer help, but is invited only to feel pain, and the more he suffers the more he approves of the author of these imaginings" (3.2; cf. Munteanu 2009). But even if the emotions elicited by literature are not quite real emotions, they are nevertheless analogous to such emotions and do not constitute a distinct aesthetic feeling; nor are they anywhere described as responses to the beauty of a work.

Seneca believed that our reactions to theatrical spectacles are almost instinctive, like shivering when we are sprayed with cold water or experiencing vertigo when we look down from great heights, or blushing when we hear obscenities. He meant that we do not give rational approval to any of these reactions: we no more judge that a battle we read about is cause for fear than we decide to feel ashamed when someone tells a bawdy story. Seneca calls these automatic responses "the initial preliminaries to emotions" (*On Anger*, 2.2.6), and other Stoics refer to them as "pre-emotions." One of Seneca's examples, indeed, is the feeling of pity we may experience even for evil characters who are suffering. This runs counter to the classical definition of pity, adopted by Aristotle and the Stoics, which holds that we feel pity at the sight of undeserved suffering, not suffering per se.[8] In any case, whether emotion or pre-emotion, Seneca does not include in his ample list of such preliminary sentiments the response to beauty itself: there is no such pre-emotion, any more than there is a genuine emotion, as the Stoics understood the term, that is elicited by the sight of something beautiful.

Still another response that a work of art or a phenomenon of nature may induce is awe, the feeling we experience upon encountering something that is sublime or "lofty," in the root sense of the Greek word (*hupsos*), the term of art in the essay by Longinus that is conventionally translated as *On the Sublime*.[9] Longinus writes that "what is extraordinary draws listeners not to persuasion but rather to ecstasy [*ekstasis*]" (1.4), and he affirms that what is marvelous (*thaumasion*) and accompanied by shock (*ekplêxis*) overwhelms all else.[10] Insofar as Longinus speaks of beauty, it is as a feature of style that can have good effects or ill (5.1), and it is associated with figures of speech (17.2, 20.1) and the choice of appropriate words, which can contribute, when properly deployed, to the effectiveness of the whole work. In this respect, Longinus is in accord with the major writers on style in antiquity, who regarded beauty as one feature of rhetoric (see Chapter 4). Demetrius, the author of the treatise *On Style* (perhaps as early as the third century BC), identified four basic styles: plain, elevated, elegant, and forceful.[11] Beautiful effects, according to Demetrius, can be in tension with and undermine forcefulness (252, 274). Hermogenes of Tarsus (second century AD) expanded the number of styles to seven: clearness, grandeur, beauty, poignancy, characterization, truth, and mastery (the last is the combined virtue of the first six; the translations of the technical terms are those of Rhys Carpenter).[12] Beauty here is one device among others. Hermogenes defines it as "a symmetry of limbs and parts, along with a good complexion," in a clear analogy to the beauty of the human body (the passage from Hermogenes is cited more extensively in Chapter 4).

In addition to pleasure, awe, the emotions of fear and pity, and pre-emotions such as the pseudo-fear we experience upon

reading about or seeing enactments of dangers that we know
are fictional or that took place in the distant past (but can still
make our hair stand on end), classical thinkers recognized what
we might call a moral response to works of art, that is, approval
or disapproval of the their ethical content or apparent message.
This is the basis on which Plato excluded certain art forms, such
as epic and tragedy, from his ideal republic: they provided bad
examples of comportment among gods and heroes, and would
corrupt young minds. Plutarch too was aware of the potentially
corrupting effect of art but sought rather to immunize young
students against the deleterious aspects of literature (which were
unavoidable in a good story) by training them to read critically
and to resist, as he put it, the immoral implications of the text.[13]
The moral evaluation of works of art has been the prevailing
attitude for most of the period since antiquity. Carole Talon-
Hugon, in her important study *Morales de l'art*, remarks on "the
massive and enduring presence of a moralizing intention in art,
an intention that, across artistic categories and genres, pertains
to poetry as much as to painting, to tragedy as much as to the
novel; an intention that is manifest in mediaeval art, powerfully
affirmed in the course of the Renaissance, and still largely present
up to the end of the eighteenth century" (2009, 29). Even Hume
maintained that an ethical response to art is inevitable, though it
caused him no little perplexity; as he affirms in his essay, *Of the
Standard of Taste*:

> The poet's *monument more durable than brass*, must fall to the ground
> like common brick or clay, were men to make no allowance for the
> continual revolutions of manners and customs, and would admit
> of nothing but what was suitable to the prevailing fashion.... But
> where the ideas of morality and decency alter from one age to
> another, and where vicious manners are described, without being

marked with the proper characters of blame and disapprobation, this must be allowed to disfigure the poem, and to be a real deformity. I cannot, nor is it proper I should, enter into such sentiments; and however I may excuse the poet, on account of the manners of his age, I never can relish the composition. The want of humanity and of decency, so conspicuous in the characters drawn by several of the ancient poets, even sometimes by Homer and the Greek tragedians, diminishes considerably the merit of their noble performances, and gives modern authors an advantage over them.[14]

The eighteenth century thus marks the end of a very long period during which "la production littéraire et picturale était sous l'autorité de l'éthique." Talon-Hugon specifies that she is deliberately avoiding, as much as possible, the use of the term *art*, since it is precisely when the various artistic practices are classified under the rubric or concept of the beaux-arts that the ethical perspective will lose its authority, as it comes into competition with other ends, finally to be abandoned entirely (29). As the headnote to her book's second chapter, "The Independence of Art and Ethics," Talon-Hugon quotes Oscar Wilde: "The first condition of creation is that the critic should be able to recognize that the sphere of art and the sphere of ethics are absolutely distinct and separate" (93).[15]

We may briefly note two other responses to art that are related to the moral view. There is a long tradition in ancient Greece of allegorical interpretation that seeks to rescue revered works, such as the Homeric epics, from accusations of immorality and impiety. A certain Heraclitus composed, probably around the beginning of the second century AD, a treatise on Homer that begins: "It is a weighty and damaging charge that heaven brings against Homer for his disrespect for the divine. If he meant nothing allegorically, he was impious through and through, and sacrilegious fables, loaded with blasphemous folly, run riot through both epics."[16] Allegory was the chief, but not the only, method for inquiring into what today we might call the meaning of a text. This style of interpretation usually looked not to the significance of a work as a whole but rather to brief episodes or even single words.

Independent of allegory, interpretation (*hermêneia*) might simply identify the back story of a given text or artwork, which required special or local knowledge. Thus, at the beginning of Longus's *Daphnis and Chloe*, the narrator asks a resident informant for an exegesis of a painting, which, as it happens, records the story of the protagonists that will form the substance of the novel. Pausanias, in his *Description of Greece*, often inquires of local exegetes what is going on in a given work, sometimes dissenting from their explanations, for example, in regard to the identity of the rival armies in the third panel of the famous Chest of Cypselus (5.18.6–8). Philostratus the Elder, in the preface to his book of ecphrases (*Eikones* or the more familiar Latin title *Imagines*), exploits the fiction of explaining (*hermêneuein*) to a ten-year-old boy the scenes represented on paintings hung in the portico of his father's villa, since the images often present a new take on what are otherwise familiar stories. Thus, Philostratus supposes that the child has heard how Theseus abandoned Ariadne on Naxos and Dionysus rescued her, but he may not perceive that, in this picture, Dionysus is portrayed as very much in love (1.14). Again, Philostratus assumes that the boy is familiar with various stories about the origin of centaurs, but he points out that here they are represented in a domestic context, with the young creatures just beginning to acquire some of the roughness or fierceness of adults. The lad, he remarks, might well find their life attractive, perhaps with the implication that he too is on the cusp of becoming tougher as he grows up (2.3).[17]

I have reviewed, all too briefly, several of the responses to art that were acknowledged in classical antiquity in order to show that the appreciation of beauty was only one among many, and not necessarily the primary one, as Arthur Danto observes (see Chapter 1). True, certain features of style might be called beautiful or, more precisely, "beauties," and the same is true for certain colors and other devices in painting, but it was very rare to ascribe *kállos* to a work of art as such, and where this seems to be the case, it would appear that it was most often conceived of as a property of the figure represented in the work rather than of the artwork itself. For this reason, the kind of problem associated with a painting like *Blue Nude* seems never to have been a subject of inquiry in classical criticism. Beauty, and the desire that it characteristically inspired, never rose to the dominant position it would acquire in the Renaissance and more so in the eighteenth century, when the modern discipline of aesthetics was invented and took beauty for its subject.

II. Beauty Ascendant   There is a history that remains to be written of how the modern notion of beauty evolved, along with the paradoxes to which it has given rise (see Chapter 1), and what relation it bears to the ancient Greek conception. I will not attempt to trace this history through the Middle Ages, whether in the Latin West or in the Byzantine world, although there were important developments in both regions that contributed to the classicizing revival of art, and attitudes toward art, in the Renaissance.[18] To take but a single example, Michael Psellos, the brilliant polymath who lived in Constantinople in the eleventh century, offered reflections on the beauty of icons and other images that approach the level of an aesthetic theory of art. In a letter recording his experience with one such icon, Psellos writes:

> I am a most fastidious viewer of icons; but one astonished me
> by its indescribable beauty [*kállos*] and like a bolt of lightning

it threatened to disable my senses and my power of judgment regarding the thing. It has the Mother of God as its model and has been painted in regard to her. But if a likeness has come to be in that supernatural image, I do not quite know how. I know this much and just this much, that the corporal nature has been faithfully imitated by means of the mixing of colors. Yet the form [*eidos*] is incomprehensible to me and is sometimes apprehended visually and sometimes conceptually. I do not therefore write about what I have beheld, but what I have experienced. For it seems that having completely exchanged its nature, it was transformed into the beauty of divine form [*theoeides...kállos*] and surpassed visual perception. There she is neither someone stern nor again decked out in a singular beauty [*kállos*], rather she is beyond both these measures. She does not descend into knowledge insofar as her shape [*morphê*] is perceived, but insofar as she astounds the viewer.[19]

Psellos would seem almost to be offering a way out of the dilemma posed by Roger Scruton concerning spiritual and corporeal beauty (see Chapter 1); for instead of regarding the Virgin's beauty as unapproachable and beyond desire, Psellos is clear that her form is beyond the visible, and if her transcendent nature is expressed in visible form, it is experienced, rather than viewed, as a shock comparable to a lightning bolt. Psellos's debt to Neoplatonism, with its vision of abstract entities beyond the mundane world of matter, is evident, and yet, in his minute attention to the impact of a concrete image, Psellos draws Plotinus's theory into the sphere of art.[20]

Newly and passionately engaged with classical civilization, the Renaissance witnessed a revival of both Neoplatonism and the rules of proportion first outlined by Polyclitus. Among the earliest Renaissance writers to compose a theoretical treatise

on art was the fifteenth-century architect and painter Leon
Battista Alberti. Alberti was fascinated by science as well as
by the classics, and his essay *On Painting* (composed in Latin in
1435 and rendered a year later into Italian) relies heavily on the
mathematics of his time. He writes:

> The primary parts of painting, therefore, are the planes. That grace
> in bodies which we call beauty is born from the composition of the
> planes. A face which has its planes here large and there small, here
> raised and there depressed—similar to the faces of old women—
> would be most ugly in appearance. Those faces which have the
> planes joined in such a way that they take shades and lights agreeably
> and pleasantly, and have no harshness of the relief angles, these we
> should certainly say are beautiful and delicate faces. (1970, 24)[21]

Alberti distinguishes beauty from accuracy of representation, and
insists that beauty is essential to great art.[22] Although Alberti was not
given to metaphysical speculation, his predilection for mathematics
was not incompatible with Neoplatonism. Anthony Blunt, in his
study of theories of art in the Italian Renaissance, affirms that
Michelangelo was still more of a Neoplatonist than Alberti, since for
Michelangelo "beauty is the reflection of the divine in the material
world" (Blunt 1962, 62). Michelangelo left little record of his views
on art in writing, but Blunt perhaps had in mind his sonnet, "*Veggio
nel tuo bel viso, Signor mio*," addressed to Vittoria Colonna:

> *A quel pietoso fonte, onde siam tutti,*
> *S'assembra ogni beltà che qua si vede,*
> *Più c'altra cosa alle persone accorte.*

> To the wise, every beauty that is seen here resembles that
> merciful source whence we all come, more than anything else.

The language of Neoplatonism, its transcendental idealism, was the common property of Renaissance thinkers and artists.[23]

The transition from the Renaissance to the eighteenth century, during which aesthetics and art history assumed for the first time the status of independent disciplines, exhibits both continuities and changes.[24] According to Jeremy Tanner, the pietistic theology of "love and sympathy for God and one's fellow men" was transferred to the Kantian notion of a disinterested appreciation of the artwork. With this shift, moreover, "feeling was placed at the center of an adequate aesthetic response rather than the intellect, *intellegere*, characteristic of Hellenistic-Roman high cultural discourses" (Tanner 2010, 23). Thus, for all the resemblances between classical and modern culture, there is a decided change in aesthetic sensibility.[25] Now, reason was not a necessary element in classical responses to artworks: I use the plural *responses* here, because, as I have been arguing, there was no single, specifically "aesthetic" way of reacting to a work of art. Although the pleasure we feel upon recognizing a mimetic likeness may have a cognitive basis, as would a moral evaluation of the subject matter, the desire that may be aroused by an attractive image or image of an attractive object does not necessarily involve rational appraisal. But desire is not so much an emotion as an appetite, and does not correspond to the kind of feeling that Tanner rightly identifies as characteristic of modern theories of the aesthetic experience.

David Hume, for example, affirms in his *Enquiry concerning Human Understanding*, published in 1748: "Beauty, whether moral or natural, is felt, more properly than perceived."[26] The modern critic Jesse Prinz, in turn, asserts categorically that "when we appreciate a work, the appreciation consists in an emotional response."[27] In a more popular vein, Howard Gardner notes that "in the not-too-distant past, the primary standard applied to works of art—whether music, dance, literature, drama, or the graphic or plastic arts—was that of beauty," and thus, "in the past, viewers were disturbed by scenes or features that were deemed unbeautiful, ugly, or inexpertly wrought."[28] Gardner glosses over the distinction between the representation of a beautiful object ("scenes . . . deemed unbeautiful") and an accurate or accomplished reproduction of whatever object, whether beautiful in itself or not ("inexpertly wrought"). But he is confident that the response to beauty of any kind is a feeling—pleasurable, no doubt, but otherwise sui generis. "In stipulating beauty, we indicate that we gain pleasure, a warm and positive feeling, a 'tingle' if you will, from the beholding of the object—or, if you prefer, a neurophysiological reference, a rush of serotonin" (41). The vague "tingle"—equally vaguely specified as "warm and positive" and identified, no more informatively, with the neurotransmitter serotonin—is as close as Gardner comes to defining the nature of the principal aesthetic response, though in this respect he is not more nebulous than Hume himself. For the aesthetic emotion is defined entirely with reference to what elicits it, which is understood in the aesthetics of the eighteenth century to be beauty. At all events, this feeling most certainly is not desire: "Importantly, in apprehending the object as beautiful, we are satisfied to maintain a *distance* from the object; that is, we don't try to hug it, eat it, or slam it to the ground" (41).[29] Despite the colloquial formulation, Gardner's view of aesthetics has its roots in the analyses of Immanuel Kant.

In a curious way, Kant himself signals the passing of beauty as the central concept in aesthetics, even as he provides its most influential defense. One threat to the priority of beauty resides in the very idea of distance, with its implication of a dispassionate relation to the aesthetic object (more on this below); another is the relocation of beauty in feeling as opposed to the objective qualities of the aesthetic object. Baumgarten, who invented the word *aesthetics*, took a step toward locating beauty in the beholder when he wrote: "The goal of aesthetics is the perfection of sensory knowledge as such; this is beauty" (para. 14).[30] But the perfection of such knowledge was at the same time an awareness of perfection in the object. As Frederick Beiser notes, "Following Wolff, Baumgarten's central thesis is that beauty consists in the intuition of perfection," and this takes the form of unity-in-variety, which is a property manifested in the object.[31] Thus, one was expected to be able to give a rational account of why an object was beautiful, consisting in "the perceptual features of the object itself" (Beiser 2009, 5), including verisimilitude (that is, mimesis). Kant, however, took issue with Baumgarten over just this premise. As Alexander Nehamas observes, "One of Kant's most telling observations about beauty is that it 'pleases universally without a concept,' which is to say that 'there can . . . be no rule in accordance with which someone could be compelled to acknowledge something as beautiful.'"[32] Nehamas illustrates the problem with the following example: "I can specify the particular shades of red whose combination and contrast I so admire in Botticelli's Uffizi *Annunciation* . . . as finely as I want, but what I tell you can't possibly convince you that you should judge it the same way: only looking for yourself will move you one way or another."[33]

One point of continuity between the rationalists and Kant is the relationship between beauty and pleasure. Much earlier, Leibniz had affirmed, "We seek beautiful things because they are pleasant, for I define beauty as that, the contemplation of which is pleasant." Leibniz goes on to claim that "everything which is loved is beautiful, that is, delightful to a sentient being," but it is not the case "that everything beautiful is loved. For we do not really love nonrational beings, since we do not seek their good in itself."[34] Leibniz, then, associated beauty with desire, and to this extent the perception of beauty would not be dispassionate, at least in relation to human beings. His formulation leaves room, however, for kinds of beauty in nature and in art that do not inspire love, though they are pleasing to contemplate. Baumgarten and Kant were in agreement on the central role of pleasure in the perception of the beautiful.[35] If beauty inspires pleasure but is beheld in a wholly disinterested way, then pleasure itself is no longer a stimulus to desire, and the bond that Leibniz perceived between beauty and love is ruptured. Thanks to Kant, beauty was deprived of the ability to inspire passion as well as of the possibility that there should ever be general agreement about aesthetic judgments (cf. Beiser 2009, 133, 136).

Modern (or postmodern) critics have exposed the underlying assumptions, not to say prejudices, that inform Kant's affirmation of standards of taste in the absence of objective criteria of what constitutes a beautiful object, together with his insistence that aesthetic appreciation must be disinterested. Jacques Derrida, in *The Truth in Painting*, affirms that not to care even about the existence of the aesthetic object is a peculiar way of appreciating it (1987, 45). Derrida expands upon the theme with characteristic panache:

> Almost nothing remains (to me): neither the thing, nor its existence, nor mine, neither the pure object nor the pure subject, no interest of anything that is in anything that is. And yet I like: no, that's still going too far, that's still taking an interest in existence, no doubt. I do not like, but I take pleasure in what does not interest me, in something of which it is at least a matter of indifference whether I like it or not. (Derrida 1987, 48)

But Pierre Bourdieu goes beyond merely observing a tension between pleasure and disinterest and discloses the class nature of Kant's haughty disdain for the baser kind of enjoyment. In the Postscript, entitled "Towards a 'Vulgar' Critique of 'Pure' Critiques," to his influential book *Distinction: A Social Critique of the Judgement of Taste*, Bourdieu argues that "Kant's principle of pure taste is nothing other than a refusal, a disgust—a disgust for objects which impose enjoyment and a disgust for the crude, vulgar taste which revels in this imposed enjoyment" (490).[36] Kant's idealization of the response to beauty, liberating it from the immediacy of desire and even of interest (albeit in a special sense of "interest"), is conditioned by his devaluation of the pleasures that arise precisely from the appetites, which Kant equates with animal instinct. As Bourdieu puts it, "In Kant's text, disgust discovers with horror the common animality on which and against which moral distinction is constructed: 'we regard as coarse and low the habits of thought of those who have no feeling for beautiful nature . . . and who devote themselves to the mere enjoyment of sense found in eating and drinking.'"[37] The pure pleasure that Kant idealizes, Bourdieu concludes, is an "ascetic, empty pleasure which implies the renunciation of pleasure, pleasure purified of pleasure"; but this hollow kind of pleasure serves a social function, insofar as it is a sign of the ethical superiority, the "moral excellence," of the beholder (493). We see here the germ of Roger Scruton's affirmation that "beauty is not just an invitation to desire, but also a call to renounce it" (Scruton 2009, 54, quoted more fully in Chapter 1), and we must wonder whether the cultivated appreciation of art shorn of appetite does not harbor a trace of that smugness that is born of privilege.

III. Beauty Dethroned

Bourdieu surely put his finger on the elitist nature of Kantian aesthetics, with its privileging of refinement and taste. But a critique of Kant's conception of beauty became less important to the degree that beauty itself was gradually being displaced as the essential quality of art. Kant led the way here, too, by elevating the sublime as an independent and equal aspect of art. With the advent of romanticism, the sublime came to be the senior partner, as it were. As Peg Zeglin Brand puts it, "The sublime came to replace beauty as the stronger of the two" (2000, 9). It is as though beauty, which was seen as mere prettiness, was too insipid a quality for the grand vision of artistic genius that took hold in the nineteenth century.[38] Jeremy Gilbert-Rolfe dates the radical distrust of beauty to the late twentieth century but opines that that beauty has always been "what serious people want to get beyond as quickly as possible when discussing works of art," and he cites Schiller for the view that "beauty is inferior to the sublime because the latter leads to a condition of thought which is 'independent of all sensuous affects.'" If beauty was still valued as a secondary attribute of art, inasmuch as "it was what got you to look at the sublime subject in the first place," it was stripped even of this virtue by the mid-seventies of the last century. Beauty lost all relevance, according to Gilbert-Rolfe, once art was itself subsumed under the broader category of "cultural object."[39] Arthur Danto locates a radical change in the attitude to beauty in roughly the same period: "Beauty had disappeared not only from the advanced art of the 1960s, but from the advanced philosophy of art of that decade as well" (2003, 25). But beauty was not simply dismissed as merely ornamental or trivial; it was also attacked from a political or moral position. By the middle of the twentieth century, J. A. Passmore had caustically remarked, "'Beauty' is always nice; always soothing; it is what the bourgeoisie pay the artist for . . . it is the refuge of the metaphysician finding a home for art in his harmonious universe, attempting to subdue its ferocity, its revelations of deep-seated conflict, its uncompromising disinterestedness, by ascribing to it a 'Beauty' somehow akin to goodness" (1951, 331). Elaine

Scarry observes that "the banishing of beauty from the humanities in the last two decades has been carried out by a set of political complaints against it" (1999, 39).[40] Scarry identifies two kinds of political reproach to beauty. One of them holds that beauty simply distracts us from attending to social ills: "It makes us inattentive, and therefore eventually indifferent, to the project of bringing about arrangements that are just." The second critique is based on the notion that a gaze (to use a term that has become quasi-technical in feminist criticism) is inherently asymmetrical: when a man looks at a beautiful woman, he inevitably objectifies or reifies her. Scarry notes that this complaint "has given rise to a generalized discrediting of the act of 'looking'" (39–40).[41]

But the wholesale political attack on beauty in art was already in full swing by the beginning of the twentieth century, when various forms of modernism assailed beauty as a means of diverting attention from the ugliness and violence of the contemporary world.[42] The often gauzy, pastel quality of impressionism as practiced by Renoir, Monet, Pissarro, Manet, Cézanne, and their contemporaries has often been described as a reaction to Academic painting, replacing the preternatural sharpness of its figures and scenes with a representation of how things actually look, with all the blurriness and lack of focus that is characteristic of human vision. But the prettiness of impressionists' paintings might also be seen as a kind of escapism or refusal to behold what was in fact before their eyes. While Renoir and Monet were depicting rustic haystacks catching the sun or women strolling gaily in elegant parks, carrying their parasols, factory smoke was turning whole cities sooty, and poor neighborhoods were zones of ugliness and suffering.[43] Artists were not exempt from having a social conscience; on the contrary, it was their duty to call attention to the evils of modern society and make their canvases reflect the glum reality of the masses rather than charming landscapes untouched by industry or exploitation. The horrors of the First World War also contributed to the revolt against beauty. Arthur Danto quotes the Dadaist Manifesto of July 1918, which denounced the "aggressive, complete madness of a world abandoned to the hands of bandits," and he comments, "Hence Tzara's dream to assassinate beauty" (49).

IV. Beauty Reinstated   Recently, it seems, beauty has been recovering from the stigma of being politically incorrect and is making something of a comeback in writings on art and culture. Wendy Steiner wrote at the beginning of this millennium: "More and more, artists and writers such as Mario Vargas Llosa are insisting that beauty is 'a legitimate appetite.' Indeed, the opposite claim is beginning to sound absurd" (2001, 192). Peg Zeglin Brand notes in the introduction to the volume she edited on beauty that, although beauty was for a long time almost absent from the scene, it is now again being treated seriously (2000, 6). A major contribution to this recuperation of beauty, with a special emphasis on the interpretation of classical literature, is Charles Martindale's book *Latin Poetry and the Judgement of Taste*. Martindale observes, "It is indeed a bold classicist today who dares publicly to call a Latin poem 'beautiful'—the very word causes us embarrassment" (2005, 10). But he goes on to note that in other branches of the humanities, "there are increasing signs of a certain dissatisfaction with an impoverished aesthetic vocabulary," and he is optimistic that an "aesthetic turn" is in the offing. Along with a critique of a narrowly anthropological approach to literature, which treats it as nothing more than a reflection of ideology, Martindale offers a defense of Kantian aesthetics, which he applies or illustrates by way of subtle and elegant readings of Roman poetry that reveal its special charms. In discussing Horace's *Ode* 2.5, for example, Martindale remarks on the way a kind of "lingering in memory annihilates the difference between past, present, and future on which the poem's logic depends, creating what I would call a poetic 'epiphany'. By this I mean a moment when an artist concentrates so intensely on something that, for the time being, it totally engrosses our attention, inducing a moment of reverent stillness which I have had to resort to religious language to describe." Martindale allows that the poem, in which the poet discourages his addressee from pursuing a girl who is still too young for marriage, may not be "sensible and humane," but he is nevertheless disposed "to call it beautiful and to grant it a distinctively Horatian virtue" (52–53).

I myself have read classical literature with a view to understanding the social values that inform it (and which literature may also undercut or challenge), but I think I am sensitive as well to the kinds of subtle resonances and imagery that seize the reader by their special grace and style. I too delight in Horace's well-turned odes, executed so neatly or, as the Romans might have put it, *pulchre* (equivalent to the Greek adverb, *kalôs*). I also welcome a greater attention to beauty in all its forms, and would wish especially to undo the breach or cordon sanitaire that certain aesthetic theories have installed between beauty and passion, including erotic passion. But it would be regrettable if the new attention to beauty were simply a return to eighteenth-century aesthetics, in which beauty was considered the sole value and very essence of art, the one and only characteristic by which a painting or a poem might be deemed successful or even recognized as an instance of art as such, rather than one among a variety of features that elicit our interest and appreciation. Of course, modern aesthetics will not reproduce ancient attitudes toward art, any more than our conception of beauty corresponds to the Greek idea of *kállos*. I have no desire to legislate the uses of the words *beauty* and *beautiful* in English (or the corresponding terms in other languages). But Greek *kállos*, as I have attempted to understand it in this book, may—and I believe should—enter into a constructive dialogue with modern efforts to come to terms with beauty, suggesting ways to circumvent some of the dilemmas that have plagued contemporary aesthetics.

Viewed from the longer historical perspective, it may turn out that the last couple of centuries, in which beauty seemed to be the core question of aesthetics even when it came under suspicion, represent not the high point of aesthetic theory but rather an interlude. In the eighteenth century, bourgeois realism came to define the novel and haughtily disparaged previous narrative fictions as mere "romances" (at least in the English-speaking world), only to give way in the twentieth century to modernist versions of the genre in which realism constitutes only one of a variety of literary values and techniques. In aesthetics too, there is room for beauty as a feature of art, even if it is no longer its defining quality. The ancient Greek conception of beauty may help to show how beauty, suitably understood and delimited, can cohabit with other, equally important aesthetic values. It may also encourage attention to the profound and still mysterious connection between beauty and desire, and this would, I think, be all to the good. Through all its permutations, ancient Greek *kállos* was never divorced from passion, not even in its most etherealized and metaphysical conception. In appreciating the nature and power of beauty in all its dimensions, the Greek idea remains a fertile starting point.

NOTES

Chapter 1

1 Bradley 2011 illustrates the multiple and sometimes contradictory meanings that body shape in Roman art might convey; corpulence, for example, could indicate wealth and power or else self-indulgence and moral corruption.

2 But cf. Stewart 1979, 111: "That the Greeks had no word for 'art' or 'artist' has clearly little or no bearing on the problem at hand," that is, the development of aesthetic terminology in classical Greece.

3 Gabrielle Starr (2013, xii) frames the question still more broadly: "It might seem natural and simply logical to group under one banner all the things we might, for example, call 'beautiful,' just as it might seem natural to group together all of the arts. But the beautiful as a category of experience or objects has been dismissed from and restored to the Western canon repeatedly, and indeed, the very idea of beauty has been insufficient historically to describe how the world and the objects in it move us."

4 Porter 2010, 30. See also Porter 2009 and Prettejohn 2012, 99, who cites the latter article.

5 Simon Goldhill and Robin Osborne, "Introduction," in Goldhill and Osborne 1994, 7, quoted by Porter 2010 on 38.

6 Porter 2010, 39.

7　The idea of an embedded economy was first proposed by Karl Polanyi
(2001; originally 1944). His view was immensely influential in
anthropology, and was developed and applied to the classical Greek and
Roman world by Moses Finley (1999; originally 1973).

8　Cf. Cohen 1992, 4: "The Athenians functioned through a market
process in which unrelated individuals . . . sought monetary profit
through commercial exchange (*allagê*). Not only were these
transactions 'disembedded from' society: they were seen by
theoreticians in their writings and litigants in their court cases
as threatening traditional social and familial methods of handling
production and consumption."

9　For recent attempts in this direction, see Davies 2001 and Oliver
2006, 282–283. Note also Tanner 2010, 271: "Of course, the Greeks
and Romans did not have a concept of . . . art, but this objection seems
to me a bit of a red herring. They had no concept of the economy,
but we are able to recognize analytically the economic dimensions of
ancient societies, and even, it can be argued, analyze certain economic
processes within the ancient economy that would have been beyond the
scope of contemporaries' understanding."

10　Lessing 1962, 14 (originally 1766).

11　Cf. Danto 2003, xiii: "It has often been noted that the Greeks, with
whom the philosophy of art began in the west, did not have a word for
art in their vocabulary. But they certainly had a concept of art."

12　For an overview of linguistic relativism, see Kay and Kempton 1984;
Swoyer 2010.

13　Levinson (2011, 198) agrees in part: "There is admittedly human
beauty of other kinds, such as that displayed by young children, which
is presumably non-sexual. Such beauty can be assimilated, I suggest,
to natural beauty of an *animate* sort, such as that exhibited by swans or
gazelles . . . But there is also the human beauty of a wizened sage or kindly
grandmother, which fits under neither physical beauty nor natural beauty.
If admitted, those are examples of what I will here label *moral beauty*." For
Levinson, however, the several kinds of beauty are irreducibly distinct.

14　Cf. Dickey 2010, 57, quoting Paolo Lomazzo's *Trattato della pittura*
(1584) in B. Haydocke's translation (1598), on how representations
of laughter or grief produce the same feelings in the viewer (here

citing the famous lines in Horace's *Art of Poetry*), "and . . . will cause the beholder to wonder, when it wondreth, and to desire a beautifull young woman for his wife, when he seeth her painted naked." In all the other examples, one is moved to share the sentiment in the painting; here only the image elicits a passion that is not necessarily understood to be that of the woman on view. Dickey notes that representations of women vulnerable to harm may evoke a split response in the male viewer, both erotic desire and an impulse to act as savior. Dickey remarks too that representations of Mary Magdalene evoked a divided response: "As a reformed prostitute (at least in legend), Mary Magdalene is typically portrayed as the most voluptuously feminine of disciples" (69). Dickey writes: "The association between earthly and spiritual beauty can be embodied in the visual analogy between Mary Magdalene and Venus, wittily addressed in two poems by Jan Vos," one on a painting by Govert Flinck, who "paints Venus into a Saint Magdalen," the other on one by an unknown artist, who paints "from Mary Magdalene a beautiful blushing Venus" (quoted on 69–70). Dickey observes that Van Hoogstraten too wrote of a painting of Mary Magdalene by Titian: "Casting her red-rimmed, weeping eyes to heaven, although she is beautiful she moves the viewer more to a similar penitence than to lust" (quoted on 70; translations by Dickey).

15 Jastrow based his cartoon on one originally published in *Harper's Weekly* (November 19, 1892, 1114), which was derived in turn from an illustration in the German humor magazine, *Fliegende Blätter* (October 23, 1892, 147). See Wolfram Mathworld online at http://mathworld.wolfram.com/Rabbit-DuckIllusion.html.

16 See Konstan 2009c, 2009b, 2010; Konstan and Ramelli 2014.

17 See Shaw 1996, 271, whose translation I have adopted.

18 So too, in the anonymous epistolary novel about the tyrannicide Chion of Heraclea, Chion declares, "Know that I have become the kind of man, thanks to philosophy, whom Clearchus will never make a slave, even if he ties me up, even if he does the most terrible things to me; for he will never conquer my soul, in which slavishness and freedom reside, since the body is always at the mercy of fortune, even if it is not subject to a tyrannical man" (14.4).

19 For text and commentary, see Moretti 2006.

20 See Eyl 2012.

21 Some early Christian writers—such as Justin Martyr, Tertullian, and Cyprian—argued that Christ himself was not beautiful. See Freedberg 1989, 211.

22 Cf. Freedberg 1989, 63, who observes that ethical issues in relation to painting "proceed from two deep-rooted assumptions and prejudices: First, from the Platonic and Neo-Platonic notion—with which we are all to some extent imbued—that the highest form of beauty is spiritual and therefore severed from the earthly and the material; and second, on the grounds that beauty softens and corrupts."

23 Gorky 1932, 161–164.

24 Unlike English, which distinguishes (or used to distinguish) between adjectives describing beauty in men and women ("handsome" vs. "pretty" or "beautiful"), Spanish, or at least peninsular Spanish, employs the same term for both (*guapo/a*, but also *bello/a, hermoso/a*). A great many languages use separate terms, e.g., German (*hübsch* and *schön* are typically applied to women rather than to men), and French (one speaks of a women as *jolie*, less often of a man). In Turkish, *güzel* is used of women but not of men (though it can be applied to art or weather, like the English *beautiful*); *yakışıklı*, however, is used only for men, like the English *handsome*. There are similar distinctions, according to my informants, in Swedish, Hindi, Bengali, Slovenian, Hungarian, Serbian, and many other languages. Analogous to Spanish are Italian (*bello* and *bella* are used of both genders), Portuguese, and Modern Greek, in which one can use the terms *omorphos* and *omorphê*, or *ôraios* and *ôraia*, of a man or woman with no offense to ordinary usage (in Mexican Spanish, however, *lindo* said of a man normally refers to his character rather than his physical appearance).

25 For the history of this apocryphal work, the earliest version of which appears in Greek in the Septuagint, see the articles in Brine, Ciletti, and Lähnemann, 2010; Gera 2013.

26 If I may be permitted to cite, in this context, a more mundane instance of the tension between carnal and spiritual beauty, Joe Cochrane and Sarah Lyall, writing from Jakarta, Indonesia, report: "The billionaire organizer of the Miss World pageant declared Thursday that there would be no bikinis this year. 'It has been misunderstood by some

people that Miss World is a beauty competition focusing on the physical
attractiveness of a woman's body,' the organizer, Hary Tanoesoedibjo,
an Indonesian media tycoon, said. 'This is absolutely misleading,' Mr.
Tanoesoedibjo said, adding that the pageant is also about 'inner beauty,
which includes intelligence, manners and achievement'" (Cochrane and
Lyall 2013).

27 Accessible at http://en.wikipedia.org/wiki/Agalmatophilia; cf. Scobie
1975, 49–54.

28 Verity Platt (2002, 37) observes of an epigram by Evenus (*Greek
Anthology*, 16.166) on Praxiteles's Cnidian Venus: "So close is the
relationship between goddess and statue that the boundary between
art and divine 'reality' is blurred, and the viewer of the *Knidia*, it is
implied, actually has an epiphany of the goddess."

29 Lucian, it is true, draws a distinction between comparing human
beauty to that of a statue of a god and to the deity itself; statues are
manmade, and so there is no sacrilege or exaggeration involved (*In
Defense of Images* [*Pro Imaginibus*], 23. But he promptly has his character
insist that tradition permits direct comparisons with gods as well,
so the distinction remains blurred. See Platt 2011, 12: "Greek
literature is riddled with examples in which gods appear to their
viewer-worshippers in the form of their images."

30 See Bussels 2012, 9–12, 26–36, 147–159, on statues and other
artworks perceived as animated or in some sense alive, especially in
connection with cult images, and the rationalistic responses to this
attitude.

31 Scruton 1981, 590. For discussion, see King 1992, who argues that
"some photographs can be interesting in the way that paintings can
be" (264), that is, aesthetically. Cf. Anna Quindlen's *Still Life with
Breadcrumbs: A Novel* (Quindlen 2014, 119): " 'That's a beauty,' he
said, and she wasn't certain if he meant the photograph or the bird,
or both."

32 Middeldorf 1947, 67 (partially quoted by Gombrich in his review).
Middeldorf's letter is in response to Brendel 1946. In his reply to
Middeldorf (which appeared in the same issue as Middeldorf's own
letter), Brendel wrote: "That Titian was an avid reader of Ficino may
be difficult to prove. There is no reason why we should fancy him as

a philosopher, though certainly he was not an illiterate. But in order to be acquainted with the common theory which we here call the "hierarchy of the senses," no more philosophy was needed than what many of his intellectual friends could easily communicate to him by letter or conversation if he did not care to read the books. Should we be so much surprised at discovering in his paintings allusions to the intellectual interests and favorite topics of this group which he knew so well?" (67).

33 So too, Elaine Scarry (1999, 7) writes: "Beauty is sometimes disparaged because it gives rise to material cupidity and possessiveness; but here, too we may come to feel we are simply encountering an imperfect instance of an otherwise positive outcome. If someone wishes all the Gallé vases of the world to sit on his own windowsills, it is just a miseducated version of the typically generous-hearted impulse" of enjoying a beautiful object and wanting to keep it in view. The desire in question, then, is simply to repeat the experience, not to own it; Scarry speaks of "the requirement beauty places on us to replicate"; as a result it is more a spur to creation than to possession. Zadie Smith's novel, *On Beauty* (Smith 2005), is something of a riposte to Scarry's confidence in the positive nature of beauty.

34 In the novel, *The Man of Feeling* (2009), first published in 1771 by the Scottish lawyer, Henry Mackenzie, the narrator drily observes: "Harley's notions of the καλov, or beautiful, were not always to be defined . . . ; notwithstanding the laboured definitions which very wise men have given us of the inherent beauty of virtue, we are always inclined to think her handsomest when she condescends to smile upon ourselves" (14).

Chapter 2

1 In this book, I indicate the accent in this word, which falls on the second syllable, save when I am quoting modern scholars who omit it; I omit accents when transliterating other Greek words, save for the noun *kállos* (see below).

2 Eco 2004, 37, 39. Crispin Sartwell, in his informal and personal study, *Six Names of Beauty* (2004), discusses words for "beauty" or its nearest equivalent in six languages; the thumbnail definitions he provides in the chapter titles are as follows: English *beauty*, defined as

"object of longing"; Hebrew *yapha*, "glow, bloom"; Sanskrit *sundara*, "holiness"; Greek *to kalon*, "idea, ideal"; Japanese *wabi-sabi*, "humility, imperfection"; and Navajo *hozho*, "health, harmony."

3   Pollitt 1974, 193. Cf. Most 1992, 1343: "noch weniger als beim deutschen Wort 'schön,' dessen Verwendung zur Bezeichnung moralischer Phänomene erst im 18. Jh. aufkam, beschränkte sich der Gebrauch des Adjektivs *kalós* auf den Bereich des die Sinnesorgane angenehm Affizierenden (nicht so der des fast ausschliesslich ästhetisch funktionierenden Substantivs *kállos*)." By "asthetisch" here is meant "by perception" or "visibly."

4   A single-line fragment of the bucolic poet Bion (fragment 17) reads: "For women, form [*morpha*] is *kalón*, for a man it is strength." There is perhaps a deliberate play on the sense of *kalós* as "beautiful" and "fine," but more likely we have here the same kind of contrast between beauty and *kalós* that we find in the Theocritean poem. Edmonds 1912 renders the verse: "The woman's glory is her beauty, the man's his strength."

5   For a similar distinction between a noun and an adjective that share a common root, cf. English "fine" and "finery"; the latter specifically denotes expensive and elegant clothing or jewelry. When pressed to provide an adjective that corresponds to the noun *kállos*, a Greek would naturally have offered the adjective *kalós* (as Critias does in Plato *Charmides* 169E); but *kalós* has a far wider semantic range, as this same dialogue makes clear (my thanks to Carlo Scardino for drawing my attention to this passage).

6   When Agamemnon dons his armor, his cloak or chiton and sandals are described as *kalós* (2.42–44; cf. Hercules's golden *poludaidalon* breastplate in Hesiod, *Shield of Hercules*, 125), and the term is applied to newly wrought chariots (5.193–194, 22.154), bread baskets (9.216, 24.626), and washing stones (22.153–154), as well as to the golden yoke on a divine chariot and the golden straps on the horses (5.730–731; cf. *kallithrix* of horses' manes, 5.323). The adjective also modifies a *temenos* (6.194–195), gifts (*xeinêïa*, 6.218), and abstract things like actions (*erga*, 5.92) and the voice of the Muses (1.604; *kalón* is used adverbially in reference to singing, 1.473).

7   The diction of the *Odyssey* in respect to *kállos, kalós*, and compounds is roughly similar to that of the *Iliad*, save for a couple of usages. The

Odyssey employs the term *kállimos*, which does not occur in the *Iliad*. More interesting, perhaps, is that the neuter comparative *kállion* is employed in the *Odyssey* in the sense of "preferable," that is, the better of two options (e.g., 3.69, 3.358, 6.639, 8.543, 8.549), though it is not used in the *Iliad*. *Kállion* may also bear the moral sense of "decent" (*Odyssey*, 7.159), and for this there is a parallel in the *Iliad*, Apollo says that dragging the corpse of Hector behind his chariot "is neither nobler [*kállion*] nor better [*ameinon*]" for Achilles (24.52; but this *kállion* here perhaps shades into the sense of "preferable").

8   Holy deeds, performed in accord with law or custom, may be described as *kalá* (*Theogony*, 417), and *perikallês* is applied to deeds (*erga*) in a fragment of the poem on women (fr. 23a.4, etc.). In the same fragment (23a.13), Agamemnon is said to have married Clytemnestra "on account of her *kállos*" (cf. fr. 215.1).

9   In the *Hymn to Apollo, kalós* is applied to Apollo's song or the Muses' voices (164, 189), a common enough usage. It is used as well for a chariot (232, 270) and in combination with *eratos* ("lovely") to describe land and a city or *polis* (cf. *kalá* of a house [*dômata*], 477). So too *kallirrhoos* is used for water (380), and *perikallês* modifies a ship (247, 258, etc.; a common formula in the *Odyssey*). As an adverbial accusative, we find *kalón* often used for singing (e.g., *Hymn to Hermes*, 38, 54), which is not atypical; it is employed also for light (*Hymn to Hermes*, 141), and *perikallês* is applied to Zeus's children (*tekna*, i.e., Hermes and Apollo, 323, 397, 504; cf. 244, of *huion*, "son").

10   Cf. Montemayor García 2013, 108 on the frequent association in the Homeric poems of beauty with the brilliance or sheen emitted by objects.

11   Hipponax, often paired with Archilochus for his sharp tongue, applies *kalê* along with *tereina* ("shapely") to a maiden (*parthenos*, fr. 119.1).

12   Simonides advises that it is good to distinguish *kalón* from what is shameful (*aiskhron*, 36.1.1) and affirms that all things are *kalá* to those who have no admixture of *aiskhra* (37.1.39). Applied to a person's face or appearance (*prosôpon*, 38.1.7), it presumably means "fair" or "attractive." In his epigrams, preserved in the *Palatine Anthology*, Simonides affirms that it is the part of virtue to die nobly (*kalôs*, adverb, 7.253), whereas in a clearly erotic context the term is applied to the youth Bryson (13.20.4). Of the young Olympian victor Theognetus,

Simonides exclaims that he is *kalliston* to see, and no worse in the competitions than his figure (*morphê*, 16.2.3): his skill evidently complements his good looks.

13 Alcman seems mainly to use *kalós* in connection with music, but the fragments offer pretty slim evidence; Stesichorus too employs some of the formulaic compounds, but as for *kalós* itself, the surviving fragments are hard to construe.

14 Cf. 1004, where *kalliston* signifies the best option, a usage familiar from the *Odyssey*.

15 For *kalós* in the moral sense, cf. also 282, 589 (adverb), 609, 683–684, 1106.

16 At 1217, a city is said to be *kalós*, in the sense, it would seem, of "fine" or "noble."

17 The sayings of the seven wise men, ostensibly dating to the sixth century BC, are later redactions, and one cannot assume that the language reflects whatever original pronouncements they may have made, but we may note briefly that the emphasis in these lists is on proper comportment, as in the Delphic saying, "nothing in excess." Thus, *ta kalá* depends on the proper moment (*kairos*); one ought not to beautify oneself (*kallôpizein*) but rather be *kalós* in fulfilling one's responsibilities; one ought not to look *kalós* but rather do things that are *kalá*; and peace (*hêsukhia*) is accounted a fine thing (*kalón*).

18 *Kalós* modifies, in the positive or superlative, such items as *erga* (e.g., *Olympians*, 2.97; *Pythians*, 7.19; *Nemeans*, 6.30 and 7.14; *Isthmians*, 6.22); *aethla* or prizes (*Olympians*, 3.15); a *hednos* or dowry (*Olympians*, 9.10); a *prooimion* (*Pythians*, 7.1); and a city (*Pythians*, 9.69).

19 When the Graces are credited for a man's being wise or *kalós* or brilliant (*aglaos, Olympians*, 14.7), the middle term perhaps refers to physical beauty. When Ixion attempted to rape Hera, Zeus created a phantom that Pindar calls "a lovely calamity" (*kalón pêma, Pythians*, 2.40), clearly in reference to her beauty—presumably what attracted Ixion, though sheer arrogance seems to have been part of his motive. It is natural enough for a chorus of the Muses to be described as *kalós*, perhaps reflecting their own good looks (*Nemeans*, 5.24), and so too for the goddess Hebe, who is the personification of youth (*Nemeans*, 10.18–19).

20 Cf. Demosthenes, *Olynthiac*, 3.25, for *kállê* (plural of *kállos*) in reference to the wonderful public monuments that earlier generations had left behind.

21 Cf. *Seven against Thebes*, 1011, on Eteocles dying where it is *kalón* for the young to die; Sophocles, *Antigone*, 72; Euripides, *Orestes*, 781. In *Agamemnon*, we read that it is wrong to report (*legein*) fine things that in fact are false (620; cf. *Seven against Thebes*, 581, on hearing things that are *kalá*). The adverb *kalôs* is often employed in the sense of "well," for instance with *phronein*, "think" (*Persians*, 725) and *prattein*, "do" (*Prometheus Bound*, 979).

22 Cf. Hippolytus's invocation of Artemis as *kallista* of all maidens and all deities, Euripides, *Hippolytus* 66, 70–71; but in *Iphigenia in Aulis*, 553, the superlative is applied to Aphrodite. In the fragments, *kállos* is found once, and there is the expression *kalê morphê*, but without context it is hard to say much about these uses.

23 The adverb *kalôs* remains very common in the sense of "well" or "properly."

24 On spectacle as especially associated with the Persians in Herodotus, see Konstan 1987.

25 Even temple gates are described as biggest and *kallista* (2.36), a frequent pairing in Greek literature generally; we may note that *kallista* is common too in the adverbial accusative plural.

26 At 7.36, the word *kallonê*, which commonly means "beauty," is used of ropes or cables.

27 See 1.37, 1.196 (of *nomos*, "law" or "custom"; cf. 3.38), 3.80, 3.155, 5.6, etc.; sometimes of natural features, e.g., pastures, 4.53; groves, 4.157; land or region, 5.42; a city, 6.24, 7.209; the spring season, 7.50; a victory, 9.64.

28 The verb *kallisteuô* is used in the *Histories* to describe marriageable women at a kind of beauty auction among the Babylonians (1.196), the Spartan woman who became fairest after having been born ugly (6.61), the fairest of maidens (4.180, in connection with a barbarian ritual), and the Ionian maidens carried off by the Persians (6.32). It is also used of horses selected for sacrifice (4.72, but some manuscripts read *kallistous*); of a bull (4.163); and of a chariot, 8.124. Conceivably, the term carries some ritual connotation; cf. *kallisteuma*, s.v., in Liddell and Scott 1940;

Euripides, *Orestes*, 1639, where Helen's beauty is said to have been part of the gods' plan. In Euripides's *Medea*, Medea affirms that the poisoned garments she is sending Jason's new bride will make her "the prettiest [*kallisteuetai*, 947] of all human beings," a clear suggestion that Jason is motivated by *erôs* in his desire for Creon's daughter. Hippolytus protests that he had no amorous interest in Phaedra: it is not as though her body *ekallistueto* more than all other women's (*Hippolytus*, 1009–1010); see also Euripides, *Bacchae*, 408, of the Pierian spring.

29 E.g. 1.38.5, "it would be fine"; cf. 1.81.5, 3.55.4, 3.94.3l, 5.69.1, 7.56.2, 7.70.7, 8.2.1, 8.12.2; 1.93.3; of a *logos* or speech, 2.53.4.

30 Cf. *Alcestis*, 648, 698; *Hippolytus*, 610; *Iphigenia in Aulis*, 305; *Andromache*, 617, of fine armor as opposed to genuine courage.

31 Cf. Aristophanes, *Frogs*, 1255; contrast the straightforward description of a song "finer than that of Orpheus" (*Medea*, 543). *Kalós* is paired with *lôista* (*Medea*, 572); on moderation as the "finest gift of the gods," see *Medea*, 636, and compare Euripides, *Bacchae*, 1150–1151.

32 Cf. 442, of her *kalá* eyes (so too *Troades*, 772); at 635–637, Helen is the fairest (*kallista*) of those the sun sees; cf. *kállos* of Helen in *Orestes*, 129, 1287.

33 In *Electra*, *kalliston* describes the flute's music, in an erotic context (Atreus's seduction of Thyestes's wife, 716–717).

34 Cf. 236–237, 261–263, 304–305, 383 (*kallosunê*), 886, 1097; at 301, *kalón* is paired with "noble" or *eugenes*. There is a similar wordplay on *kalós* itself at 952, where Menelaus observes that a noble man may shed tears, it's said, but he refuses this benefit (*kalón*), if indeed it is *kalón* (cf. *Orestes*, 819: the *kalón* is not *kalón*). In *Phoenissae*, Eteocles argues that what is *kalón* is not always the same as what is clever (*sophon*), and hence there arises strife among people (499–500; cf. *Orestes*, 492–493); indeed, if one is going to do wrong, it is *kalliston* to do so for the sake of tyranny (524–525). The irony is palpable, and the chorus register it at once when they exclaim that one should speak well only of *kalá erga* (527–528; cf. 535, also 814).

35 For these inscriptions, see Shapiro 1987; Lissarrague 1999.

36 For the features associated with feminine beauty, or at least sexual attractiveness, in Aristophanes, see Robson 2013, 45–53; Robson discusses dress, perfumes, and other enticements practiced by women in the comedies.

37   The compound expression is often translated as "noblemen" or "gentlemen," and there is no indication that *kalós* in this context refers to physical beauty as opposed to qualities of character.

Chapter 3

1   Isocrates applies *kalós* to *ergon* (*Demonicus*, 3) and to *oikeion* (*Demonicus*, 9.2), and contrasts the adjective with *aiskhros* (15.3); *kállos*, on the contrary, is rare and mostly confined to the *Helen*, as at 16.7, where her beauty is said to outclass the strength of Hercules.

2   Cf. Lucian *Imagines*, 22, for Aphrodite's *kállos* vs. Athena's *erga* or "deeds." Of course, a perverse or particularly hard-up male might be aroused sexually by Athena—Hephaestus is one unlucky example (Apollodorus, *Library of Mythology*, 3.187; Pausanias, *Description of Greece*, 3.18.13; Hyginus, *Fabulae*, 166)—but this was plainly regarded as an inappropriate response to the virgin deity. The mythographer Apollodorus informs us as well that, "according to some," Medusa was defeated by Athena because she presumed to be compared with her for beauty (2.46).

3   Cf. Plutarch, *Life of Aratus*, 32.1–2, where a girl outstanding for her *kállos* and height dons a helmet and is mistaken for an epiphany of Artemis.

4   Squire 2011, 105; cf. 108.

5   E.g., Ovid, *Heroides*, 17.118; Propertius 2.2.13–14; Lucian, *Judgment of the Goddesses,* 9. For the iconography, see Kossatz-Deissmann 1994.

6   I proposed the *Cypria*, an archaic epic poem that survives only in fragmentary condition, as the possible source; see Konstan 2014c.

7   Von Arnim 1903–1905 = *SVF*; quoted by Clement of Alexandria in his miscellany entitled *Stromateis* (8.9).

8   On sight and erotic passion, cf. Pindar, fr. 123.10–12; Euripides, *Trojan Women*, 891–892 and *Hippolytus* 27–28; Gorgias, *Helen*, 15–18; Plato, *Phaedrus*, 251B–C; Bartsch 2006, 67–83.

9   Omitting a corrupt passage.

10   See Konstan 2012a. It is worth noting, in this context, Darwin's theory of sexual selection, according to which certain traits are overdeveloped because they are attractive to the opposite sex and

hence favor reproduction; this is the natural origin, according to Darwin, of the human conception of beauty. See Darwin 1871, 64, and cf. Grammer et al. 2003; Prum 2012, 2254: "The most revolutionary and challenging feature of Charles Darwin's proposed mechanism of evolution by mate choice is that it was explicitly aesthetic. Darwin repeatedly wrote of mating preferences as an 'aesthetic faculty' and described them as 'a taste for the beautiful.'"

11 Tarrant 2000, 175; various examples are cited on pp. 175–177, e.g., Achilles Tatius 6.6.3, 6.7. Note that Longus's novel begins with the narrator explaining that he came across a painted illustration of a love story while he was hunting in a handsome [kalón] grove full of trees and flowers and watered by a spring (Prologue 1.1); the preface concludes with the exclamation about no one having escaped love. At one point, a garden is said to be en kállei, that is, flourishing or "in a beautiful condition" (4.13.4), but apart from this single exception, the noun kállos is used in Daphnis and Chloe only of physical attractiveness as a stimulus to erôs (cf. 1.15.4, 1.24.1, 1.32.1, 1.32.4, 2.2.1, 2.71, 3.23.3, 3.34.2, 4.17.3–4, 4.17.7, 4.18.1, 4.32.1, 4.33.3–4). When Chloe first sees Daphnis naked as he bathes, we are told that then, for the first time, he seemed kalós to her, "and because he first seemed kalós to her then, she assumed that the bath was responsible for his beauty [kállos]" (1.13.2); kalós clearly means beautiful in the sense of erotically attractive, even if Chloe does not yet know how to name her feelings (cf. 1.13.4).

12 Tarrant inquires whether other senses might stimulate erôs, whether one could love the unattractive, and whether a person has any choice about falling in love (178), and in this connection considers Plato's Gorgias (474D) and Hippias Major (297E); the latter dialogue is discussed in Chapter 4, where I argue that its subject is not kállos but to kalón. In Chapter 4, I discuss a passage in Aristotle that has been interpreted as dissociating beauty from desire, but which, I argue, in fact does nothing of the sort.

13 I wish to thank Gabriella Moretti for raising this problem with me.

14 See Plato's criticism of people who have an indiscriminate desire to see sights, whom he dubs philotheamones (Republic 5, 476B; so, too, those with a passion for sounds he labels philêkooi). Morales 2004, 18–20,

discusses the passage in Plutarch's *On Love* (as excerpted by Stobaeus, 4.20.34), in which he takes Menander to task for supposing that sight has no discrimination, for otherwise all people would love the same person (the most beautiful), but in fact they do not. Plutarch argues that vision is trained: an expert can view things better than an amateur and is in a superior position to judge their qualities; beauty remains a stimulus to *erôs*. Morales notes (20–21) that Lucian too, in his essay, *On the Hall*, affirms that sight requires *paideia*; that is, it must be educated.

15 This view of the asymmetrical nature of Greek *erôs* was developed particularly by Kenneth Dover, John J. Winkler, and David Halperin, and in its broad outline correctly describes the prevailing attitude in classical Greece. But this is not to say that Greek males necessarily felt threatened by female desire, or that they always represented women as submissive; cf. Toscano 2013, 11–12: "Since the vase painters often present female participation as a vital part of erotic pleasure, everyday vase paintings provide evidence that the Athenians valued heterosexual eroticism and enjoyed the reciprocity of female desire. Apparently, the men of ancient Athens wanted women to want them sexually." Philostratus, *Epistle*, 26, invites a woman not to be shy about exhibiting herself to the view of the writer, which is treated as a natural desire on the part of women; Morales 2004, 23, discusses the letter as "a stark example of the gaze as a technology of gender."

16 See Aeschines, *Against Timarchus*, 29–32; Dover 1989, 19–22; Fisher 2001 for translation and commentary.

17 Vérilhac 1978 includes a chapter entitled "Éloges de la beauté" (55–72), although only a few inscriptions bear on the topic of this study. In #33, from Praeneste (now in the Vatican = *Corpus Inscriptionum Graecarum* 3.6228, Peek 1955 = *GV,* 1.1057), the deceased is made to say that men from her city of Smyrna called her Euthales, "Flourishing," "on account of my youth (*hôrê*) and my attractive stature" (*megethous eratou*, v. 2), but death took her anyway. In #36 (*GV,* 1.1900), death is said to have extinguished a lit lamp of beauty (*kallosunê*). In #39 (*GV,* 1.575), a child who died at the age of eight is compared to a rose, "the *kalón* flower of the Erotes" (v. 2); so too in #40, a child named Eros who died at four years of age is compared to a rose (cf. #4 for another reference to a flower, of a three year old). In #43 (*GV,* 1.583), Mênophilos, who

died at eight years and five months, is described as having the lovable appearance of the Graces (*Kharitôn trissôn panepêraton eidos ekhonta*, v. 2). For other references to Eros, see #44 (*GV*, 1.409, died at four years and four months); #45 (*AP*, 7.628), by Crinagoras, which states that Eros himself gave the child his name and form (*morphê*); #46 (*GV*, 1.2045) for comparison with Eros. Eros is clearly a favored figure in funerary inscriptions for small children, which is unsurprising, given the common representation of the deity as a child in this period (all are AD, with the possible exception of Crinagoras's poem, which might be late first century BC); but a child named Eros may well have been a slave. In #47 (*GV*, 1.1280), a ten month old is compared to Iacchus, Hercules, and *kalós* Endymiôn (v. 6), with whom the Moon fell in love (for the Moon's passion for Endymion, cf. Apollodorus, *Library*, 1.56). On young girls, compare Aeschylus, *Suppliant Women*, 996–1009.

18 Similar insinuations of effeminacy were leveled against Julius Caesar; see Suetonius, *Life of the Divine Julius*, 2, 22, 45 (on Caesar's practice of plucking his body hair), 49 (on his alleged affair, as a young man, with the king Nicomedes), 50–51 (on his debaucheries with women), and the notorious remark of Curio to the effect that Caesar was "every man's wife and every woman's husband." On men, including emperors (in particular, Otho, but also Galba), primping themselves even in time of war, see Juvenal, *Satires*, 2.99–116.

19 For text and discussion of the hymn, see Marcovich 1988.

20 Plutarch, however, says that when Theseus and Pirithous were about to engage in combat, they each admired the *kállos* and boldness of the other to such a degree that they left off fighting and ultimately became the closest of friends (*Life of Theseus*, 30.2). I cannot tell whether there is a hint of erotic attraction in this description.

21 We may note that there are no examples of *kállos* in Lysias's speeches and that *kalós* in the positive and superlative are mainly applied to fine actions, e.g., in his *Funeral Oration*, the noblest culmination of previous dangers, 2.47 (cf. 2.55 and 2.65); with *ergon* 2.53; with *doxa* 2.53; with *onoma* 12.78; with *kairos* 13.16 (cf. also 2.79 and 24.23).

22 Contrast Cope 1877, 88: "Personal beauty has no absolute standard or uniform expression, manifesting itself in the same forms at all periods and under all circumstances. It is relative, not only to the three stages

of human life, youth, prime (*akmê*) and old age, but also to the habits and functions natural and appropriate to each of those stages; manly and athletic exercises, in the way of training, to youth; military service, the imperative duty of an active and able-bodied citizen, to middle age; sedentary and intellectual pursuits, to old age, yet so that strength and vigour remain adequate to the endurance of ordinary or necessary labours, extraordinary exertions, as in athletic exercises and service in the field, being no longer required. The habit of body which is fitted to the exercise of these several functions at the corresponding period of life is a constituent element of its personal beauty." Xenophon, in *The Education of Cyrus* (1.3.2), has Cyrus exclaim that his grandfather, Astyages, is *kallistos* among the Medes, just as his father is among the Persians; whether this means "most handsome" or "noblest" is difficult to determine.

23 E.g., Isocrates, *To Demonicus*, 6; [Plutarch], *On the Education of Children*, 5D; Achilles Tatius, 2.36–38; Theocritus, 23.32, noting that "a boy's beauty [*kállos*] is a fine thing [*kalón*], but it endures a short while."

24 For seven years as an age at which sexual characteristics emerge, cf. Petronius, 25.1–2: "'Right,' Quartilla said, 'good advice: why shouldn't our Pannychis lose her virginity, since this is an excellent opportunity?' And at once a quite pretty girl was led out, who seemed to be no more than seven years old." Laes 2011, 84, notes that "seven years was commonly seen as a threshold age."

25 Ovid relates that Liriope, a most beautiful (*pulcherrima*) nymph, gave birth to an infant who even then could inspire love (*iam tum qui posset amari*, 3.344–345), a hint that his future beauty was already evident; his name was Narcissus.

26 Thornton 1997 makes the most forceful case for the dangers of *erôs* as the classical Greeks conceived of it.

27 Cf. Xenophon, *Memorabilia*, 4.2.35: "Many have been destroyed on account of *kállos*." In Lucian's essay, *Images* (*Eikones*), the beauty of Panthea, mistress (it may be) to the emperor Lucius Verus, is evident to a passerby, but only someone who is personally acquainted with her is in a position to describe her virtues.

28 But it is possible that Telemachus is represented in the *Odyssey* as the object of Helen's amorous sentiments, just as Paris had been; see Konstan 2014c. For youth associated with beauty, cf. *Odyssey* 10.395–396, where

Odysseus's companions are rejuvenated (*neôteroi*) and rendered *kalliones* upon regaining their human form in Circe's house.

29 When the gods gave Bellerophon "beauty and love-inspiring manliness" (*Iliad*, 6.156), it got him into trouble with his host's wife, just as his beauty brought disaster on Paris and all of Troy. There is, I think, a certain irony in the collocation of the terms *ênoreên* ("manliness") and *erateinên* ("love-inspiring"), since the two ideas are as likely to be contrasted.

30 Byzantine writers noted that physical beauty might be a source of envy and was one reason why women might hide or deny their beauty; see Hinterberger 2013, 129–130.

31 In a recent novel for adolescents (Durst 2007), an infatuated young man cries out: "Surely she is some princess from a faraway land. Look at her grace, her beauty, her poise!"

32 Helen Morales 2011, 99, remarks: "In the scopic economy of the Greek novels, beauty is an index of status." In Heliodorus's novel *Aethiopica*, the heroine, Chariclea, proves to be a princess, the daughter of the king and queen of Ethiopia; the leader of a bandit gang, upon seeing her, is struck by "the impression of noble birth [*emphasis eugeneias*] and the sight of beauty [*kállos*]" (1.4.3). But the two traits are distinct: beauty is not said to be the sign of her status (cf. 8.17.2; 10.7.4). Indeed, royal pride (*phronêma*) may be contrasted with beauty, as in the case of Arsace, the wife of the Persian satrap in Egypt (7.17.4); contrariwise, a courtesan named Rhodopis can be described as second only to Chariclea in beauty (2.25.1). The protagonist Theagenes's size and beauty testify to his descent from Achilles (4.5.5), and his "masculine beauty" (*andreiôi tôi kállei*) is said to "flower" (*anthein*, 1.2.3), a sign of his youth (cf. 3.3.7 for the association between youth and beauty). Thus, in a novel in which beauty as a sign of royal status might have been a leitmotif, the connection seems moot.

33 The remark is in fact dubiously attributed to Cromwell; the earliest mention is Horace Walpole 1871: 226 (originally published in 1761).

34 Cf. D'Ambra 1998, 26–28, on the Roman realistic style: "With such clinically observed, toughened faces, the style of the portraits surpasses realism to become a form of hyper-realism, for which the term verism

is used. Despite the apparently close description of individual traits, the portrait heads share many features, whose repetition undermines the notion that the portraits record the physical appearance of individuals. The signs of age indicated that the subjects were men who had devoted their lives to public service in the pursuit of politics."

35 The scene in Terence's *Eunuch* in which Chaera falls in love instantly with a woman he takes to be a slave (but who is in fact a citizen girl) is a partial exception to the rule; she is indeed described as beautiful, but she has been raised to be a hetaera, even though she is still a virgin, and presumably she looks the part.

36 There was a theory, rather than a tradition, according to which primitive peoples chose their leaders for their strength and looks; cf. Lucretius, 5.1110–1116; Aesop, 244.2, on birds choosing their king on the basis of *kállos*.

37 Vv. 1009–1019, trans. Ian Johnston, available at http://records.viu.ca/~johnstoi/aristophanes/clouds.htm.

38 For discussion of this and related passages on male attractiveness in Aristophanes, see Robson 2013, 53–59.

39 Ebert (1969) proposed that Thersites was in fact a kind of decadent noble, basing his view at least in part on the late antique Greek poet, Quintus of Smyrna, who described Thersites as a relative of Diomedes (*Post-Homerica*, 1.741–781). The view has not won general acceptance among scholars, with some treating him as a representative precisely of the lower classes, but Thersites's precise social status in the *Iliad* is difficult to specify. Blok 1995, 202–209, sees Thersites's role as determined by his words, which have a structural function in early epic.

40 Masséglia 2012, 415. I suspect that *kalós* in the expressions *kalôn agalmatôn* (v. 20), *kalôn ergôn* (v. 26), and *kalón prêgma* (39–40; cf. *kalá*, vv. 58, 79, 83) in Herodas's mime means "well done" rather than "beautiful," as Masséglia renders the term, suggesting a modern, more narrowly aesthetic value.

41 On old age and sex, especially in the case of women, see Richlin 1992, 109–115.

42 Cf. *Ephesiaca*, 2.6.3, where under torture the hero's "blood flows and his *kállos* withers."

43 In Chariton's novel *Callirhoe*, the Greek aristocrat Dionysius exclaims upon hearing that a slave woman excels in beauty (she is in fact Callirhoe,

the novel's heroine, who has been abducted from her home country): "It is impossible, Leonas, that a body [*sôma*] should be *kalón* if it has not been born [or is not by nature, *pephukos*] free" (2.1.5), and he goes on to suggest that his foreman was judging her only in comparison to rustics. Barbarians (non-Greeks) may be represented as especially astonished at the novelistic heroine's beauty (Xenophon, *Ephesiaca*, 2.2.4), but their deficiency is a symptom of their lack of culture rather than of social status.

44 Compare Charles Dickens, who in the preface to *Oliver Twist* defends the description of characters "in all their deformity, in all their wretchedness," as "a service to society" (Dickens 1992, lxii). An ancient astrology manual by Dorotheus, dating to the mid- first century AD, testifies to a prevalent anxiety over the possibility of enslavement, especially as a result of shipwrecks; see Konstan 1997.

45 Hellenistic art delighted in grotesque representations not just of monsters such as the Gorgon or slapstick characters like the satyrs and sileni but also of old women and other types from daily life as well. Whether or not these images represented a class bias is uncertain; see the preceding discussion of the drunken old woman.

46 A speech by Themistius called *Erôtikos*, bearing the subtitle *On Royal Beauty* (*Peri kallous basilikou*), celebrates the beauty of the young emperor Gratian; it is discussed in detail in Chapter 4, but it may suffice to note here that it does not provide evidence for the good looks of emperors in general.

Chapter 4

1 Animals: sheep and bulls, Diodorus Siculus 40.26.2, 40.27.1; the peacock, in a highly erotic context, Achilles Tatius 1.16.2, 1.19.1–2. Landscapes: Diodorus Siculus 2.35.3 of India, 30.10.1 of the Nile region, 30.69.1 of a large cave; Hermogenes *Peri heureseôs* 2.2 of rivers, cf. Plutarch *Life of Timoleon* 22.1, etc. Cities: Plutarch, *Life of Marcellus*, 19.2; *Life of Cato the Elder*, 12.5, etc.

2 For texts and translations, see Russell and Wilson 1981.

3 For *kállos* in its usual sense, cf. *Politics*, 1282b37, 1284b10, 1290b5; *Nicomachean Ethics*, 1123b7, 1231a2. *Kállos* is frequently associated in Aristotle and other writers with stature (*megethos*) and strength (*iskhus*), e.g., *Rhetoric*, 1361a2; Isocrates, *Evagoras*, 22 (with *rhômê*, "strength").

For the application of the term to a mountain, see *De mundo*, 391a20; to property, Aristotle, *Rhetoric*, 1361a13. Indeed, Aristotle is quoted by Philoponus as maintaining that beauty is precisely not an attribute of the soul (fr. 1.4.45 Rose, quoted by Philoponus in his commentary on *De anima*, 1.4). Aristotle argues here that the soul cannot consist in a harmony of elements of the sort that obtain in a fine body, since Thersites is ugly but he has a soul: hence beauty is not a property of the soul. Polystratus, in Lucian's *Imagines* (11), insists that the beauty of Panthea's soul is much greater than that of her body, but in the next sentence affirms that he esteems virtues and cultivation more than *kállos*.

4   Cf. Clement of Rome, *Homilies*, 13.16.1; Galen, *On the Opinions of Hippocrates and Plato*, 5.3.19–21, 5.4.9; Themistius, *To Theodosius*, 198B. John Chrysostom, *Homilia de capto Eutropio*, 52.412.52–53: "There is soul, there is body, and they are two essences; there is *kállos* of the body and there is *kállos* of the soul." Gregory of Nazianzus, in his funeral oration for Basil, affirms that Basil was second to none in *kállos*, strength, and stature (10.4), but later he makes it clear that "Basil's *kállos* was his virtue, his stature [or greatness, *megethos*] was his theology," etc. (66.2). An inscription on a funeral stone for a certain Asclepiodote, found on the Athenian acropolis, bids the viewer to "behold the beauty of her immortal soul and her body, for nature bestowed unadulterated beauty on both" (*GV*, 1282).

5   Cf. Plato, *Charmides*, 153D on *kállos* of the body versus *sophia* or wisdom and 154C on *kállos* inspiring erotic desire. Critias affirms that *kalós* is the adjective corresponding to the noun *kállos* (169E), but Socrates inserts a wedge between the moral associations of *kalós* and mere physical attractiveness (I am grateful to Carlo Scardino for these references). Gorgias in the *Encomium of Helen* affirms that *kállos* is the ornament (*kosmos*) of the body, wisdom that of the soul. Anaximines in his *Rhetoric* speaks of strength, beauty, and health as advantages of the body, whereas courage, wisdom, and justice are those of the soul (1.10); cf. Aristotle, *Rhetoric*, 1361a2–6; Themistius, *Erôtikos* on Gratian's *kállos* and the *eumorphia* of his soul (176C); also Lucian, *Imagines*, 23, for beauty of the body and virtue of the soul. Aspasius, commenting on Aristotle's *Nicomachean Ethics*, speaks of the health

and beauty of the soul (111.22–13); cf. also Plotinus, *Enneads*, 1.6.1, discussed in greater detail in Section 3 of this chapter.

6   The passage is quoted in Demetrius, *On Style*, 173. For discussion of Theophrastus's treatise, see Innes 1985. Diogenes Laertius (9.13) cites a work by Democritus, "On the Beauty [*kallosunê*] of Words [or Verses *epea*]"; his aesthetic theory will have been based on atomism, but the details are difficult to reconstruct; for discussion, see Brancacci 2007.

7   See Fortenbaugh and Schütrumpf 1999. The matter is still debated, and some scholars continue to defend the attribution to Demetrius.

8   Cf. Hermogenes, *On Style*, 1.10; also *On Interpretation*, 4.7, on alliteration (*parêkhêsis*) as the beauty of similar sounds (this latter treatise is doubtfully attributed to Hermogenes). For the combination of beauty and arrangement of words, see also Plutarch, *On How a Youth should Listen to Poems*, 30D. On Dionysius's notion of beauty, see de Jonge 2008, 84–88.

9   Hermogenes, *Peri ideôn*, 1.12.20–28, my translation; the translation in Wooten 1987 amplifies Hermogenes's compressed account for the sake of clarity, and I reproduce it here for the reader's convenience: "To use an analogy with the human body, beauty generally consists of symmetry and harmony and proportion in the various parts and limbs of the body, combined with a fresh and healthy complexion. That is also how the style is produced, whether you mix all the types together or concentrate on each one individually—for these are, as it were, the 'parts and limbs of the body.' At any rate, if the passage is going to be beautiful, whether that beauty is varied or of one kind, there must be a certain harmony and proportion that exists, either among all the styles that are being used, if the beauty is of the mixed kind, or among all the elements that make up the style being employed, if it is of the simple kind. It is also necessary that a certain healthy complexion, as it were, bloom in it, a uniform quality of expression appearing throughout, which some critics naturally call the complexion of the speech."

10   Isocrates advises Nicocles to adorn his city with the beauty of his possessions and the benefactions of his friends (*To Nicocles*, 19). For horses differing in *aretê*, arms in *kállos*, and women in *kosmos*, see Xenophon, *Hierocles*, 2.2.

11 References to this treatise are collected in the appendix to Montemayor García 2013.

12 Cf. Barker 2010, 407, on appeals to symmetry, and in particular Plato, *Timaeus*, 87 C–E and *Philebus* 64D–65A; Barker underscores the relative vagueness of symmetry as used in these contexts. Netz (2010, 428) notes that "the unique relevant use of the word 'beautiful' by a Greek mathematician" occurs at Apollonius, *Conics*, Book 3. The word here however is *kallista*. In the *Harmonics*, Claudius Ptolemy observes that whoever contemplates the harmony of the world, if he is moved by any sort of beautiful thing (*kalón*), will desire (*pothein*) to behold this type as well by virtue of a kind of divine *erôs* (3.3), clearly a nod to the Platonic tradition. Cf. his the preface to the *Almagest*, where Ptolemy affirms that his science, by revealing the order of universe, makes of its followers lovers (*erastai*) of this divine beauty (*kállos*, 1.1 H1.7). Also cf. Tolsa 2013.

13 For beauty as symmetry, see among many other texts Cicero, *De officiis*, 1.98: "The beauty [*pulchritudo*] of the body moves the eyes by means of a fitting [*apta*] composition of its limbs"; Dyck (1996, 257) cites as parallels Aristotle, *Topics*, 1162b21, "the *kállos* of limbs seems to be a kind of symmetry"; *SVF*, 3.122.19 and 154.34: "*kállos* resides in a symmetry of the parts [*moriôn*]"; Clement of Alexandria, *Paed.*, 272.7–8.

14 On the meaning of ecphrasis in classical rhetorical texts, see Webb 2009.

15 On Lucian's concern with technique, cf. Pretzler 2009; on the question of novelty, d'Angour 2011, 151–56; on the narrative technique, Billault 2006.

16 For the story and its afterlife (viewed from a psychoanalytic perspective), see Mansfield 2007.

17 In the same paragraph, Polystratus says that *kállos* must be adorned not with clothing and jewelry but with the several virtues.

18 At 2.2.5, Chiron prophesies a "fine [*kalós*] and auspicious" future for the young Achilles; cf. the ironic use in reference to the mad Heracles's "excellence" with the bow as he is on the point of slaying his son (2.23.1).

19 Cf. 1.24.1, of Hyacinth; 2.9.1, of Xenophon's Panthea; 2.10.1, of Cassandra; 2.25.1, of the remains of Abderus's half-eaten body; also 2.25.2.

20 For the contrast between beauty (*kállos*) and youth (*hôraios*), cf. Aristotle, *Rhetoric*, 1406b36–07a2: "The one [i.e., simile] about poets'

verses, which are like people who are without beauty [kállos] but are youthful [hôraioi]—for they lose their bloom, just as the meter, when undone, does not seem the same."

21 Kállos is applied to music in the elder Philostratus's description of Olympus experimenting with his flute.

22 For discussion, see Bäbler and Nesselrath 2006, 109.

23 The phrase has a paradoxical ring, since plasma often signifies "fiction"; see Bäbler and Nesselrath 2006, 106, n. 6.

24 Squire (2011, 11) cites Vitruvius 3.1.1–2 for the view that the "visual ideology" of the classical world, even in respect to architectural monuments such as temples, "was derived from a certain conceptualisation of the human body." The passage reads: "The design of Temples depends on symmetry, the rules of which Architects should be most careful to observe. Symmetry arises from proportion. . . . Proportion is a due adjustment of the size of the different parts to each other and to the whole; on this proper adjustment symmetry depends. Hence no building can be said to be well designed which wants symmetry and proportion. In truth they are as necessary to the beauty of a building as to that of a well formed human figure, which nature has so fashioned, that in the face, from the chin to the top of the forehead, or to the roots of the hair, is a tenth part of the height of the whole body. From the chin to the crown of the head is an eighth part of the whole height, and from the nape of the neck to the crown of the head the same. From the upper part of the breast to the roots of the hair a sixth; to the crown of the head a fourth. A third part of the height of the face is equal to that from the chin to under side of the nostrils, and thence to the middle of the eyebrows the same; from the last to the roots of the hair, where the forehead ends, the remaining third part. The length of the foot is a sixth part of the height of the body. The fore-arm a fourth part. The width of the breast a fourth part. Similarly have other members their due proportions, by attention to which the ancient Painters and Sculptors obtained so much reputation" (trans. Gwilt 1826).

25 Cf. 283A8, and the use of kallista as "best" (superlative adverb with the verb "know") at 284A3–4, 285B8; also 287D10 with comparative adverb.

26 Heitsch 2011, 54, in dividing the text into subsections, places 286c3–287e1 under the heading: "Die thematische Frage: Was ist das Schöne?"; but this seems at the very least premature. As Albert Joosse notes in his review of this work (Joosse 2012), in the course of his translation Heitsch employs "eight different words in German ('hübsch,' 'recht,' 'Erfolg,' 'schön,' 'am besten,' 'passend,' 'angemessen' and 'geeignet') for ten instances of *kalós* (281a1, 282b1, d6, 282e9, 283a9, 285b8, 286a4, a5, b1, b4). The last four of these are particularly close to each other, and immediately precede the question 'what is *to kalón?*'"

27 Readers interested in the details may consult Tarrant 1928, Sider 1977, Woodruff 1982, Vancamp 1996 (cf. Slings 1998), Hazebroucq 2004, Balaudé 2004, and Pradeau and Fronterotta 2005.

28 This is the case, I believe, with the discussion of love or desire in Plato's *Lysis*, which sets the stage for the deeper analysis in the *Symposium* (see Konstan 2000); this may be an argument in favor of the ascription of the *Hippias Major* to Plato himself.

29 Ludlam (1991, 73) rightly observes: "Were the *Hippias Major* simply a treatise on aesthetic beauty, we would have expected the discussion to dwell upon the nature of *to kállos*, 'beauty.' Instead, its cognate adjective is used substantivally—*to kalón*—to the extent that *kállos* appears only twice in the entire dialogue (289b5, and 292d3). The two terms are not synonymous." Ludlam cites Ast 1835–1838, where *to kállos* is defined as "pulchritudo; splendor, decus," whereas *kalós* has a much broader range of meanings, including "pulcher, venustus; honestus, decens; laudabilis, praeclarus; bonus, opportunus; utilis; etiam Atticae est urbanitatis blandimentum (et saepenumero in irrisione ponitur)." Ludlam notes that Woodruff (1982) had challenged the idea that the treatise is primarily about aesthetics, but goes too far in dismissing aesthetic beauty entirely (74). Ludlam argues that the author of the dialogue "believes the two terms should be synonymous. The discrepancy between the two terms is a fault which is seen to be in need of correction. By referring to *to kállos*, the dramatist wants us not to strip *to kalón* of all aesthetic connotations, but rather to develop *to kállos* to the extent already attained by *to kalón*" (75); but such a motive would have been quixotic, and so far as I can see without much point, whether within or outside the dialogue.

30 Cf. Yunis 2011, 10–11: "The presence of beauty among the Forms, indeed among the essential ones such as justice, moderation, and

wisdom . . . , makes the aesthetic and affective aspects of life as essential as knowledge and ethics. . . . Divine *erôs* explains how an individual forms a commitment to philosophy and acquires the motivation to pursue it. . . . Ultimately, the *erôs* that attracts a soul to beauty is the same force that draws a soul to all the Forms and that motivates the individual to pursue wisdom through dialectic and any other means."

31 Cf. Desmond 1986, 124: "Contact with the beautiful, Plato implies, may crystallise in man a certain absolute dimension in that it may release in him his deeper eros. Eros fuels man's surpassing and transcendence. . . . Platonic eros carries man outside himself, beyond himself." Desmond observes further that Kantian aesthetics "captures the modern emphasis on the subject, defining the significance of the object in terms of the self's constitutive contribution. The Platonic encapsulates the ancient emphasis on the intrinsic character of the beauty of the thing itself, defining the aesthetic attunement of the psyche in response to this character" (101).

32 Whitehead 1979, 39.

33 Aristotle, interpreting the ideas as universals, argued that they could not possess the attributes that they impart to material things, since in that case the ideas would be one more member of the class of things that have this property in common, and one would need a further idea or universal to account for this new class, and so forth ad infinitum; this argument, referred to as "the third man," need not concern us here. See *Metaphysics*, 990b15–17, 1038b34–39a3.

34 Published in two volumes (in Latin) in 1750 and 1758.

35 The fifth-century Neoplatonic philosopher Proclus too sees the higher beauty as beyond symmetry and harmony; cf. Terezis and Polychronopoulou 2000, 202: "Proclus presents a clear distinction between the superior hyperempirical and empirical beauty." See also Proclus, *On Plato's Theology*, 1.106.6–10, and esp. 1.107.3–9: *eraston esti to kállos* ("beauty is erotically desirable").

36 Ramelli (2010, 356) notes that "Gregory very much relied on the Bible, where *kalós* is a counterpart of *agathos* and means both 'beautiful' and 'good'" (356). Ramelli observes (361) that transcendental beauty, including that of the incorruptible human body after the resurrection, is described as *erasmion* or "loveable" by Gregory. Divine beauty, however, is sharply distinguished from physical attractiveness; Ramelli

cites (361) Gregory's *Commentary on the Song of Songs* 6 (in Langerbeck 1986, 191, lines 7–9): "Divine beauty [*theion kállos*] seems to have its lovability [*to erasmion*] in what is fearful [*en tôi phoberôi*], deriving its manifestation from the characteristics opposite to corporeal beauty [*tôn enantiôn tôi sômatikôi kállei*]."

37   Cf. Squire 2011, 173. Squire notes that icons and other images were ultimately defended as leading to an intuition of the divine; thus Aquinas (*Summa Theologica*, II.II.q.81.3.3) writes: "Religious worship is not directed to images in themselves, considered as mere things, but under their distinctive aspect as images leading on to God Incarnate" (quoted on p. 189). See also O'Sullivan 2011, 137–154.

38   Dio places the emphasis on the awe-inspiring quality of Phidias's statue of Zeus, which causes "shock" or awe (*ekplêxis*) in viewers—indeed, even in animals (51)! Gregory of Nazianzus maintains the beauty and order of creation testify to the hand of the Creator (*On Theology*, 13), just as we can infer the role of an artist from any work of art.

39   For a discussion of the historical circumstances of this speech, see Vanderspoel 1995, 179–184, and Kelly 2013, 383–385, who observes: "In going to Rome, Themistius was serving the interests both of Valens and of Gratian" (384).

40   The speech has received relatively little scholarly attention, and most of that has been devoted to its date and the historical circumstances under which it was delivered. The only work devoted exclusively to this discourse, to my knowledge (apart from a one-page article on a textual point), is Audergon 2001, containing text, translation, and commentary; the only copy seems to be located in the library of the University of Fribourg, and I am immensely grateful to Mr. Audergon for kindly sending me an electronic version of his book. Translations of the speech are available in French, German, Italian, and Spanish, but not in English—unless some early version has escaped me.

41   The description of a long journey was a common topic in rhetorical compositions; we may compare John Chrysostom's account of the difficulties endured by the bishop Flavian on his voyage to Constantinople to defend the people of Antioch (*On the Statues* or *Ad populum Antiochenum homilia*, 3). Themistius has put this topic to a new use, by comparing it to a lover's travails.

42 The praise of cities was, as we have seen, a standard rhetorical topic and earns a chapter in Menander Rhetor's handbook (342–351); Libanius calls Theodosius the *erastês* or lover of Antioch (*Oration*, 19.1).

43 Themistius notes that there are different beauties (*kállê*, 167b), and he dwells at some length, as we have seen, on the visual attractiveness of Constantinople.

44 Richlin 2006; Williams (2012, 250) observes that their "language fits smoothly into longstanding textual traditions not only of *amor* but also of *amicitia*."

45 For a model of a different sort, see the famous hymn the Athenians sang in honor of Demetrius Poliorcetes (quoted in Chapter 3). If there was a latent irony in that eulogy, as I suspect, it would hardly suit the context of Gratian's speech.

46 On cosmopolitanism, see Konstan 2009a, on which this paragraph draws.

Chapter 5

1 Both nouns are in the dative case (*eidei* and *kállei*).

2 John Nelson Darby et al., trans., *The Darby Translation Bible (DBY)* (rev. edition; Addison, IL: Bible Truth Publishers, 1961).

3 One may think of a fine sword as well made in the sense that it serves its function well, is durable, is balanced, and so on, but not necessarily consider it beautiful in the sense of attractive.

4 See Macwilliam 2009, 267: "One of the common words for expressing physical beauty in the Hebrew Bible is *yapeh* and its related forms. While not confined to a human application, *yapeh* often refers to human beauty that excites sexual desire in the onlooker; or, as Ringgren rather optimistically expresses it, 'we are told with surprising frequency how beauty awakens love in the opposite sex' [citing Botterweck and Ringgren 1974–1993]. Although *yapeh* is not the only way of describing physical attractiveness, it provides a convenient means of exploring the varying significations of beauty in the Hebrew Bible." Cf. Penchansky 2013, 47: "Western philosophers regard beauty as one of the 'transcendentals,' along with truth and goodness. In the Hebrew Bible, *yapeh* and other corresponding words are more geared to

physical appearance. Although the Western tradition tends to disparage physical appearance, in the Hebrew Bible a character described as beautiful has power." Loader (2011, 652, n. 4) provides a list of over a dozen different roots that express the idea of beauty; a thorough investigation of how each of these is rendered in the Septuagint would be desirable, but there is a danger in equating beauty with notions such as "pleasing" or "important." I am grateful to Françoise Mirguet for bringing these papers to my attention.

5 In the Vulgate, *quaerantur regi puellae virgines ac speciosae—speciosus* refers unambiguously to physical beauty; cf. Esther 2:3, 2:7; Genesis 2:9 (of trees) and 3:6; 24:16 (of Rebecca), 26:7; 2 Samuel 11:2 (of Bathsheba); Daniel 1:4 (of boys), where the Septuagint gives *eueideis*, but Theodotion has *kalous têi opsei*; Daniel 1:15.

6 In the Vulgate, *formosae*; cf. 41:24 and 41:26, with Latin *pulcher*.

7 Cf. Song of Songs 1:3, 4:10, 7:10, where beauty is compared to fragrant oils or wine. Loader (2012a, 337) suggests that the tree of knowledge in Genesis 3:6, which is described as *ṭôb*, inspires an "aesthetic desire," and thus the real reason for Adam and Eve's disobedience "was their inclination towards the beautiful." This interpretation is something of a stretch.

8 Cf. Avioz 2009, 347: "In the commentaries, as well as in Bible research, it is customary to interpret the adjective 'good' in this verse with the meaning of physical beauty, apparently because of the reference to Saul's height here in Samuel's words to the people (10:23–24). However, when the word 'good' appears by itself, without explicit connection to external appearances, it can be interpreted as moral good. Thus, in his commentary to 1 Samuel 9, Rabbi Joseph Kaspi proposes the 'good in shape' as well as 'good before God.' The NJPS translates it as 'an excellent young man,' i.e. in the spiritual sense" (347). So too, Macwilliam (2009, 278) notes in reference to the description of Saul in 1 Samuel 8–10, "The key word is *ṭôb*, the meaning of which is rather more vague than *yapeh*. It can mean good in the sense of good-looking, but rarely does so on its own. The reference to Saul's great height suggests that *ṭôb* does refer to his appearance, but it may be that NIV's choice of 'impressive' is more convincing than the more sexually charged 'handsome' (e.g. NRSV, JPS)."

9   On *yapeh*, see Brown et al. 1953, 421, s.v., where it is defined as
    "fair, beautiful"; examples are offered of its application to women,
    to kine (a couple of instances), and, "less oft. of boy, young man," for
    instance of Joseph, along with a few examples of its application to cities
    (Jerusalem), trees, and occasionally to actions. Penchansky (2013, 54)
    observes: "The Hebrew term *yapeh* does not refer to God but is rather a
    unisex adjective that refers both to men and women . . . We look in vain
    to find anything feminizing or demeaning in the word when it refers to
    men." This is true, but the tendency to restrict the application of the
    word to young men should be taken into account.

10 E.g., Genesis 29:17, where the Septuagint describes Rachel as *kalê*
    tôi eidei kai hôraia têi opsei; Genesis 39:6, of Joseph; Genesis 41:2,
    of cows; 1 Samuel 25:3, of Abigail; Esther 2:7, of Esther: *kalón tôi*
    eidei; cf. Genesis 12:11, where the Septuagint has *euprosôpos*, "fair in
    appearance."

11 Cf. Deuteronomy 21:11, where the reference is to captive wives; 1
    Samuel 25:3; 1 Samuel 16:12, where beauty of eyes is rendered as
    kállos; 1 Samuel 17:42; 2 Samuel 13:1, of Tamar.

12 Ezra 16:14, on Jerusalem: *en tôi kállei sou*, Vulgate *propter speciem tuam*;
    Ezra 16:15 (Latin *pulchritudo*, as also at 27:11, 28:7), and, of a cedar
    tree, 31:8 and 31:9, Latin *pulchritudo* and *speciosus*, respectively; Psalm
    45:3, of a man, and 45:12, of the king's lover; Proverbs 6:25, of
    adulterous women, and cf. Proverbs 11:22 and 31:30, of the vanity of
    beauty, consistently rendered as *pulchritudo* or *pulchra* in Latin; Esther
    1:11 of Vashti.

13 E.g., Genesis 12:14, *hoti kalê ên sphodra*, Vulgate *quod esset pulchra*
    nimis; cf. 2 Samuel 14:27, of Tamar, although "in appearance" is in the
    Hebrew; Ezekiel 16:13, on Jerusalem as an unfaithful wife.

14 The girl is described as "very beautiful" (*kalé . . . sphodra*) in the
    following verse (1:4); the scene is an odd one, in which a girl is sought
    throughout Israel to "warm up" the aged King David.

15 As at 1:8, 1:15, 4:1, 4:7, 5:9, 6:1, 6:4, 6:10, all rendered as *pulcher* or
    pulcherrima in Latin, 2:10 (Latin *formonsa*), 2:13 (Latin *speciosa*); at 1:16,
    kalós is said of the male lover.

16 Cf. Jeremiah 46:20, a description of Egypt as a heifer; Jeremiah 11:6,
    of an olive tree, where the Greek gives *hôraios* or "in season": *elaian*

hôraian euskion tôi eidei; Vulgate *olivam uberem pulchram fructiferam speciosam*; Proverbs 31:3 and 31:7, where a tree is described as *kalós*; Ezra 33:32, of a voice, where the Greek has *hêduphônou* and Latin *suavi dulcique sono*; Ecclesiastes 5:18, of what is good to eat and drink, rendered naturally enough as *kalón* (cf. 3:11).

17 Cf. Lamentations 2:15, of Jerusalem.

18 Cf. also Isaiah 53:2, where again the Latin is more faithful; it is possible that the Greek translators had a different text, or understood the Hebrew term differently.

19 For details, see Thiele 1987–2005.

20 The Latin version adds a further pair of verses (9:10–11) that seem to be a doublet of the preceding and may reflect the use of an alternate Greek version, for which there is some evidence: *omnis mulier quae est fornicaria quasi stercus in via conculcatur / speciem mulieris alienae multi admirati reprobi facti sunt conloquium enim illius quasi ignis exardescit*; at Ecclesiasticus 11:2, *kállos* is applied to an adult male, as in Psalm 45:3.

21 Loader (2012a, 337) argues, on the contrary, that "the dangers of erotic beauty are well attested" in the Hebrew Bible. That a woman's beauty may attract the unwelcome attention of men (as in the case of Sarah's beauty when she and Abraham descend into Egypt) is indeed evident in various episodes, but seems not to be construed as a fault of the woman herself, nor do women consciously exploit their beauty for their own gain (cf. the case of Joseph and Potiphar's wife); of course, Esther and Judith are examples of women who use their beauty in the service of their own people (339). Many of Loader's examples, however, speak of seductive words or dress, with no specific mention of beauty as such.

22 Loader (2012a, 335) affirms that old age is "presented as a sign of blessing" and that its "physical manifestation must therefore be beautiful"; Loader cites 2 Samuel 23:1 in support of the idea that even in his decrepitude David is "the beautiful one in the songs of Israel." However, this is perhaps a tendentious translation; the RSV gives "the sweet psalmist of Israel," which corresponds better to the Hebrew *noim*, defined as "pleasant, delightful" in Brown et al. 1953, 653, s.v., although "lovely, beautiful (physically)" is given as a secondary sense, with a cross reference to *yapeh* (2 Samuel 23:1 is cited as an illustration of this latter sense). In an earlier paper, Loader notes that descriptions

of male beauty and female beauty share many features, and he adduces as examples precisely young men such as Joseph; see Loader 2011, 655–656.

23 The case of Absalom involves a similar tension between a positive appreciation of male beauty and a sense that it presages disaster; thus Macwilliam suggests that one might read the description of him at 2 Samuel 14:25–26 "as a deliberate ploy by the narrator, who, taking the theme of male beauty as signifying hero, deliberately undercuts the reader's expectations by gradually revealing Absalom as villain. This is not only a neat interpretation in itself, but it also encapsulates proper masculine suspicion and unease at the confrontation with male beauty."

24 Loader (2012b) argues that various kinds of human work are regarded as beautiful and as exercising charm or attraction in the Hebrew Bible, but the varied terminology employed to describe such items makes it questionable whether there existed a notion of aesthetic beauty (no distinction is drawn between terms for "beautiful" and for "fine" or "excellent," for example).

25 Stróżewski 2002, 280, trans. Sonek.

26 For the absence (or near absence) of a concept of beauty as "Seiendes," that is, as an entity in its own right, in the Hebrew Bible, see Westermann 1984, 479–481.

27 Monteil 1964, 233; cf. Monteil's summary of the meaning of the term (240): "Comme diminutif 'de petitesse,' il désignait la grâce inhérente aux êtres de petite taille, et équivalait au fr. 'joli, gracieux.' Comme diminutif 'de modeste,' il minimisait à dessein la beauté d'êtres adultes ou de grande taille, et équivalait aux tours français 'tout juste beau, un peu beau, à peu près beau, assez beau. . . . *Bellus*, en effet, dans la gamme des vocables latins exprimant l'idée de beauté, occupe à l'opposé de *pulcher* une position extrême: exprimant soit la beauté d'un être insuffisamment développé, soit la beauté insuffisamment développée d'un être, *bellus* se situe à l'échelon le plus infime de la beauté. Il est le *terminus a quo*, comme *pulcher* en est le *terminus ad quem*. C'est entre ces deux extrêmes que s'échelonnent tous les autre termes."

28 Fontanier 1998, 36; the same is true of Ambrose. I do not mean to suggest that there were hard and fast boundaries between the several terms for beauty in Latin; in the interest of variation of expression,

writers might very well employ them interchangeably, as Quintilian does in *Education of the Orator*, 8.3.9–11, where he is describing what he calls a "strong and virile kind of ornamentation" (*ornatus... uirilis et fortis*, 8.3.6). Comparing rhetoric to trees, Quintilian insists that they must have beauty (*decor*) as well as utility (8.3.9), and be arranged in precise intervals. There is nothing, he says, *speciosius* [comparative of *speciosus*] than the *quincunx*, a pattern that permits visibility along a number of axes. So too, olive trees trimmed into a spherical shape are *formosius* in appearance as well as more practical (8.3.10), and a horse slim in the loins is handsomer (*decentior*) as well as swifter, just as an athlete is *pulcher* when his muscles are developed. Never, Quintilian concludes, is *species* separate from utility (8.3.11).

29   "Sans doute *pulchritudo* exprime-t-il une idée de beauté; mais elle est moins physique et anatomique (*forma*) que surnaturelle et symbolisant la prospérité."

30   *Diem pulcrum et celebrem et venustatis plenum / dignum Venere pol quoi sunt Aphrodisia hodie!* (v. 255).

31   Plautus has 32, Cicero 180, of which 91 are in the speeches, 78 in the philosophical works, and 11 in the letters; the figure of 34 given for Tacitus, who employs the word of things such as a great deed or a noble death (e.g., *pulchrum facinus, Histories*, 1.44; *pulchrior mors, Histories*, 2.47), is a mistake and should read 13; Monteil 1964, 71.

32   "Déjà au niveau des plus anciens textes, *pulcher* paraît fréquemment exprimer la beauté en general" (Monteil 1964, 94).

33   "Sauve, toi que bénit le ciel, cette femme parfaite" (95), rendered on page 78 as "sauve, en te montrant propice, cette femme si parfaite."

34   "La *pulchritudo* de Pyrgopolinice est, nous l'avons vu, une sorte de faveur divine, dont la beauté physique (*forma*) n'est qu'un aspect."

35   "C'est un bien grand malheur qu'un excès de faveur divine... Pyrgopolinice ne se trouve point trop beau, lui qui est fier de son physique (*formast ferox*, 1390), mais déplore ses trop nombreuses bonnes fortunes" (p. 80, with similar interpretations of vv. 59, 959, 968).

36   Cf. Gardin Dumesnil 1825, 473, no. 2074, who renders: "Born of the courageous Hercules."

37   Conceivably, the word evokes the workmanship of the weavers and the desirability of the object; the context is the night raid by Euryalus and

Nisus, who, as the sun begins to rise, leave behind in the enemy camp *multa uirum solido argento perfecta relinquunt / armaque craterasque simul pulchrosque tapetas (Aeneid,* 9.358–359). The proximity of the word *crateras* suggests that Virgil may just possibly have had in mind here Homer's attribution of *kállos* to a *krêtêr* in *Iliad,* 23.

38 The text is uncertain here; I have assumed the intrusion of the intrusion of *bonis* after *animi et formae*; cf. 26.19: *nam quae apud eundem Democritum inuenitur compositio medicamenti, quo pulchri bonique et fortunati gignantur liberi.*

39 Pliny does not employ the adjective *formosus,* but *speciosus* occurs four times, in reference to a kind of food (13.45, a date, according to the *Oxford Latin Dictionary*), a flower (25.116), metal that looks "prettier" from a distance, and a precious stone (35.159); the adverb occurs at 35.49, where it means "glamorously" or "handsomely." No form of *pulcher* occurs in Vitruvius, but *formosus* occurs once, of boys (*catlastri,* 8.3.25), and *speciosus* twice: at 2.8.1, of brickwork that is more solid than pretty, and at 6.5.2, where it is paired with *commodiora* and contrasted with *elegantiora* and *spatiosiora.*

40 The compound phrase "pleasant and fine" is virtually a formula in Dionysius's treatise; cf. 4.145, 5.68, 6.3, 10.6, 11.22, 18.83, 19.6–7, 19.57–58, 20.125, etc.

41 Roberts (1910, 304–305) defines *kalós* as "noble."

42 For commentary, see Mankin 2011, 269–272.

43 Fontanier 1998, 17: "Augustin ne traite jamais de la beauté artistique comme d'un problème autonome."

44 Fontanier (1998, 35) also cites Aristotle, *Rhetoric,* 1366a, 1390a, on *kalón* as an end in itself, as opposed to the relative nature of what is *sumpheron* (advantageous), a distinction that is echoed in Cicero's *De inventione* in the contrast between *honestum* (which renders *kalón,* as usual in moral contexts; see Setaioli 2008) and *utile* (26); but this seems foreign to the question of beauty. Fontanier notes that in Psalm 44:5, *pulchritudo* and *species* render the Greek words *kállos* and *hôraiotês* respectively, and that *hôraios* signifies the beauty of youth at its acme (n. 27).

45 In the following section (16), Augustine notes that God is his own magnitude and beauty, but body is not large or beautiful by virtue of being body, since even if it is smaller and less beautiful, it is still

body: *cum tua magnitudo et tua pulchritudo tu ipse sis, corpus autem non eo sit magnum et pulchrum, quo corpus est, quia etsi minus magnum et minus pulchrum esset, nihilominus corpus esset.*

46   Cf. 2.1.61: *plurima signa pulcherrima, plurimas tabulas optimas and duo signa pulcherrima*; also of statues, 2.2.3, 2.2.85, 2.4.4, 2.4.7, 2.4.36, 2.4.69, 2.4.72, 2.4.82, 2.4.83, 2.4.93, 2.4.94, 2.4.110, 2.4.119, 2.4.127, 2.4.128–129, 2.5.184; of other objects, 2.1.87, 2.3.186, 2.5.44, 2.5.67 (boats), 2.4.29 (*phalerae*), 2.2.154 (ironically of a festival that Verres had named for himself), 2.4.37 (a table), 2.4.39 (the necklace that so inflamed the desire of Eriphyla that she betrayed her husband), 2.4.62–63 (vases), 2.4.64–65 (a candelabrum), 2.1.133, 2.4.108 and 2.5.184 (temples), 2.4.119 (a portico), 2.4.123 (*tabulae*), 2.4.124 (a door and the Gorgon face that adorns it), 2.4.125 (spears), 2.4.131 (*crateres*), 2.5.77 (a triumph).

47   Fontanier (1988, 34) remarks that Augustine virtually never employs the term *forma* in the sense of beauty as such (for which *pulchritudo* or sometimes *species* are the usual designations), "save to indicate the beauty of a woman who arouses desire and, analogously though rarely, that of the virtues, such as wisdom or justice, that are personified as women" ("Du reste, hors même de ce contexte paulinien [that is, a citation of the *Vetus Latina*], Augustin n'use guère de *forma* au sens de 'beauté,' sinon pour désigner la beauté d'une femme qui attire le désir, et, par analogie mais exceptionnellement, celle de vertus de sagesse ou de justice personnifiées fémininement").

48   Trans. Yonge, modified.

49   Cf. Lapatin 2010, 255: "What made works famous in antiquity and provided their enduring histories was often the circumstances of their creation and the message(s) they were fashioned to communicate in particular circumstances, whether to a local audience or one further afield, through their materials, imagery, author (artist or patron), placement, or some other factor"; Squire 2010, 150–151 on Apelles's Aphrodite Anadyomene, which was located in a temple complex dedicated to Julius Caesar: "The painting's context, and therefore its significance, vacillates (un)easily between that of temple, picture gallery, and victory monument"; Tanner 2010, 273–274: "The Hellenistic and Roman periods saw the creation of spaces—picture galleries and sculpture gardens—that lent themselves to aestheticizing and

cultivated modes of viewing, distinct from the political and religious settings characteristic of the classical period . . . Settings and displays that were materially structured to encourage an autonomously aesthetic gaze seem to have been largely restricted to the private sphere"; cf. 280: "Autonomous art . . . was, of course, a phenomenon of great cultural and some social significance. But it remained a marginal phenomenon by comparison with the overwhelming preponderance of art production and consumption in the Roman world." Talon-Hugon (2009, 109) puts it pithily: in antiquity, "l'expérience esthétique ne contitue pas un philosophème," even if there was a certain awareness of it here and there.

50   For a popular, informed account, see Taylor 1948, 18–32, also Laurence 2009, 141–150. Rutledge (2012, 184) observes of the golden statue that Caesar commissioned of Cleopatra, placed next to that of Venus: "Not only was Cleopatra a desirable object to be conquered, but also one, in light of the material in which the statue was cast, literally to be desired." Dwyer (2012, 308) remarks: "Because of the profound differences in personal identity that separate the moderns from the ancients, there is hardly any benefit to be gained from calling individual Romans or Pompeians 'private collectors.'" He also observes that "envy and its counterpart, envy avoidance, together constitute a powerful dynamic in the private life of the Roman. At Rome, it could be very dangerous for even leading citizens like Scaurus and Lucullus to be in the vanguard among collectors" (309).

51   Berry (2012) argues that Cicero had a finer sense for *decorum*, that is, what was suitable décor for an aristocratic villa, than he had for quality in art as such, and certainly his focus is generally on workmanship rather than what we might call aesthetic values. In dealing with a passionate collector such as Verres, however, Cicero found himself confronted with a kind of taste that was new to him, and which he tried to account for even as he vilified it.

52   For the corresponding beauty of natural features such as the sea, cf. 2.110; Cicero also applies *pulcher* to landscapes, productive farms, towns, and the like. On Seneca's conception of beauty, see Setaioli 2007.

53   For Greek examples, cf. Aristotle, *Politics*, 1254b38–39: "[It is] not equally easy to perceive the *kállos* of the soul and that of the body"; Plato, *Symposium*, 210B; other examples cited in Chapter 4.

54   *Calamidis dura illa quidem, sed tamen molli ora quam Canachi; nondum Myronis satis ad veritatem adducta, iam tamen quae non dubites pulchra dicere;*

pulchriora Polycliti et iam plane perfecta, ut mihi quidem videri solent. similis in pictura ratio est: in qua Zeuxim et Polygnotum et Timanthem et eorum, qui non sunt usi plus quam quattuor coloribus, formas et liniamenta laudamus; at in Aetione Nicomacho Protogene Apelle iam perfecta sunt omnia.

55   Later representations of the Gorgon sometimes showed a relatively pretty face, albeit surrounded by a serpentine coif; see Avaliani 2012.

56   Compare Xenophon of Ephesus 1.1.6, where the handsome young hero Habrocomes is said to be more beautiful than a statue of Eros; the comparison is with the beauty of Eros, not that of the statue per se.

Chapter 6

1   Halliwell (2002, 5) defines two types of mimesis: "first, the idea of mimesis as committed to depicting and illuminating a world that is (partly) accessible and knowable outside art . . . ; second, the idea of mimesis as the creator of an independent artistic heterocosm, a world of its own." The first of these views is judged by the standard of realism, the latter by that of internal coherence or congruity (23). Halliwell argues that both alternatives "were present in the tradition of thought about mimesis from a very early stage" (5), and that the "history of mimesis is the record of a set of debates" precipitated by this polarity (23). I am inclined to see the first view as the prevailing one in antiquity, though there are intimations of the second as well.

2   As Aristotle puts it, we recognize that "this one is that one" (*houtos ekeinos, Poetics* 4, 1448b17). Cf. Philostratus's *Life of Apollonius of Tyana,* in which Apollonius affirms that painting is imitation (*mimêsis*) and that no one would admire a painting of a bull or horse unless he had an idea of the animal it resembled (2.22); indeed, even in the case of more abstract forms, like clouds, people instinctively organize them so as to represent known objects. Aristotle, however, was well aware that sometimes we do not or cannot recognize a likeness. In this case, he adds, we take pleasure in nonrepresentative features of a work, such as craftsmanship, color, and the like. Here, perhaps, is the germ of what would become, in the Hellenistic period, a debate between those who supposed that the proper response to literature necessarily involved an

appreciation of its content, and those (called "euphonists") who insisted that only strictly formal elements, such as sound and rhythm, were relevant to the quality of a work. Janko (2000, 120–121) notes that the second-century BC critic Crates of Mallus "advocated a method of literary judgement . . . in which sound is the sole criterion for excellence in verse. This is the natural excellence of a poem, inherent in the verse and recognized intuitively by the ear . . . the critic is aware of the content without judging it in itself." Cf. Seamus Heaney 2002, 373, "A poet's biography is in his vowels and sibilants, in his meters, rhymes and metaphors . . . With poets, the choice of words is invariably more telling than the story they tell."

3   Cf. Plutarch, *Quaestiones Convivales*, 5.1: "When we see emaciated people we are distressed, but we look upon statues and paintings of them with pleasure because our minds are captivated by imitations which we find endearing," cited in Bradley 2011, 11. References in non-philosophical literature to the pleasure of viewing works of art do not normally explain the cause, but the lifelikeness of the representation is often implicit (cf. Euripides *Iphigenia in Aulis* 231–234).

4   Cf. Cicero's *On the Orator*, 3.178–181, cited in Chapter 5. On *pulchritudo*, Mankin (2011, 271 ad section 179) compares *On the Nature of the Gods* 2.58 (Balbus speaking), and notes that in Balbus's account of human anatomy (2.120–121, 133–145), "the emphasis is on *utilitas*, not *venustas*."

5   For references and further discussion of pleasure in response to art, see Konstan 2005. Destrée 2013 argues that, according to Aristotle, the pleasure we take in watching tragedy results from the educated spectator's reflection on the quality of the play and its success at evoking pity and fear in a safe context.

6   That pity and fear are aroused by the entire plot of tragedy rather than individual episodes is argued in detail in Konstan 2008.

7   In Cicero's *On the Orator*, Crassus argues that even those who are not masters of an art can judge whether a work succeeds or fails (3.195–196), for "all people distinguish what is right [*recta*] from what is distorted [*prava*] in arts and in arguments [*in artibus ac rationibus*] by a kind of implicit sense [*tacito quodam sensu*] without the use of art or reasoning [*sine ulla arte aut ratione*]" (3.195). This is evident in the

judgment of pictures and still more so in the appreciation of language, rhythm, and tone [*verborum, numerorum vocumque iudicio*]. Mankin (2011, 286 ad section 195) renders *tacito quodam sensu* as "a kind of inarticulate feeling," following May and Wisse 2001, and compares Cicero's *The Orator*, 203, on the composition of verses, where art (or technique) establishes the method, but the ears on their own, by "a kind of implicit sense [*tacito enim sensu*]" determine it without the help of art (*sine arte definiunt*; cf. also *Brutus* 184). Büttner (2006, 119) sees in the expression *sensus tacitus* an anticipation of Kant's conception of an aesthetic response and takes it for granted that Kant knew and was inspired by Cicero's text: "Man darf wohl vermuten, dass Kant, der rein guter Cicero-Kenner war, sich von Passagen wie diesen beim Schreiben seiner *Kritik der Urteilskraft* und der Bestimmung des Kunst- und Naturschönen hat inspirieren lassen." But this is reading too much into Crassus's argument; he means simply that a person can recognize a well-made speech or other artifact (there is no mention of beauty in this passage) without having professional or scientific knowledge of the art in question. *Sensus* is better rendered as "awareness" than as "feeling."

8   For discussion, see Konstan 2012c; Staley 2010, 95: "The vividness of tragedy's images may arouse our emotions, but these are only preliminary and involuntary; we can in the end judge their truth value." This view legitimates, according to Staley, Seneca's own composition of tragedies. "If the emotional pull we feel in response to vivid events is not really emotion in the full Stoic sense of that word, then it cannot really be harmful" (74).

9   Veneration or awe may have its own emotional valence. Keltner and Haidt (2003, 304) note that awe has been little studied as an emotion, and they affirm, "Beautiful people and scenes can produce awe-related experiences that are flavoured with aesthetic pleasure"; cf. Pearsall 2007. Woodruff (2001, 8) in turn defines reverence as "the well-developed capacity to have the feelings of awe, respect, and shame when these are the right feelings to have." In classical sources, responses of awe, identified by terms such as *ekstasis, ekplêxis, thambos, thauma, phrikê*, and the like, are more commonly elicited by impressive or sublime events and scenes than by beauty (for *phrikê* as a sign of awe, see Cairns 2014, 96–100); see de Jonge 2012, 290–301 on the Augustan debate and the connection between the sublime and the rise of Atticism.

10 See Heath 2012. Halliwell (2011, 337) argues that Longinus has "a cognitivist model of the sublime, a model in which thought and emotion . . . work in close harness." That is why music ultimately produces mere "simulacra and illegitimate surrogates of persuasion" (*On the Sublime*, 39.3) and lacks "any determinate content" (339). Therefore it is incapable of producing emotion or *pathos* in the strict sense of the term. Dio Chrysostom speaks of the awe (*ekplêxis*) that viewers, even animals, of Phidias's statue of Zeus experience (*Orations*, 12.51), but perhaps this response should rather be classified among the proto-emotions described by Seneca.

11 On Demetrius's date, see Grube 1964.

12 Carpenter 1902, 263–210 ("Glossary").

13 For further discussion of Plutarch's important essay *How a Youth Should Listen to Poems* see Konstan 2004; full commentary in Hunter and Russell 2011.

14 Hume 1757, section 32; cf. Talon-Hugon 2009, 187.

15 Wilde 1966, 1048. Talon-Hugon's own view is that, although criticism cannot be "exclusivement éthique, " there is nevertheless, within certain limits, "une place légitime pour le jugement moral" (204). Kivy (2011, 67) argues that novels in particular elicit moral rather than aesthetic responses (the latter being more characteristic of arts such as music), and he defends the ethical value of art by observing that "for most of their history the fine arts have been understood as moral instruments: as major sources of moral knowledge and moral improvement." Cf. Plutarch, *On How a Youth Should Listen to Poetry*, 16b2–5: "For not meter nor figure of speech nor loftiness of diction nor aptness of metaphor nor proportion and word-order has so much allure [*haimulia*] and charm [*kharis*] as the well-woven disposition of mythical narrative," where "narrative" (*muthologia*) perhaps refers less to content as such than to the disposition of the parts of the story.

16 Russell and Konstan 2005, 3; for a brief overview of the allegorical tradition, see the introduction to this volume.

17 Michael Squire (2013, 111) argues eloquently that Philostratus's work "probes the parameters of both the visual and verbal imagination." I do not mean to reduce Philostratus's project to the mere filling-in of details, but he clearly takes it for granted that this is one of the tasks of the critic.

18 Cf. Desmond 1986, 132: "Aquinas defines beauty as "that which being seen, pleases" (*id quod visum, placet*). According to Desmond, Aquinas regards beauty as an objective quality, which involves "unity or integrity, consonance, and finally radiance" (133; Desmond finds the same elements in Hegel, 136). Brand (2000, 8) notes that "Plato linked beauty with love," but adds, "Common to both Beauty and beautiful things is the complex human act of *contemplation*: a component retained from Plato and elaborated in a cognitive-based notion of beauty by Saint Thomas Aquinas. For Aquinas . . . , 'the beautiful is that which calms the desire, by being seen or known'" (9).

19 Psellus 1941, 220.19–221.18 (letter 194), trans. Barber 2014 (very slightly modified). I refer the reader to Barber's full discussion and am deeply indebted to him and Stratis Papaioannou for permission to see the essay prior to its publication. See also Papaioannou 2013 for an excellent introduction to Psellos's writings.

20 Barber concludes his essay with these words: "It would be wrong to interpret Psellos's discussions of art and aesthetics in light of modern conceptions of these terms, but it would be equally wrong to deny the play of these terms in his texts and thereby ignore the possibility of this author's discourse on both art and aesthetics." For the influence of Byzantine art on the Italian Renaissance, see Bloemsma 2013, 37: "Byzantine art and artefacts had a great appeal for late medieval and early Renaissance Italian culture. The reasons for this fascination are diverse. Icons, relics, manuscripts and ivories were valued as venerable objects with miraculous powers; they were prized for their technical extravagance and their costly materials; and they offered the possibility to appropriate the prestige of the Byzantine Empire through its art." Although Giotto introduced a new stage of realism, it did not displace the older forms more influenced by Byzantine precedents; rather, "Byzantine means and forms now became an alternative mode available to artists to counter the ever-increasing realistic tendencies of contemporary painting" (58).

21 Cf. Squire 2011, 9: "Polyclitus' legacy lies in the *idea* of the ideal. Two particular points are important: first, the Polyclitan body was understood to manifest abstract, numerical calculations, second, this materialized ideal of immaterial beauty was thought to hold universally. . . . At no time was the idea of this ideal more influential than in the Italian Renaissance." Squire affirms, however, "For all our

abiding attempts to conflate the two, the images of fifth-century Athens are not those of fifteenth-century Italy" (60).

22 Cf. Sinisgalli 2011, 78.

23 When Leonardo da Vinci mentions painting, it is primarily in connection either with proportion or with the values of certain colors; see da Vinci 2005. The so-called *Treatise* is in fact a posthumous compilation of Leonardo's writings on painting.

24 Cf. Tanner 2010, 23: "Notwithstanding the importance of A. G. Baumgarten's articulation of the concept of 'the aesthetic' and J. J. Winckelmann's development of a more systematically historical orientation towards art, eighteenth-century developments in certain key respects are continuous with and elaborations upon those of the Renaissance." Winckelmann's conception of beauty was firmly tied to the human form, above all that of the male; he was in a way even more "Greek" than the ancient Greeks in this regard. As North (2012, 15) observes: "Winckelmann begins his *Gedanken* with the statement that Greek sculpture was based on the beauty of the male physique of the local citizens"; the reference to *Gedanken* is to Winckelmann's *Reflections on the Imitation of Greek Works in Painting and Sculpture* (1987; orig. 1756 Winckelmann).

25 Cf. Squire 2011, 153, on the Roman habit of fusing together parts, particularly heads and bodies, of different statues. Although such combinations may strike the modern viewer as incongruous, "Roman viewers seem to have looked to the body rather differently: they could read it as much as a corpus of semiotic signs as a mirage of verisimilitude. Instead of simply mirroring the sight of a 'real' figure, the Roman portrait could simultaneously work in more *symbolic* ways, as a series of amalgamated parts that together added up to more than the whole." Plutarch, in his treatise on the *daimôn* of Socrates (*Moralia*, 575B6–8), praises viewers who examine each detail of a work (whether visual or literary) as opposed to those who take it in uncritically at one glance; the better class of observers miss nothing in respect to whether a work is done well (*kalôs*) or the reverse. But contrast Strabo's injunction to his readers at the beginning of his *Geography*: "Just as with colossal works we do not seek exactitude in each particular but rather consider generally whether the whole is well done, so too must one

form a judgment in the case of the present work. For it too is a kind of colossus and it shows how whole and large things fare" (1.1.23).

26 Hume 1999, 210; cf. Gracyk 1994.

27 Prinz 2011, 71. Starr (2013, 7) affirms that "all aesthetic experiences involve pleasure or displeasure and some degree of emotional response" (cf. p. 33: "Emotion is the key to aesthetic experience") and provides some neurological evidence in support of the claim (41–53, 151–157), but pleasure and emotion are not necessarily the same thing, and in any case the responses measured are not "exclusively attributable to beauty" (24).

28 Gardner 2011, 40, particularly the chapter "Beauty," 39–76.

29 Cf. 54: "The feeling of awe is, importantly, not the same thing as the 'tingle' that announces an experience of beauty," since with beauty, one keeps control and "maintains one's distance," whereas with awe "one feels overpowered, overwhelmed."

30 *Aesthetices finis est perfectio cognitionis sensitivae, qua talis. Haec autem est pulcritudo*; cf. Böhme 2001, 13.

31 Beiser 2009, 145. Beiser remarks of Baumgarten that even if his originality is exaggerated (Wolff was an important predecessor), he "was the first to give the discipline its modern name, and to conceive it as 'a science of the beautiful' (*Wissenschaft des Schönen*), which is close to some modern understandings of the term" (119). The reference to Wolff is to his *Psychologia empirica* (1732).

32 Nehamas 2007, 47; the citations are from Kant's *Critique of the Power of Judgment* (Kant 2000, 104, sec. 9 and 101, sec. 8).

33 Nehamas quotes Isenberg 1973, 164: "There is not in all the world's criticism a single purely descriptive statement concerning which one is prepared to say beforehand, 'If it is true, I shall like that work all the better.'"

34 Leibniz 1989, 137; cf. Beiser 2009, 35–36. Leibniz's essay dates to 1670–1671.

35 Cf. Beiser 2009, 144: "Although he is a cognitivist, Baumgarten does not underrate or conceal the role of pleasure in aesthetic judgment. No less than Kant, he holds that something can be beautiful only if it is pleasing to perceive it."

36 Bourdieu cites Kant: "One kind of ugliness alone is incapable of being represented conformably to nature without destroying all aesthetic delight, and consequently artistic beauty, namely, that which excites

disgust. For, as in this strange sensation, which depends purely on the imagination, the object is represented as insisting, as it were, on our enjoying it, while we still set our face against it, the artificial representation of the object is no longer distinguishable from the nature of the object itself in our sensation, and so it cannot possibly be regarded as beautiful" (Kant 1952, 174–175; cf. Bourdieu 1984, 490). Disgust, then, signals the point at which it is impossible to distinguish the representation from the object itself; art merges with reality.

37 Bourdieu 1984, 491, quoting Kant 1952, 162.

38 Cf. Scarry 1999, 58: "The sublime (an aesthetic of power) rejects beauty on the grounds that it is diminutive, dismissible, not powerful enough."

39 Gilbert-Rolfe 2000, 3; the reference is to Schiller's "On the Sublime" (Schiller 1980, 198). Cf. Prettejohn 2005, 161: "Perhaps it could be argued that by dropping the word 'beauty,' twentieth-century writers were simply widening the range of objects that might be described as having aesthetic value."

40 Contrast the notorious attack on Picasso's art by Carl Jung, who affirmed that the painter "follows not the accepted ideals of goodness and beauty, but the demoniacal attraction of ugliness and evil" (Jung 1932). T. J. Clark (2013) identifies an influence of Nietzsche on Picasso, which, unlike Jung, he regards as positive.

41 Scarry sees the two critiques as mutually incompatible, since the first wishes precisely to direct our gaze toward social ills in the hopes of ameliorating, not reifying, them.

42 Danto (2003, 7) notes the additional factor of the aesthete's disdain for the business side of art: "Beauty had almost entirely disappeared from artistic reality in the twentieth century, as if attractiveness was somehow a stigma, with its crass commercial implications."

43 In Iris Murdoch's novel, *Nuns and Soldiers* (2001: 125–126), the outspoken character Daisy Barrett exclaims, "Prettification, that's what your friends Titian and Veronese and Botticelli and Piero and Perugino and Ucello and all that famous old gang are on about. They take what's awful, dreadful, mean, grim, disgusting, vile, evil, nasty, horrid, creepy-crawly in the world and they turn it into something sweet and pretty and pseudo-noble. It's such a lie. Painting is a lie, or most of it is. No wonder Shakespeare never mentions a single painter."

BIBLIOGRAPHY

Alberti, Leon Battista. 1970. *On Painting*. Translated with Introduction and Notes by John R. Spencer. New Haven: Yale University Press (originally published in 1435).

Ast, Friedrich. 1835–1838. *Lexicon Platonicum*. 3 vols. Leipzig: Weidmann.

Audergon, Sébastien. 2001. *Themistios: Discours 13, Sur l'amour ou la beauté du prince*. Fribourg: Université de Fribourg (Mémoire de Licence, Faculté des Lettres de l'Université de Fribourg, Suisse).

Avaliani, Eka. 2012. "МОНСТРЫ ЭЛЛИНСКОГО МИФАИ ИХ ПЕРИФЕРИЙНЫЕ ВАРИАНТЫ" ("Monsters of the Hellenic Mythology and their Peripheral Counterparts"). 2012. *Skhole* 6.2: 306–322.

Avioz, Michael. 2009. "The Motif of Beauty in the Books of Samuel and Kings." *Vetus Testamentum* 59: 341–359.

Bäbler, Balbina, and Heinz-Günther Nesselrath, eds. and trans. 2006. *Ars et verba: die Kunstbeschreibungen des Kallistratos*. Berlin: De Gruyter.

Balaudé, Jean-François, trans. 2004. *Platon: Hippias mineur, Hippias majeur*. Paris: Livre de Poche.

Barber, Charles. 2014. "An Introduction to Michael Psellos on Art and Aesthetics." In *Psellos and Aesthetics*. Edited by Charles Barber and Stratis Papaioannou. Notre Dame, IN: University of Notre Dame Press.

Barker, Andrew. 2010. "Mathematical Beauty Made Audible: Musical Ethics in Ptolemy's *Harmonics*." *Classical Philology* 105: 403–425.

Barney, Rachel. 2010. "Notes on Plato on the *Kalon* and the Good." *Classical Philology* 105: 363–377.

Bartsch, Shadi. 2006. *The Mirror of the Self: Sexuality, Self-Knowledge, and the Gaze in the Early Roman Empire*. Chicago: University of Chicago Press.

Baumgarten, Alexander Gottlieb. 1750–1758. *Aesthetica*. Frankfurt an der Oder: I. C. Kleyb.

Beiser, Frederick C. 2009. *Diotima's Children: German Aesthetic Rationalism from Leibniz to Lessing*. Oxford: Oxford University Press.

Berry, D. H. 2012. "Cicero and Greek Art." *Papers of the Langford Latin Seminar* 15: 1–19.

Billault, Alain. 2006. "Very Short Stories: Lucian's Close Encounters with Some Paintings." In *Authors, Authority, and Interpreters in the Ancient Novel: Essays in Honor of Gareth L. Schmeling* = *Ancient Narrative* supplement 5. Edited by Shannon N. Byrne, Edmund P. Cueva, and Jean Alvarez. Groningen: Barkhuis Publishing, 47–59.

Bloemsma, Hans. 2013. "Byzantine Art and Early Italian Painting." In *Byzantine Art and Renaissance Europe*. Edited by Angeliki Lymberopoulou and Rembrandt Duits. Farnham, UK: Ashgate, 37–59.

Blok, Josine H. 1995. *The Early Amazons: Modern and Ancient Perspectives on a Persistent Myth*. Leiden: E. J. Brill.

Blunt, Anthony. 1962. *Artistic Theory in Italy, 1450–1600*. 2nd edition. Oxford: Oxford University Press.

Böhme, Gernot. 2001. *Aisthetik: Vorlesungen über Ästhetik als allgemeine Wahrnehmungslehre*. Munich: Wilhelm Fink Verlag.

Botterweck, G. Johannes, and Helmer Ringgren, eds. 1974–1993. *Theological Dictionary of the Old Testament*. Translated by John. T. Willis. 14 vols. Grand Rapids, MI: Eerdmans.

Bourdieu, Pierre. 1984. *Distinction: A Social Critique of the Judgement of Taste*. Translated by Richard Nice. London: Routledge.

Bradley, Mark A. 2011. "Obesity, Corpulence and Emaciation in Roman Art." *Papers of the British School at Rome* 79: 1–41.

Brancacci, Aldo. 2007. "Democritus' *Mousika*." In *Democritus: Science, The Arts, and the Care of the Soul*. Edited by Aldo Brancacci and Pierre-Marie Morel. Leiden: E. J. Brill, 181–206.

Brand, Peg Zeglin. 2000. "Introduction." In *Beauty Matters*. Edited by Peg Zeglin Brand. Bloomington: Indiana University Press, 1–24.

Brendel, Otto. 1946. "The Interpretation of the Holkham Venus." *The Art Bulletin* 28: 65–75.

Brine, Kevin R., Elena Ciletti, and Henrike Lähnemann, eds. 2010. *The Sword of Judith: Judith Studies across the Disciplines.* Cambridge: OpenBook Publishers.

Brown, Francis, S.R. Driver, and Charles A. Briggs, eds. 1953. *Hebrew and English Lexicon of the Old Testament.* Oxford: Clarendon Press.

Burke, Edmund. 2004. *Reflections on the Revolution in France.* Edited by Connor Cruise O'Brien. London: Penguin Books (originally published in 1790).

Büttner, Stefan. 2006. *Antike Ästhetik: Eine Einführung in die Prinzipien des Schönen.* Munich: Beck.

Bussels, Stijn. 2012. *The Animated Image: Roman Theory on Naturalism, Vividness and Divine Power.* Berlin: Akademie Verlag.

Cairns, Douglas. 2014. "A Short History of Shudders." In *Unveiling Emotions II. Emotions in Greece and Rome: Texts, Images, Material Culture.* Edited by Angelos Chaniotis and Pierre Ducrey. Stuttgart: Franz Steiner Verlag, 85–107.

Carpenter, Rhys, ed. 1902. *Demetrius: On Style: The Greek Text of Demetrius De elocutione.* Cambridge: Cambridge University Press.

Clark, T. J. 2013. *Picasso and Truth: From Cubism to Guernica.* Princeton, NJ: Princeton University Press.

Cochrane, Joe, and Sarah Lyall. 2013. "Emphasizing Inner Beauty, Pageant Says No to Bikinis." *New York Times / International Herald Tribune* (Global Edition Asia Pacific), June 6, Section A, p. 6.

Cohen, Edward E. 1992. *Athenian Economy and Society: A Banking Perspective.* Princeton, NJ: Princeton University Press.

Cope, Edward Meredith. 1877. *Aristotle: Rhetoric.* Vol. 1. Revised by John Edwin Sandys. Cambridge: Cambridge University Press.

D'Ambra, Eve. 1998. *Art and Identity in the Roman World.* London: Weidenfeld and Nicolson.

d'Angour, Armand. 2011. *The Greeks and the New: Novelty in Ancient Greek Imagination and Experience.* Cambridge: Cambridge University Press.

Danto, Arthur C. 2003. *The Abuse of Beauty.* Chicago: Open Court.

Darwin, Charles. 1871. *The Descent of Man, and Selection in Relation to Sex.* London: John Murray.

Davies, John K. 2001. "Hellenistic Economies in the Post-Finley Era." In *Hellenistic Economies.* Edited by Zofia H. Archibald, John Davies, Vincent Gabrielson, and Graham J. Oliver. London: Routledge, 7–43.

da Vinci, Leonardo. 2005. *A Treatise on Painting.* Translated by John Francis Rigaud. Mineola, NY: Dover (original date of translation, 1877).

de Jonge, Casper C. 2008. *Grammar and Rhetoric: Dionysius of Halicarnassus on Language, Linguistics and Literature*. Leiden: E.J. Brill.

de Jonge, Casper C. 2012. "Dionysius and Longinus on the Sublime: Rhetoric and Religious Language." *American Journal of Philology* 133: 271–300.

Derrida, Jacques. 1987. *The Truth in Painting*. Translated by Geoff Bennington and Ian McLeod. Chicago: University of Chicago Press.

Desmond, William. 1986. *Art and the Absolute: A Study of Hegel's Aesthetics*. Albany: State University of New York Press.

Destrée, Pierre. 2013. "Aristotle on the Paradox of Tragic Pleasure." In *Suffering Art Gladly: The Paradox of Negative Emotion in Art*. Edited by Jerrold Levinson. Basingstoke, UK: Palgrave Macmillan, 3–27.

Dickens, Charles. 1992. *Oliver Twist*. London: Penguin.

Dickey, Stephanie S. 2010. "Damsels in Distress: Gender and Emotion in Seventeenth Century Netherlandish Art." In *The Passions in the Arts of the Early Modern Netherlands / De Hartstochten in de Kunst in de Vroegmoderne Nederlanden*. Edited by Stephanie S. Dickey and Herman Roodenburg. Zwolle: Waanders Publishers, 53–81.

Dover, Kenneth J. 1989. *Greek Homosexuality*. 2nd edition. Cambridge, MA: Harvard University Press.

Durst, Sarah Beth. 2007. *Into the Wild*. London: Penguin Books.

Dwyer, Eugene. 2012. "Collectible Singletons." *Arethusa* 45: 305–318.

Dyck, Andrew R. 1996. *A Commentary on Cicero, De officiis*. Ann Arbor: University of Michigan Press.

Ebert, Joachim. 1969. "Die Gestalt des Thersites in der *Ilias*." *Philologus* 113: 159–175.

Eco, Umberto. 2004. *History of Beauty*. Translated by Alastair McEwen. New York: Rizzoli.

Edmonds, J. M. 1912. *Greek Bucolic Poets*. Cambridge, MA: Harvard University Press.

Eyl, Jennifer. 2012. "Why Thekla Does Not See Paul: Visual Perception and the Displacement of Eros in the Acts of Paul and Thekla." In *The Ancient Novel and Early Christian and Jewish Narrative: Fictional Intersections = Ancient Narrative* supplement 16. Edited by Marília P. Futre Pinheiro, Judith Perkins, and Richard Pervo. Groningen: Barkhuis Publishing, 3–20.

Fairbanks, Arthur, trans. 1931. *Elder Philostratus, Younger Philostratus, Callistratus*. London: Heinemann.

Finley, Moses I. 1999. *The Ancient Economy*. Revised edition with a forward by Ian Morris. Berkeley: University of California Press (originally published in 1973).

Fisher, Nick. 2001. *Aeschines, Against Timarchos*. Oxford: Oxford University Press.

Fontanier, Jean-Michel. 1998. *La beauté selon saint Augustin*. Rennes: Presses Universitaires de Rennes.

Ford, Anton. 2010. "Response to Irwin." *Classical Philology* 105: 396–402.

Fortenbaugh, William W., Pamela Huby, Robert Sharples, and Dimitri Gutas, eds. 1992. *Theophrastus of Eresus: Sources for his Life, Writings, Thought and Influence*. 2 vols. Leiden: Brill.

Fortenbaugh, William W., and Eckart Schütrumpf, eds. 1999. *Demetrius of Phalerum: Text, Translation and Discussion*. New Brunswick, NJ: Transaction Publishers.

Freedberg, David. 1989. *The Power of Images: Studies in the History and Theory of Response*. Berkeley: University of California Press.

Furley, William D., ed. 2009. *Menander: Epitrepontes*. London: Institute of Classical Studies = *BICS* Supplement 106.

Gardin Dumesnil, M. J. B. 1825. *Latin Synonyms with their Different Significations and Examples*. Translated and augmented by J. M. Gosset. 3rd edition. London: George B. Whittaker.

Gardner, Howard. 2011. *Truth, Beauty, and Goodness Reframed: Educating for the Virtues in the Twenty-First Century*. New York: Basic Books.

Gera, Deborah Levine. 2013. *Judith: Introduction, Translation, Commentary*. Berlin: de Gruyter.

Gilbert-Rolfe, Jeremy. 2000. "Beauty." *X-Tra* 2.3: 3–5 (corrected version online at http://www.strikingdistance.com/xtra/XTra100/v2n3/jgr.html, accessed 6 April 2013).

Gombrich, Ernst. 1990. Review of Freedberg 1989. *New York Review of Books* 15: 6–9.

Gorky, Maxim. 1932. *My Apprenticeship*. Translated by Margaret Wettlin. Moscow: Foreign Languages Publishing House.

Gracyk, Theodore A. 1994. "Rethinking Hume's Standard of Taste." *The Journal of Aesthetics and Art Criticism* 52: 169–182.

Grammer, K., B. Fink, A. P. Møller, and R. Thornhill. 2003. "Darwinian Aesthetics: Sexual Selection and the Biology of Beauty." *Biological Reviews of the Cambridge Philosophical Society* 78: 385–407.

Green, R. P. H., trans. 1997. *Saint Augustine: On Christian Teaching*. Oxford: Oxford University Press.

Grube, G. M. A. 1964. "The Date of Demetrius 'On Style.'" *Phoenix* 18: 294–302.

Gwilt, Joseph. 1826. *The Architecture of Marcus Vitruvius Pollio*. London: Priestley and Weale. Available (in modified version) at http://penelope.uchicago.edu/Thayer/E/Roman/Texts/Vitruvius.

Hazebroucq, M.-F. 2004. *Hippias Majeur*. Paris: Ellipses.

Halliwell, Stephen. 2002. *The Aesthetics of Mimesis: Ancient Texts and Modern Problems*. Princeton, NJ: Princeton University Press.

Halliwell, Stephen. 2011. *Between Ecstasy and Truth: Interpretations of Greek Poetics from Homer to Longinus*. Oxford: Oxford University Press.

Heaney, Seamus. 2002. *Finders Keepers: Selected Prose, 1971–2001*. London: Faber and Faber.

Heath, Malcolm. 2012. "Longinus and the Ancient Sublime." In *The Sublime: From Antiquity to the Present*. Edited by Timothy M. Costelloe. Cambridge: Cambridge University Press, 11–23.

Heitsch, Ernst. 2011. *Platon, Größerer Hippias*. Göttingen: Vandenhoeck and Ruprecht.

Hinterberger, Martin. 2013. *Phthonos: Mißgunst, Neid und Eifersucht in der byzantinischen Literatur*. Wiesbaden: Dr. Ludwig Reichert Verlag.

Hume, David. 1757. *Of the Standard of Taste*. London: A. Millar.

Hume, David. 1999. *An Enquiry concerning Human Understanding*. Edited by Tom L. Beauchamp. Oxford: Oxford University Press.

Hunter, Richard, and Donald Russell, eds. 2011. *Plutarch: How to Study Poetry (De audiendis poetis)*. Cambridge: Cambridge University Press.

Hyland, Drew A. 2008. *Plato and the Question of Beauty*. Bloomington: University of Indiana Press.

Innes, Doreen. 1985. "Theophrastus and the Theory of Style." In *Theophrastus of Eresus: On his Life and Work*. Edited by William F. Fortenbaugh. New Brunswick, NJ: Transaction Books, 251–268.

Irwin, Terence. 2010. "The Sense and Reference of *Kalon* in Aristotle." *Classical Philology* 105: 381–396.

Isenberg, Arnold. 1973. "Critical Communication." In *Aesthetics and the Theory of Criticism: Selected Essays of Arnold Isenberg*. Edited by William Callaghan et al. Chicago: University of Chicago Press (originally published in *Philosophical Review* 58 [1949]: 330–344).

Janko, Richard. 2000. *Philodemus: On Poems Book One*. Oxford: Oxford University Press.

Jeremiah, Edward T. 2012. *The Emergence of Reflexivity in Greek Language and Thought: From Homer to Plato and Beyond*. Leiden: Brill = Philosophia antiqua 129.

Joosse, Albert. 2012. Review of Heitsch 2011. *Bryn Mawr Classical Review* 2012.03.56.

Jung, Carl. 1932. "Picasso." *Neue Zürcher Zeitung* 153, no. 2,107 (November 13): 2.

Jowett, Benjamin. 1908. *The Republic of Plato*. 3rd ed. Oxford: The Clarendon Press.

Kant, Immanuel. 1952. *Critique of Judgement*. Translated by J. C. Meredith. London: Oxford University Press.

Kant, Immanuel. 2000. *Critique of the Power of Judgment*. Translated by Paul D. Guyer. Cambridge: Cambridge University Press.

Kay, Paul, and Willett Kempton. 1984. "What Is the Sapir-Whorf Hypothesis?" *American Anthropologist* n.s. 86: 65–79.

Kelly, Gavin. 2013. "The Political Crisis of AD 375–376." *Chiron* 43: 357–409.

Keltner, Dacher, and Jonathan Haidt. 2003. "Approaching Awe, a Moral, Spiritual and Aesthetic Emotion." *Cognition and Emotion* 17: 297–314.

Ker, Walter C. A. 1919. *Martial: Epigrams*. 2 vols. London: Heinemann.

King, William L. 1992. "Scruton and Reasons for Looking at Photographs." *British Journal of Aesthetics* 32: 258–265.

Kivy, Peter. 2011. *Once-Told Tales: An Essay in Literary Aesthetics*. Malden, MA: Wiley-Blackwell.

Konstan, David. 1987. "Persians, Greeks and Empire." *Arethusa* 20: 59–73.

Konstan, David. 1997. "Conventional Values of the Hellenistic Greeks: The Evidence from Astrology." In *Conventional Values of the Hellenistic Greeks*. Edited by Per Bilde et al. Aarhus: Aarhus University Press = Studies in Hellenistic Civilization 8, 159–76.

Konstan, David. 2000. "Plato between Love and Friendship." *Hypnos* 6: 154–169.

Konstan, David. 2004. " 'The Birth of the Reader': Plutarch as Literary Critic." *Scholia* 13: 3–27; Spanish version under the title, " 'El nacimiento del lector': Plutarco como crítico literario," *Praesentia* 13 (2012), available at http://erevistas.saber.ula.ve/index.php/praesentia/article/view/4229.

Konstan, David. 2005. "The Pleasures of the Ancient Text or The Pleasure of Poetry from Plato to Plutarch." In F. Cairns, ed., *Greek and Roman Poetry, Greek and Roman Historiography* = Papers of the Langford Latin Seminar 12: 1–17.

Konstan, David. 2008. "In Defense of Croesus, or Suspense as an Aesthetic Emotion." *Aisthe* 3: 1–15 (accessible online at http://www.ifcs.ufrj. br/~aisthe/vol%20II/KONSTAN.pdf). Reprinted in Fernando Santoro,

Tatiana Ribeiro, and Henrique Cairus, eds., *Pathos: A Poética das Emoções*. Rio de Janeiro: Arquimedes Editora, 2009.

Konstan, David. 2009a. "Cosmopolitan Traditions." In *A Companion to Greek and Roman Political Thought*. Edited by Ryan Balot. Oxford: Blackwell, 473–484.

Konstan, David. 2009b. "Le courage dans le roman grec: de Chariton à Xénophon d'Ephèse, avec référence à Philon d'Alexandrie." In *Roman IV: Vertus, passions et vices dans le roman grec (Actes du colloque de Tours, 19–21 octobre 2006, organisé par l'université François-Rabelais de Tours)*. Edited by Bernard Pouderon and Cécile Bost-Pouderon. Lyon: Presses de la Maison de l'Orient et de la Méditerranée, 117–126.

Konstan, David. 2009c. "Reunion and Regeneration: Narrative Patterns in Ancient Greek Novels and Christian Acts." In *Fiction on the Fringe: Novelistic Writing in Late Antiquity*. Edited by Grammatiki Karla and Ingela Nilsson. Leiden: Brill Academic Publishers = *Mnemosyne* Supplements Series 310, 105–120.

Konstan, David. 2010. "Suche und Verwandlung: Transformation von Erzählmustern in den hellenistischen Romanen und den apokryphen Apostelakten." Translated by Regina Höschele. In *Askese und Identität in Spätantike, Mittelalter und früher Neuzeit*. Edited by Werner Röcke and Julia Weitbrecht. Berlin: Walter de Gruyter, 251–268.

Konstan, David. 2012a. "Between Appetite and Emotion, or Why Can't Animals Have Erôs?" In *Eros in Ancient Greece*. Edited by Ed Sanders et al. Oxford: Oxford University Press, 13–25.

Konstan, David. 2012b. "El concepto de belleza en el mundo antiguo y su recepción en Occidente." *Nova Tellus* 30: 133–148.

Konstan, David. 2012c. "A Senecan Theory of Drama?" In *Estudios sobre teatro romano: el mundo de los sentimientos y su expresión*. Edited by Rosario López Gregoris. Zaragoza: Libros Pórtico, 179–185.

Konstan, David. 2013a. "Beauty, Love, and Art: The Legacy of Ancient Greece." *ΣΧΟΛΗ* 7: 327–339.

Konstan, David. 2013b. "Biblical Beauty: Hebrew, Greek, and Latin." In *The One Who Sows Bountifully: Essays in Honor of Stanley K. Stowers*. Edited by Caroline Johnson Hodge et al. Atlanta: Society of Biblical Literature, 129–140.

Konstan, David. 2013c. "Cómo decir 'belleza' en griego antiguo." In *Ianua Classicorum: Temas y formas del Mundo Clásico*, vol. 1. Madrid: Sociedad Española de Estudios Clásicos = Actas del XIII Congreso de la Sociedad Española de Estudios Clásicos (Logroño, julio de 2011), 441–446.

Konstan, David. 2013d. "Themistius on Royal Beauty." In *The Purposes of Rhetoric in Late Antiquity: From Performance to Exegesis*. Edited by Alberto Quiroga. Tübingen: Mohr Siebeck, 179–188.

Konstan, David. 2014a. "Beauty." In *A Companion to Ancient Aesthetics*. Edited by Pierre Destrée and Penelope Murray. Malden, MA: Wiley-Blackwell.

Konstan, David. 2014b. "Beauty and Desire between Greece and Rome." In *Emotions Between Greece and Rome (Bulletin of the Institute of Classical Studies)*. Edited by Douglas Cairns.

Konstan, David. 2014c. "Wit and Irony in the Epic Cycle." In *A Companion to the Greek Epic Cycle*. Edited by Marco Fantuzzi and Christos Tsagalis. Cambridge: Cambridge University Press.

Konstan, David, and Ilaria Ramelli. 2014. "The Novel and Christian Narrative." In *The Blackwell Companion to the Ancient Novel*. Edited by Shannon Byrne and Edmund Cueva. Hoboken, NJ: John Wiley and Sons, 180–197.

Kosman, Aryeh. 2010. "Beauty and the Good: Situating the *Kalon*." *Classical Philology* 105: 341–357.

Kossatz-Deissmann, Anneliese. 1994. "Paridis iudicium." *Lexicon iconographicum mythologiae classicae*. Vol. 7.1. Zurich: Artemis Verlag, 176–188.

Krafft-Ebbing, Richard von. 1886. *Psychopathia Sexualis: Eine klinisch-forensische Studie*. 1st edition. Stuttgart: Ferdinand Enke.

Kristeller, Paul Oskar. 1951. "The Modern System of the Arts: A Study of the History of Aesthetics (I)." *Journal of the History of Ideas* 12: 496–527. Reprinted, along with part II (*Journal of the History of Ideas* 13 [1952]: 17–46), in P. O. Kristeller, *Renaissance Thought and the Arts: Collected Essays*, expanded edition. Princeton, NJ: Princeton University Press, 1990, 163–227.

Laes, Christian. 2011. *Children in the Roman Empire: Outsiders Within*. Cambridge: Cambridge University Press.

Langerbeck, H., ed. 1986. *Gregorii Nysseni Opera*. Vol. 6. Leiden: Brill.

Lapatin, Kenneth. 2010. "The 'Art' of Politics." *Arethusa* 43: 253–265.

Laurence, Ray. 2009. *Roman Passions: A History of Pleasure in Imperial Rome*. London: Continuum.

Leibniz, Gottfried Wilhelm. 1989. *Elements of Natural Law*. In *Leibniz, Philosophical Papers and Letters: A Selection*. Translated and edited with an introduction by Leroy E. Loemker. 2nd edition. Dordrecht: Kluwer.

Lessing, Gotthold Ephraim. 1962. *Laocoon: An Essay on the Limits of Painting and Poetry*. Translated by Edward Allen McCormick. Baltimore: The Johns Hopkins University Press (originally published in 1766).

Levinson, Jerrold. 2011. "Beauty Is Not One: The Irreducible Variety of Visual Beauty." In *The Aesthetic Mind: Philosophy and Psychology*. Edited by Elisabeth Schellekens and Peter Goldie. Oxford: Oxford University Press, 190–207.

Liddell, Henry George, and Robert Scott, eds. 1940. *A Greek-English Lexicon*. 9th edition. Revised by Henry Stuart Jones and Roderick McKenzie. Oxford: Oxford University Press.

Linwood, William. 1843. *A Lexicon to Aeschylus*. London: Taylor and Walton.

Lissarrague, François. 1999. "Publicity and Performance: *Kalos* Inscriptions in Attic Vase-Painting." In *Performance Culture and Athenian Democracy*. Edited by Simon Goldhill and Robin Osborne. Cambridge: Cambridge University Press, 359–373.

Loader, James Alfred. 2011. "The Pleasing and the Awesome: The Beauty of Humans in the Old Testament." *Old Testament Essays* 24: 652–667.

Loader, James Alfred. 2012a. "The Dark Side of Beauty in the Old Testament." *Old Testament Essays* 25: 334–350.

Loader, James Alfred. 2012b. "Making Things from the Heart: On Works of Beauty in the Old Testament." *Old Testament Essays* 25: 100–114.

Ludlam, Ivor. 1991. *Hippias Major: An Interpretation*. Stuttgart: Franz Steiner Verlag.

Macan, Reginald Walter. 1908. *Herodotus: The Seventh, Eighth & Ninth Books with Introduction and Commentary*. London: Macmillan.

MacKenna, Stephen, trans. 1969. *Plotinus: The Enneads*. New York: Pantheon Books.

Mackenzie, Henry. 2009. *The Man of Feeling*. Edited by Brian Vickers. New York: Oxford University Press (originally published in 1771).

Macwilliam, Stuart. 2009. "Ideologies of Male Beauty and the Hebrew Bible." *Biblical Interpretation* 17: 265–287.

Mankin, David, ed. 2011. *Cicero De oratore Book III*. Cambridge: Cambridge University Press.

Mansfield, Elizabeth C. 2007. *Too Beautiful to Picture: Zeus, Myth, and Mimesis*. Minneapolis: University of Minnesota Press.

Marcovich, Miroslav. 1988. "Hermocles' Ithyphallus for Demetrius." In *Studies in Graeco-Roman Religions and Gnosticism*. Edited by Miroslav Marcovich. Leiden: Brill, 8–19.

Martindale, Charles. 2005. *Latin Poetry and the Judgement of Taste: An Essay in Aesthetics*. Oxford: Oxford University Press.

Masséglia, Jane. 2012. " 'Reasons to be Cheerful': Conflicting Emotions in the Drunken Old Women of Munich and Rome." In *Unveiling Emotions: Sources and Methods for the Study of Emotions in the Greek World*. Edited by Angelos Chaniotis. Stuttgart: Franz Steiner, 413–430.

May, James M., and Jakob Wisse, trans. 2001. *Cicero on the Ideal Orator*. Oxford: Oxford University Press.

Middeldorf, Ulrich. 1947. "Letters to the Editor." *The Art Bulletin* 29: 67.

Monteil, Pierre. 1964. *Beau et laid en latin*. Paris: Klincksieck.

Montemayor García, Alicia. 2013. *La trama de los discursos y las artes: El Canon de Policleto de Argos*. Mexico City: Conaculta.

Morales, Helen. 2004. *Vision and Narrative in Achilles Tatius' Leucippe and Clitophon*. Cambridge: Cambridge University Press.

Morales, Helen. 2011. "Fantasising Phryne: The Psychology and Ethics of Ekphrasis." *Cambridge Classical Journal* 57: 71–104.

Moretti, Francesca Paola. 2006. *La Passio Anastasiae: introduzione, testo critico, traduzione*. Rome: Herder.

Moscoso, Javier. 2011. *Historia cultural del dolor*. Madrid: Taurus.

Moscoso, Javier. 2012. *Pain: A Cultural History*. Translated by Sarah Thomas and Paul House. Houndmills: Palgrave.

Most, G. W. 1992. "Schöne (das)." In *Historisches Wörterbuch der Philosophie*. Vol. 8. Edited by Joachim Ritter and Karlfried Grunder. Basel: Schwabe Verlag, 1343–1351.

Munteanu, Dana. 2009. "*Qualis Tandem Misericordia in Rebus Fictis?* Aesthetic and Ordinary Emotion." *Helios* 36: 117–147.

Murdoch, Iris. 2001. *Nuns and Soldiers*. New York: Penguin Books (originally published in 1980).

Murray, A. T., trans. 1924. *Homer: The Iliad*. Cambridge, MA: Harvard University Press.

Nehamas, Alexander. 2007. *The Promise of Happiness: The Place of Beauty in a World of Art*. Princeton, NJ: Princeton University Press.

Netz, Reviel. 2010. "What Did Greek Mathematicians Find Beautiful?" *Classical Philology* 105: 426–444.

North, John Harry. 2012. *Winckelmann's "Philosophy of Art": A Prelude to German Classicism*. Newcastle upon Tyne: Cambridge Scholars Publishing.

O'Donnell, James J., ed. 1992. *The Confessions of Augustine: Text and Commentary*. Oxford: Oxford University Press.

Oliver, Graham J. 2006. "The Economic Realities." In *A Companion to the Classical Greek World*. Edited by Konrad H. Kinzl. Malden, MA: Blackwell, 281–310.

Olyan, Saul M. 2008. *Disability in the Hebrew Bible: Interpreting Mental and Physical Differences*. Cambridge: Cambridge University Press.

O'Sullivan, Patrick. 2011. "Dio Chrysostom and the Poetics of Phidias' Zeus." In *The Statue of Zeus at Olympia: New Approaches*. Edited by Janette McWilliam et al. Newcastle upon Tyne: Cambridge Scholars Publishing, 137–154.

Papaioannou, Stratis. 2013. *Michael Psellos: Rhetoric and Authorship in Byzantium*. Cambridge: Cambridge University Press.

Passmore, J. A. 1951. "The Dreariness of Aesthetics." *Mind* n.s. 60: 318–335.

Pearsall, Paul. 2007. *Awe: The Delights and Dangers of our Eleventh Emotion*. Deerfield Beach, FL: Health Communications Inc.

Peek, Werner. 1955. *Griechische Vers-Inschriften*. Berlin: Akademie-Verlag.

Penchansky, David. 2013. "Beauty, Power, and Attraction: Aesthetics and the Hebrew Bible." In *Beauty and the Bible: Toward a Hermeneutics of Biblical Aesthetics*. Edited by Richard J. Bautch and Jean-François Racine. Atlanta: Society of Biblical Literature, 47–65.

Perrin, Bernadotte, trans. 1916. *Plutarch: The Parallel Lives*. Vol. 3. Cambridge, MA: Harvard University Press.

Platt, Verity. 2002. "Evasive Epiphanies in Ekphrastic Epigram." *Ramus* 31: 33–50.

Platt, Verity. 2011. *Facing the Gods: Epiphany and Representation in Graeco-Roman Art, Literature and Religion*. Cambridge: Cambridge University Press.

Polanyi, Karl. 2001. *The Great Transformation: The Political and Economic Origins of Our Times*. Boston: Beacon Press (originally published in 1944).

Pollitt, Jerome. 1974. *The Ancient View of Greek Art: Criticism, History, and Terminology*. New Haven, CT: Yale University Press.

Porter, James I. 2009. "Is Art Modern? Kristeller's 'Modern System of the Arts' Reconsidered." *British Journal of Aesthetics* 49: 1–24.

Porter, James I. 2010. *The Origins of Aesthetic Thought in Ancient Greece: Matter, Sensation, and Experience*. Cambridge: Cambridge University Press.

Pradeau, J.-F., and F. Fronterotta. 2005. *Platon: Hippias majeur, Hippias mineur*. Paris: Flammarion.

Prettejohn, Elizabeth. 2005. *Beauty and Art: 1750–2000*. Oxford: Oxford University Press.

Prettejohn, Elizabeth. 2012. *The Modernity of Ancient Sculpture: Greek Sculpture and Modern Art from Winckelmann to Picasso*. London: I. B. Tauris.

Pretzler, Maria. 2009. "Form over Substance? Deconstructing Ecphrasis in Lucian's *Zeuxis* and *Eikones*." In *A Lucian for our Times*. Edited by Adam M. Bartley. Newcastle upon Tyne: Cambridge Scholars Publishing, 157–172.

Prinz, Jesse. 2011. "Emotion and Aesthetic Value." In *The Aesthetic Mind: Philosophy and Psychology*. Edited by Elisabeth Schellekens and Peter Goldie. Oxford: Oxford University Press, 71–88.

Prum, Richard O. 2012. "Aesthetic Evolution by Mate Choice: Darwin's *Really* Dangerous Idea." *Philosophical Transactions of the Royal Society B: Biological Sciences* 367 (19 August): 2253–2265.

Psellus, Michael. 1941. *Scripta minora*. Vol. 2. Edited by Edward Kurtz and Francis Drexl. Milan: Vita e Pensiero.

Pusey, Edward B. 1838. *The Confessions of Saint Augustine*. Oxford: J. H. Parker.

Quindlen, Anna. 2014. *Still Life with Breadcrumbs: A Novel*. New York: Random House.

Ramelli, Ilaria. 2010. "Good/Beauty: *agathon/kalón*." In *The Brill Dictionary of Gregory of Nyssa*. Edited by G. Maspero and L.F. Mateo-Seco. Leiden: Brill, 356–363.

Richlin, Amy. 1992. *The Garden of Priapus: Sexuality and Aggression in Roman Humor*. 2nd edition. Oxford: Oxford University Press.

Richlin, Amy. 2006. *Marcus Aurelius in Love: Marcus Aurelius and Marcus Cornelius Fronto*. Chicago: University of Chicago Press.

Roberts, Rhys W., ed. 1910. *Dionysius of Halicarnassus: On Literary Composition*. London: Macmillan.

Robson, James. 2013. "Beauty and Sex Appeal in Aristophanes." *Eugesta* 3: 43–66.

Rudd, Niall, ed. 1989. *Horace: Epistles Book II and Epistle to the Pisones ("Ars Poetica")*. Cambridge: Cambridge University Press.

Russell, Donald A. 2002. *Quintilian: The Orator's Education*. Vol. 3. Cambridge, MA: Harvard University Press.

Russell, Donald A., and David Konstan, eds. and trans. 2005. *Heraclitus: Homeric Problems*. Atlanta: Society of Biblical Literature.

Russell, Donald A., and Nigel G. Wilson, eds. 1981. *Menander Rhetor*. Oxford: Clarendon Press.

Rutledge, Steven H. 2012. *Ancient Rome as a Museum: Power, Identity, and the Culture of Collecting*. Oxford: Oxford University Press.

Sartwell, Crispin. 2004. *Six Names of Beauty*. New York: Routledge.

Scarry, Elaine. 1999. *On Beauty and Being Just*. Princeton, NJ: Princeton University Press.

Schiller, Friedrich von. 1980. "On the Sublime." In *Schiller: Naive and Sentimental Poetry and On the Sublime*. Translation, introduction, and notes by Julius A. Tobias. New York: Fredrich Ungar Publishing Co.

Scobie, A. 1975. "Perversions Ancient and Modern: I. Agalmatophilia, The Statue Syndrome." *Journal of the History of the Behavioral Sciences* 11: 49–54.

Scruton, Roger. 1981. "Photography and Representation." *Critical Inquiry* 7: 577–603.

Scruton, Roger. 2009. *Beauty*. Oxford: Oxford University Press.

Setaioli, Aldo. 2007. "Some Ideas of Seneca's on Beauty." *Prometheus* 33: 49–65.

Setaioli, Aldo. 2008. "La notion éthique de *kalós/kalón* en latin." *Prometheus* 34: 160–180.

Shapiro, Alan. 1987. "*Kalos*-Inscriptions with Patronymic." *Zeitschrift für Papyrologie und Epigraphik* 68: 107–118.

Shaw, Brent. 1996. "Body/Power/Identity: Passions of the Martyrs." *Journal of Early Christian Studies* 4: 269–312.

Sider, David. 1977. "Plato's Early Aesthetics: *The Hippias Major*." *Journal of Aesthetics and Art Criticism* 35: 465–470.

Sinisgalli, Rocco, ed. 2011. *Leon Battista Alberti On Painting: A New Translation and Critical Edition*. Cambridge: Cambridge University Press.

Slater, William J., ed. 1969. *Lexicon to Pindar*. Berlin: De Gruyter.

Slings, S. R. 1998. "Review of Vancamp 1996." *Mnemosyne* 51: 611–616.

Smith, Zadie. 2005. *On Beauty*. London: Hamish Hamilton.

Solomon, J., trans. 1984. "Eudemian Ethics." In *The Complete Works of Aristotle*. Vol. 2. Edited by Jonathan Barnes. Princeton, NJ: Princeton University Press.

Sonek, Krzysztof. 2009. *Truth, Beauty, and Goodness in Biblical Narratives: A Hermeneutical Study of Genesis 21:1–21*. Berlin: Walter de Gruyter.

Squire, Michael. 2010. "Introduction: The Art of Art History in Greco-Roman Antiquity." *Arethusa* 43: 133–163.

Squire, Michael. 2011. *The Art of the Body: Antiquity and its Legacy*. Oxford: Oxford University Press.

Squire, Michael. 2013. "Apparitions Apparent: Ekphrasis and the Parameters of Vision in the Elder Philostratus's *Imagines*." *Helios* 40: 97–140.

Staley, Gregory A. 2010. *Seneca and the Idea of Tragedy*. Oxford: Oxford University Press.

Starr, G. Gabrielle. 2013. *Feeling Beauty: The Neuroscience of Aesthetic Experience*. Cambridge, MA: MIT Press.

Steiner, Wendy. 2001. *Venus in Exile: The Rejection of Beauty in Twentieth-Century Art*. Chicago: University of Chicago Press.

Stewart, A. F. 1979. *Attika: Studies in Athenian Sculpture of the Hellenistic Age*. London: Society for the Promotion of Hellenic Studies = *Journal of Hellenic Studies*, suppl. vol. 14.

Stróżewski, Władyslaw. 2002. *O wielkości: Szkice z filozofii człowieka*. Cracow: Znak.

Swoyer, Chris. 2010. "Relativism." In *The Stanford Encyclopedia of Philosophy*. Edited by Edward N. Zalta. http://plato.stanford.edu/archives/win2010/entries/relativism (accessed March 9, 2013).

Talon-Hugon, Carole. 2009. *Morales de l'art*. Paris: Presses Universitaires de France.

Tanner, Jeremy. 2010. "Aesthetics and Art History Writing in Comparative Historical Perspective." *Arethusa* 43: 267–288.

Tarrant, Dorothy. 1928. *The Hippias Major Attributed to Plato*. Cambridge: Cambridge University Press.

Tarrant, Harold. 2000. "The Special Power of Visual Beauty in Plato and the Ancient Greek Novel." In *Greek Philosophy and the Fine Arts*. Vol. 1. Edited by Konstantine Boudouris. Athens: Ionia Publications, 175–184.

Taylor, Francis Henry. 1948. *The Taste of Angels: A History of Art Collecting from Rameses to Napoleon*. Boston: Little, Brown, and Co.

Terezis, Christos, and Kalomoira, Polychronopoulou. 2000. "Aspects of Beauty According to Neoplatonic Philosopher Proclus." In *Greek Philosophy and the Fine Arts*. Vol. 1. Edited by Konstantine Boudouris. Athens: Ionia Publications, 200–208.

Thiele, Walter, ed. 1987–2005. *Sirach (Ecclesiasticus)*. Freiburg: Verlag Herder (*Vetus latina: Die Reste der altlateinischen Bibel*, vol. 11.2).

Thornton, Bruce S. 1997. *Eros: The Myth of Ancient Greek Sexuality*. Boulder, CO: Westview Press.

Tolsa, Cristian. 2013. *Claudius Ptolemy and Self-Promotion: A Study on Ptolemy's Intellectual Milieu in Roman Alexandria*. Doctoral thesis, Departament de Filologia Grega, Universitat de Barcelona.

Toscano, Margaret M. 2013. "The Eyes Have It: Female Desire on Attic Greek Vases." *Arethusa* 46: 1–40.

Vancamp, Bruno. 1996. *Platon: Hippias maior, Hippias minor*. Stuttgart: Steiner.

Vanderspoel, John. 1995. *Themistius and the Imperial Court: Oratory, Civic Duty, and Paideia from Constantius to Theodosius*. Ann Arbor: University of Michigan Press.

Vérilhac, Anne Marie. 1978. *ΠΑΙΔΕΣ ΑΩΡΟΙ: Poésie Funéraire.* Vol. 1: Textes. Athens: Athens University Press.

von Arnim, Hans. 1903–1905. *Stoicorum veterum fragmenta.* Stuttgart: Teubner.

Walpole, Horace. 1871 (originally published 1761). *Anecdotes of Painting in England.* London: Alexander Murray (reprint of 1786 edition).

Watson, J. S., trans. 1860. *Cicero on Oratory and Orators.* New York: Harper and Brothers.

Webb, Ruth. 2009. *Ekphrasis, Imagination and Persuasion in Ancient Rhetorical Theory and Practice.* Farnham: Ashgate.

Westermann, Claus. 1984. "Das Schöne im Alten Testament." In *Erträge der Forschung am Alten Testament: Gesammelte Studien.* Vol. 3. Edited by Rainer Albertz and Claus Westermann. Munich: Chr. Kaiser Verlag, 479–497.

Whitehead, Alfred North. 1979. *Process and Reality.* New York: Free Press (originally published in 1929).

Wilde, Oscar. 1966. "The Critic as Artist." In *The Complete Works of Oscar Wilde.* Edited by J. B. Foreman. London: Collins, 1009–1059.

Williams, Craig A. 2012. *Reading Roman Friendship.* Cambridge: Cambridge University Press.

Wilson, H. A. 1893. *Gregory of Nyssa: On the Making of Man.* In Philip Schaff and Henry Wace, eds., *Gregory of Nyssa: Dogmatic Treatises; Select Writings and Letters.* Edinburgh: T. & T. Clark = Nicene and Post-Nicene Fathers, series 2, vol. 5, pp. 387-427.

Winckelmann, Johann Joachim. 1987. *Reflections on the Imitation of Greek Works in Painting and Sculpture.* Translated by E. Heyer and R. C. Norton. La Salle, IL: Open Court (originally published in 1756).

Wolff, Christian. 1732. *Psychologia empirica.* Frankfurt and Leipzig: Officina Libraria Rengeriana.

Woodruff, Paul. 1982. *Plato: Hippias Major: Translation and Commentary.* Oxford: Blackwell.

Woodruff, Paul. 2001. *Reverence: Renewing a Forgotten Virtue.* Oxford: Oxford University Press.

Wooten, Cecil W. 1987. *Hermogenes On Types of Style.* Chapel Hill: University of North Carolina Press.

Yonge, C. D., trans. 1854. *Athenaeus: The Deipnosophists.* London: Henry G. Bohn.

Yonge, C. D., trans. 1856. *The Orations of Marcus Tullius Cicero.* Vol. 1. London: Henry G. Bohn.

Yunis, Harvey, ed. 2011. *Plato: Phaedrus.* Cambridge: Cambridge University Press.

INDEX